Research Methods for Social Workers

Also Available from Lyceum Books, Inc.

Advisory Editor: Thomas M. Meenaghan, *New York University*

Using Statistical Methods in Social Work Practice with a Complete SPSS Guide
Soleman H. Abu-Bader

Social Work Evaluation: Enhancing What We Do
James R. Dudley

A Practical Guide to Social Service Evaluation
Carl F. Brun

Clinical Assessment for Social Workers: Quantitative and Qualitative Methods
Catheleen Jordan and Cynthia Franklin

Practical Tips for Publishing Scholarly Articles: Writing and Publishing in the Helping Professions
Rich Furman

Essentials of Social Work Practice: Assessment, Intervention, Evaluation
Thomas O'Hare

Toward Evidence-Based Practice: Variations on a Theme
Joel Fischer

Research Methods for Social Workers

A PRACTICE-BASED APPROACH

CYNTHIA A. FAULKNER
Morehead State University

and

SAMUEL S. FAULKNER
Morehead State University

LYCEUM
BOOKS, INC.

Chicago, Illinois

© Lyceum Books, Inc., 2009

Published by
LYCEUM BOOKS, INC.
5758 S. Blackstone Ave.
Chicago, Illinois 60637
773 + 643–1903 (Fax)
773 + 643–1902 (Phone)
lyceum@lyceumbooks.com
http://www.lyceumbooks.com

6 5 4 3 2 1   09 10 11 12

ISBN 978–1-933478–15–9

Library of Congress Cataloging-in-Publication Data

Faulkner, Cynthia A.
Research methods for social workers : a practice-based approach / Cynthia A. Faulkner and Samuel S. Faulkner.
    p.   cm.
Includes bibliographical references and index.
1. Social service—Research—Methodology.   I. Faulkner, Samuel S.   II. Title.
HV11.F37   2009
361.0072—dc22
2008020773

Contents

Figures, Tables, and Examples

Figures

Tables

Examples

Preface

If you are reading this text, chances are you are somehow involved with the Council on Social Work Education (CSWE)—either as a student who is attending a CSWE-accredited program or as a faculty member teaching in a program accredited by the CSWE. The Council on Social Work Education mandates that accredited programs teach research methods as part of their curricula. It is up to the individual programs to decide how they want to carry that out. There are important reasons why CSWE mandates that research be included. In today's changing world, it is important for practitioners to have an understanding of how to evaluate practice, be able to sort out solid research methods from shoddy science, and have the skills to stay current in the latest practices. Having a solid grounding in research methods will help you to do that.

There are many research texts on the market. Before deciding to undertake the long and arduous process of writing another one, we spent time examining and teaching from several of those texts. The most common complaints from our students were that the texts available bombarded them with complex terminology that was difficult to understand and that many of the concepts did not appear to apply to social work practice. Although students would purchase these texts, many did not find them useful and therefore used them only as a reference—or not at all—and relied predominately on the classroom instruction and examples to grasp the concepts, complex terminology, and applications of research methods as it applies to the field of social work. One of our goals, then, at the outset, was to create a text that was understandable yet contained the information needed to practice evidence-based social work. Over a three-year period, we issued drafts to our students to use in their research classes. The consistent comment from our students has been that they actually read the text. They said it is easy to understand, and we consider this high praise for a research book.

Discussion of research methods is often convoluted and difficult to understand. This book is designed to be as user-friendly as possible. We present the complicated concepts of social work research in easy-to-understand language and use numerous practice-based examples to illustrate the material and enhance readers' understanding. The text is loosely organized in three parts. The first five chapters offer a foundation for conducting a research study. The next four chapters introduce readers to several different types of research designs, the last two of which focus on specific designs used to evaluate social work practices. Following are two chapters that offer an introduction to descriptive statistics and inferential statistics. Although teaching statistical analysis was beyond the scope of this text, these chapters will provide students with a basic understanding that will improve their comprehension of the research process and will help them both to understand the findings of the literature they review and to select some preliminary analysis to include in their own research. Finally, the last chapter offers some concluding remarks, and an appendix provides an example research proposal that readers can use as a guide in structuring their own research proposals. Important vocabulary terms are boldfaced and provided in a glossary at the end of the book. At the end of each chapter we summarize the key points presented; offer applied learning activities, competency-based exercises that give readers an opportunity to practice new knowledge and allow them to develop a deeper understanding of the material; and provide a list of additional resources for students to consult to deepen their understanding of a number of research-related topics.

We suffer from no illusions that this text is the "be all and end all" of research texts. However, we do believe that this book provides social work students who have no prior exposure to research with a solid foundation in research methodology. In addition, it is our hope that this text will provide students with an understanding of the importance of research in the social work profession and will equip them with the tools they need to understand the research they come across in their studies and to conduct their own research.

Acknowledgments

As with most writings, there are many people who contributed their time and expertise to this text. A special thank-you goes to our colleague and friend Eric Swank, associate professor at Morehead State University, Kentucky, who read every chapter of two revisions to provide us with feedback on content and organization, and to our wonderful and dedicated research assistant, Lynn Embleton, who put in countless hours to see this text come to completion. We also want to thank our research students at Morehead State University (both the Morehead and Prestonsburg campuses) who provided feedback while this text was being piloted, and one student in particular, Melissa Caldwell, who took part of her summer to lend a student perspective. Our gratitude goes to David Follmer, publisher of Lyceum Books, for supporting the production of this book, to Tom Meenaghan, advisory editor, for some excellent advice prior to our final rewrite, and to Sonia Fulop, for the necessary and important developmental and copy edits. Special thanks go to our children (Wayne, Shay, Christina, Alisa, McKennzie, and Ezra) for inspiring us to be lifelong learners and our eight grandchildren (so far) for helping us stay young. *"I can do everything through God who gives me strength"* (Phil. 4.13).

About the Authors

CYNTHIA A. FAULKNER is associate professor of social work at Morehead State University in Kentucky. She received her BSSW from Kansas State University in 1984, an MSW from the University of Kansas in 1989, and her PhD from the University of Texas at Arlington in 2001. Professor Faulkner has practiced social work for over twenty years in multiple settings and is a licensed clinical social worker.

SAMUEL S. FAULKNER is associate professor of social work at Morehead State University in Kentucky. Professor Faulkner completed his PhD in social work at the University of Texas at Arlington in 2001 after receiving two master's of science degrees: one in social work from the University of Texas at Arlington and the other in counseling education from Texas A&M University–Corpus Christi.

CHAPTER ONE

What Is Research?

RESEARCH HAS BECOME AN INCREASINGLY valuable tool for social work practitioners and scholars. **Research** is a systematic and methodological approach to creating knowledge. In social work, research is instrumental in the development of effective practice outcomes, or the outcomes of professional activities that are designed to improve or change the well-being of an individual, agency, or other system. For instance, we can research an issue concerning practice accountability, such as whether an intervention is effective, or we can measure an issue related to the characteristics of an agency population, such as changes in the ages of substance abuse admissions over time. Measuring practice accountability and monitoring agency populations both provide information that can be used to create evidence-based practices. **Evidence-based practices** are practices whose efficacy is supported by evidence. In this chapter, we will discuss why research is important in social work practice and what research entails, critically examine ways of knowing, define the two fields of research, and provide an overview of four methods of research.

Importance of Social Work Research

Perhaps you are asking yourself something along the lines of "Why should I have to take a class in research? After all, I am interested in working with people. I could care less about research methods." The reality is that research is gaining an increasingly important place in the practice of social work. For instance, managed care companies, insurance companies, and consumers themselves are demanding that social workers be able to demonstrate not only that the techniques, methods, and practices that they

1

employ are useful and effective but that these practices can be used effectively in other settings and with other populations. Gone are the days when a social worker could rely on personal intuition and undocumented outcomes as proof that his or her practices were effective. In fact, the Code of Ethics of the National Association of Social Workers (see Appendix A) has an entire section on evaluation and research. Section 5.02 stresses that "Social workers should monitor and evaluate policies, the implementation of programs, and practice interventions." In addition, "Social workers should promote and facilitate evaluation and research to contribute to the development of knowledge" (National Association of Social Workers, 1999).

There are other reasons why researchers are compelled to adopt more rigorous ways of measuring the effectiveness of social work practice. In difficult economic times, as programs are experiencing a decrease in funding, it is becoming increasingly important to utilize evidence-based practices to demonstrate accountability. An increasing number of both government and private grant-funding sources are requiring evaluation components to be incorporated into grant proposals. In this age of shrinking dollars, foundations and governmental funding agencies want assurances that money is spent in the most effective way possible. Program evaluation can help agencies obtain or retain grants and other such funding by demonstrating program success. When writing proposals and developing new programs, social workers need to have at least a basic understanding of how to carry out a program evaluation.

Additionally, by researching specific social problems, social workers can become agents of macro change. Social workers can devise social policies and large-scale interventions to alter inequality and injustice in their agencies and communities. For instance, a social service agency identifies a significant amount of no-shows for job-skills training appointments. The agency conducts a telephone survey to identify barriers that prevent clients from keeping appointments and discovers that lack of access to transportation is the most significant barrier, and lack of child care the second most significant barrier. In response to these findings, an agency policy is developed to provide taxi tokens and child care vouchers to consumers with financial need.

Defining Research

With that in mind, we turn to the question "What is research?" Chances are, you are already a researcher and do not know it. We often use research methods without actually labeling what we are doing research. For example, think back to the last time you were going to see a movie. If you have ever solicited a review from a friend or read a review in a paper or magazine and then based your decision to see the film on the reviewer's opinion, you were utilizing research methodology. Similarly, if you have ever consulted a newspaper or a local television station for information about the weather so that you could decide how to dress for the day, you are utilizing research methods.

Research is, in its simplest form, the assimilation of knowledge and the gathering of data in a logical manner in order to become informed about something. We often consult with others whose opinions we value (friends, experts, etc.) and then make a decision based on our informed judgment. The process of conducting research is essentially the same, but much more thorough.

Ways of Knowing

The Code of Ethics of the National Association of Social Workers (1999) states that "Social workers should promote and facilitate evaluation and research to contribute to the development of knowledge" (section 5.02b). Have you ever wondered how we gain knowledge (how we know what we know)? Here we will discuss four ways in which knowledge can be gained.

First, we can use our own experiences to gain knowledge. Simply by trial and error we can gradually make decisions about a problem and eventually develop enough knowledge to solve a problem. For instance, you require a certain amount of sleep at night to feel rested the next day. A pattern of sleep experiences over time provides you with enough information to determine the specific amount of sleep you require. However, in social work practice, personal experiences can be misleading because our experiences and the experiences of our consumers may be different, just as others may need more or less sleep than you do.

Second, we can rely on the knowledge of others. Agency supervisors and other coworkers who have years of practice experience can be important sources of knowledge. Many have developed tried-and-true practices that have over time become evidence-based practices. For instance, a supervisor explains that a particular judge prefers for documentation on a case to be presented in a certain way and that this practice increases the possibility of a positive outcome in court. In addition, consulting an expert or some authority in a field outside our own expertise can help us make better practice decisions.

However, if we rely on faulty information, we may be taking misperceptions as truth. For instance, many self-help books are available on how to intervene with an active alcoholic. While many are reliable resources, authors without evidence-based practice experiences may be offering advice that is based on just one person's experience. Therefore, you must look at the qualifications of the person who is offering advice and ensure it has been shown to be reliable and valid through repeated positive outcomes.

Third, we can rely on traditions. Tradition provides us with knowledge passed down over time. Many new social work practitioners are indoctrinated into agency practice through the established practices of those who have worked there over time. For instance, agency traditions may include weekly team meetings to staff cases, debriefing with a supervisor after a difficult assessment, and identifying caseload counts to ensure equitable distribution. These practices have proved to increase accountability, reduce turnover rates, and monitor workloads, all of which are beneficial. However, there are traditions that are not best practices. For instance, taking consumer files home to work on, giving consumers our home or cell phone numbers, and standardized group notes are practices that can bring up issues of confidentiality, boundaries, and lack of individualized documentation.

The fourth way to gather knowledge is by using scientific methods to answer our questions. By researching our questions, we can increase our knowledge about a particular issue or population. It should be noted that one misconception about research is that studies are large experiments that are able to solve whole problems. The truth is that the research process involves small incremental steps. Each study adds a small piece of information to the whole. The process is much like painting a picture. Each brushstroke, each dab of paint, adds a small amount of detail until eventually a coherent picture emerges. Each stroke or dab of paint, standing alone, may not represent much, but when all the dabs of paint are viewed together as a whole, we see a picture. Research studies, by themselves, may only explain a small part of the whole, but when linked together with other studies, they begin to help us see a larger picture or describe an occurrence. For example, there is a plethora of child maltreatment research. Some studies may examine characteristics of the abusers, others the abused children, and still others the family dynamics of families in which child abuse is occurring. Each study is a small part that contributes to our understanding of child maltreatment.

Therefore, one study is not sufficient to apply to everyone. Different studies may have different, and sometimes opposite, findings because of the specific characteristics of the populations being researched. For instance, a child protection agency in a large urban city may report a high percentage of parents using street drugs, whereas a small rural community may report a high percentage of parents using prescription drugs. As you can see, the findings of the larger urban study do not apply to the rural study because the characteristics of the populations are different.

In summary, it is important to explore all possible ways of knowing about social work practice. The Code of Ethics of the National Association of Social Workers (1999) emphasizes that "Social workers should critically examine and keep current with emerging knowledge relevant to social work" (section 5.02c). Critical examination of personal experiences, the experiences of others, traditions, and research methods can contribute to evidence-based practices in social work. The ability to use critical thinking to determine how reliable the information is is an important skill for all social work practitioners. Incompatible findings are the result of different decisions made by researchers, and this book will teach you to determine which studies are relatively better.

Qualitative, Quantitative, and Mixed-Method Research

There are two overarching ways of gathering data, or fields of research. These are qualitative research methods and quantitative research methods. **Qualitative research** is concerned with developing knowledge where little or none exists and uses words, observations, and descriptions to develop this knowledge. **Quantitative research** is concerned with expanding knowledge that already exists and using numerical data to report the findings from the research. But, perhaps you want to use both qualitative and quantitative methods, or a mixed-method design, in your research. A **mixed-method design** allows researchers to design a study using both qualitative and quantitative methods by using numerical and textual data.

Qualitative Research

Social work is a profession that owes a large debt of gratitude to many other disciplines. Anthropology, psychology, sociology, and medicine have all contributed to the development of our profession. One of the areas in which this becomes exceedingly clear is the field of qualitative research. Qualitative research has deep roots in the fields of anthropology and sociology, where the development of rigorous and exact methods for fieldwork has long been fostered.

The use of qualitative research methods is debated among social work practitioners, faculty, researchers, and other professionals. It is generally agreed that qualitative research is employed when little or nothing is known about a subject, or when the researcher wants to gain an in-depth understanding of a person's experience. Some may argue that qualitative methods are better suited for studies on complicated topics such as a person's comfort level with death, how it feels to be unemployed, or how a child views the drinking habits of an alcoholic parent. Qualitative research primarily relies on information generated from observations of the researcher and discussions and interviews with study participants. However, researchers engaged in qualitative research might also gather some descriptive information such as the demographics of participants and their settings in order to place their experiences within a context. In their simplest form, qualitative research methods are used to help us understand the characteristics of a phenomenon. Often this type of research uncovers these characteristics by focusing on the ideas of the people involved.

As an example, let us imagine for a moment that you are a case manager at a homeless shelter and the year is 1982. You have noticed that a large number of your consumers who report being intravenous drug users are also suffering from a strange new illness that seems to impair their immune system. You may be aware that AIDS was a relatively unknown disease in 1982 and that scientists were just beginning to understand the causes of the transmission of this disease. As a case manager, you may want to design a qualitative study that will help you explore the experiences of those who are suffering from this disease by interviewing people living with AIDS (recording their own words). You may also want to collect some demographic information such as sex, age, race, and length of illness to describe their experiences within the context of the research population.

Quantitative Research

Advocates of quantitative research argue that it is only through the use of methods that report numerical representation that the social sciences can become truly valid. Quantitative research seeks to explain relationships between two or more factors. The aim of quantitative research is to determine how one thing (a variable) affects another in a population. A **variable** is any attribute or characteristic that changes or assumes different values. Variables can represent subject characteristics (e.g., age, race, sex) or the things you are really interested in (e.g., agency performance; rate of relapse in addiction treatment; physiological, psychological, or sociological causes of child maltreatment). Variables can also represent the effect of any intervention that subjects receive, such as a cultural sensitivity training.

Mixed-Method Research

Mixed-method research uses both qualitative and quantitative research designs. Using more than one research method while collecting and analyzing data in a study is called *concurrent mixed-method research*. When data collected through the use of one type of research design provides a basis for the collection of data using the other type, this is called *sequential mixed-method research*. When data are analyzed one way and then analyzed again in another way, it is called *conversion mixed-method research*.

There are several reasons to use a mixed-method design. Among these are that it can test the consistency of findings obtained through different forms of data collection. This is referred to as *triangulation*; this means that the findings from the methods used are consistent and support each other. Or a researcher might use a mixed-method design because it allows him or her to use qualitative methods to add richness and detail to the results obtained from the use of quantitative methods. Researchers may also choose a mixed-method design so they can use results from one method to shape subsequent methods or steps in the research process. This is frequently seen when a qualitative study is used to shape a quantitative study. In addition, mixed-method research can be used as a means to develop new research questions or to use one method to challenge results obtained through another method.

Developing Your Research Questions

You may be asking yourself at this point, "Where do research questions originate?" Research questions may arise from your personal experience. Thus, a person who was adopted may feel compelled to study the factors that make adoptions work well for children. Research questions may develop out of research articles or theories you are studying. A **theory** is a statement or set of statements designed to explain a phenomenon based upon observations and experiments and often agreed upon by most experts in a particular field. For example, you may want to test the credibility of the claims put forth by a developmental theory on aging that you learned about in one of your human behavior classes. Research questions may arise out of your own practice experience. Regardless of the source, most questions are born out of the researcher's personal interest in a subject.

To illustrate this process, we may begin with an observation ("This person smiles at me and goes out of her way to help me"), then we have an idea ("This person would make a good friend"), and then we develop a question ("Does this person like me?"). We can examine this question by drawing from our past experiences, by consulting others, or by asking the person directly.

When you are developing research questions, there are some issues to keep in mind. The first thing to consider is whether the question is empirical. This means the researcher must decide whether it can be quantified. For example, a question such as "What is the best religion?" is both value laden and subjective ("the best"). As a researcher, you need to be careful to remember that we can study values in order to understand what others think, but we cannot conduct research on values in order to evaluate them. Therefore, we can approach value-laden issues through qualitative methods that are meant to deal with the subjective questions that we have—this eliminates any objectivity from the research. "How many people cheat on their partner?" or "Has having an abortion prevented further unwanted pregnancies?" are both examples of questions that attempt to quantify issues of moral worth and can be measured through quantitative methods.

What Is a Hypothesis?

A **hypothesis** is a research statement about relationships between variables that is testable and that can be accepted or rejected based on the evidence. Therefore, you can only develop hypotheses that are quantifiable. To design a study to test your hypothesis, you use quantitative research methods. Hypotheses are divided into two categories: research hypotheses and null hypotheses. The research hypothesis asserts that that there is a relationship between the variables, and the null hypothesis claims that the relationship between the variables can be rejected. In other words, the null hypothesis is what the researcher is attempting to reject. For example, we may have a null hypothesis that no difference exists between a treatment group and a nontreatment group after intervention. If this is rejected, then the research hypothesis that the treatment group will be different from the nontreatment group after intervention (e.g., less sick or more educated) is supported. Hypotheses are typically abbreviated as H_o (null hypothesis), H_a (research hypothesis), and H_1, H_2, H_3 (a number is used when there is more than one research hypothesis).

Imagine that you are working at an emergency shelter with a consumer named Joe. Joe is in need of permanent housing (he has been living on the streets for the past two years). While you are collecting assessment history with Joe, he discloses that he has a long history of drug abuse. One initial hypothesis may be "A history of substance abuse is related to not having stable housing." In further discussions with Joe, you explore this hypothesis with him, and he confirms that his substance abuse has interfered with his ability to seek and keep a job—a strong factor in his being homeless. You then decide to design a research study to determine if this relationship between substance abuse and homelessness exists beyond your client. You can also test a second hypothesis that looks at the relationship between substance abuse and unemployment.

Research Designs

There are different designs that researchers can chose from to collect data in conducting qualitative, quantitative, and mixed-method research. Exploratory designs are exclusively grounded in qualitative research, and explanatory designs are exclusively grounded in quantitative research. Descriptive designs, evaluative designs, and single-subject designs can draw from either or both types of research.

Exploratory Research Designs

An **exploratory research design** is a type of research design that allows us to use our powers of observation, inquiry, and assessment to form tentative theories about what we are seeing and experiencing. It is generally used to explore understudied topics. In essence, we need to find out about a phenomenon. By asking an **open-ended question** (that is, a question that is worded in a way that allows the respondent to answer in his or her own words as opposed to merely soliciting a yes-or-no response) and observing the environment, we can begin to identify common themes from the information we gather. For instance, imagine you are a crisis call worker shortly after the 9/11 terrorist attacks. You are receiving a high volume of calls from rescue workers involved in the recovery of human remains. You have little or no knowledge about this experience; therefore, you explore the callers' experiences with them by asking questions such as "What is it like for you?" After listening to several workers, you might discover evidence of a common theme, for example, that the callers have been experiencing periods of tearfulness. Based on this evidence, you can then tell other callers that this experience appears to be common among rescue workers.

Explanatory Research Designs

An **explanatory research design** is a type of research design that focuses on examining the relationships between two or more factors and attempts to determine if they are related, and if so, in what ways and how strongly they are related.

For example, you may believe there is a relationship between the amount of time students spend studying for their research methods class and their final course grade in that class. Your hypothesis might be "The more students study research methods, the better their grades in that course will be." In fact, you would be able to find studies that have provided evidence that a relationship exists. If you were so inclined, it would be possible to design a study to examine just how strong the relationship is between hours spent studying and final course grades.

Descriptive Research Designs

In a sense, all research is descriptive by nature, as it describes how and/ or why a phenomenon occurs. Qualitative research methods do this using words, and quantitative research methods using numbers. A **descriptive research design** is a method that can be used to seek information that uses numeric language (how many, how much, etc.) to describe a population or phenomenon. This can be used in both qualitative and quantitative methods of research. For example, if you were conducting a quantitative study of victims of domestic violence, you may want to collect information on certain characteristics, such as their average age, what percentage of them have children, and the type of abuse and how frequently it occurs. You might also ask them to interpret the severity of the last abuse episode, using a scale from 1 to 5. It is important to note here that although this type of research looks at patterns such as how often an event occurs or ways that responses develop in relation to each other, it does not try to address why these patterns exist.

Descriptive information is also collected during qualitative studies to help put the experiences into context with the population reporting them. For example, while conducting interviews with 9/11 rescue workers, you might also collect information on how many of these individuals are firefighters, police officers, health professionals, volunteer civilians, and so forth. By using this mixed-method design, you may also be reporting how frequently the rescue workers reported similar textual information—for example, "Six out of ten volunteers stated they would volunteer again, regardless of the difficulties they are experiencing now."

Evaluative Research Designs

Evaluative designs can also draw from both fields of research. An **evaluative research design** draws from qualitative research methods when statements made in interviews and focus groups and written comments are used to describe outcomes. For instance, positive comments from a survey may be included in a program evaluation to demonstrate consumer satisfaction. Evaluative designs can also draw from the quantitative field of research. For instance, an evaluative design might examine how many and what type of residents were serviced at an agency over the last month.

Single-Subject Designs

Finally, a **single-subject design** uses systematic methodology to measure an individual's progress over time and measures whether a relationship exists between an intervention and a specific outcome. These designs can also draw from either or both methods of research. In a study using qualitative methods, the consumer's own statement that he or she is suicidal might be used to justify an extension for mental health treatment from an insurance company.

Strengths and Limitations of Research

A major strength of research is that it can help us gain an understanding of many social problems. Through research, we can gain knowledge of issues such as child maltreatment, domestic violence, and substance abuse. Another benefit is that research has led to the development of new agency policies, greater practice accountability, evidence-based treatment strategies, and new knowledge.

Research also has inherent limitations. First, research is conducted in small steps that are often repeated to build evidence. Each new study adds to the overall body of knowledge, which is a strength. However, knowledge is built slowly over time—not in quantum leaps. A second limitation of research is that the knowledge that it yields is confined to the questions that are asked. Only by asking enough relevant questions can we obtain useful answers. Finally, research is subject to bias. **Bias** is the unknown or unacknowledged error created during the design of the research method, in the choice of problem to be studied, over the course of the study itself, or during the interpretation of findings. This is not to say that the research is necessarily flawed—only limited. For example, if your study examines parents' use of corporal punishment with their children but all your research participants are white, your findings are racially biased. Therefore, bias can be unintentional and sometimes unavoidable but must always be identified as a limitation.

Applied Learning Activities

Activity #1

Use the four ways of knowing—your own experience, your knowledge of others, tradition, and scientific methods—to explain how you know the following statement is factual: "Americans celebrate the Fourth of July."

Activity #2

1. You are working on a presidential campaign and want to know how your classmates would vote in the upcoming election. How would you state your research question? What research design would you choose to carry out your study, and why?

2. Is the design you selected a qualitative, quantitative, or mixed-method design?

Key Points

- Research is the process of systematically gaining information.

- Research is becoming increasingly important as governing agencies demand evidence that programs and practices are effective.

- Knowledge is gained through our own experiences, through others, through tradition, and through the use of scientific methods.

- There are two types of research methods: qualitative research methods and quantitative research methods. When both research methods are used, this is called a mixed-method design.

- Research questions may arise from personal experience, out of research articles or theories under study, or out of practice experience and are born out of the researcher's personal interest in a subject.

- Hypotheses are research statements about relationships between variables that are testable and that can be accepted or rejected based on the findings from a study.

- Exploratory research designs allow the researcher to use his or her powers of observation, inquiry, and assessment to form tentative theories about what is being seen and experienced. They attempt to explain the relationship between two or more factors.

- Descriptive research designs use descriptive language to provide information about a phenomenon.

- Evaluative research designs can draw from both qualitative and quantitative research methods.

- Single-subject designs are used to measure a person's progress over time.

Additional Resources

Boas, M. (1962). *The scientific renaissance, 1450–1630*. New York: Harper and Row.
The author discusses historical topics such as the discovery of the human circulatory system, alchemy, and the effect Copernicus's telescope had on the rest of the scientific community.

Ellis, L. (1994). *Research methods in the social sciences*. Madison, WI: WCB, Brown & Benchmark.
Ellis focuses on research within psychology, sociology, social work, and other human sciences. The author utilizes a straightforward approach to explain both research methodology and statistics.

Elmes, D., Kantowitz, B., & Roediger, H. (2006). *Research methods in psychology* (8th ed.). Belmont, CA: Wadsworth/Thomson Learning.
First published in 1981, this textbook is currently in its eighth edition, which attests to the durability of the text. The book continues to expand and evolve as the authors' own idea about research change. The text, while focused on the discipline of psychology, is highly readable and understandable.

Tashakkori, A., & Teddlie, C. (2003). *Handbook of mixed methods in the social and behavioral research*. Thousand Oaks, CA: Sage.
This book has been receiving increasing attention as mixed-method designs have become more popular. It offers practical advice on how to design and conduct mixed-method research.

CHAPTER TWO

Ethical Considerations

JUST AS ETHICS IS AN IMPORTANT PART of our interactions with consumers and colleagues, and in carrying out social work practice on a daily basis, ethics is also important when we are conducting research. This chapter will introduce you to some ethical principles and applications used in research, including the protection of the rights of research participants.

Historical Overview

Today, most countries have laws in effect that require human subjects to be treated with dignity and respect in the conduct of research. The United States has regulations in place providing guidance and structure for the researcher. What is the history behind these regulations? It may surprise you to know that the impetus for these regulations and the implementation of oversight committees was research done during World War II.

In 1946, an American military tribunal opened a criminal trial in Nuremberg, Germany, against twenty-three Nazi physicians. These physicians were accused of conducting horrific medical experiments on prisoners at various concentration camps. After 140 days of proceedings during which eighty-five witnesses testified and 1,500 documents were entered as evidence, sixteen doctors were found guilty, and seven were sentenced to death. From this trial came the Nuremberg Code, ten principles for permissible medical experiments:

1. The voluntary consent of the human subject is absolutely essential.
2. The experiment should be such as to yield fruitful results for the

good of society, unprocurable by other methods or means of study, and not random or unnecessary in nature.

3. The experiment should be so designed and based on the results of animal experimentation and a knowledge of the natural history of the disease or other problem under study, that the anticipated results will justify the performance of the experiment.

4. The experiment should be so conducted as to avoid all unnecessary physical and mental suffering and injury.

5. No experiment should be conducted where there is an a priori reason to believe that death or disabling injury will occur; except, perhaps, in those experiments where the experimental physicians also serve as subjects.

6. The degree of risk to be taken should never exceed that determined by the humanitarian importance of the problem to be solved by the experiment.

7. Proper preparations should be made and adequate facilities provided to protect the experimental subjects against even remote possibilities of injury, disability, or death.

8. The experiment should be conducted only by scientifically qualified persons. The highest degree of skill and care should be required through all stages of the experiment of those who conduct or engage in the experiment.

9. During the course of the experiment, the human subject should be at liberty to bring the experiment to an end, if he has reached the physical or mental state where continuation of the experiment seemed to him to be impossible.

10. During the course of the experiment, the scientist in charge must be prepared to terminate the experiment at any stage, if he has probable cause to believe, in the exercise of the good faith, superior skill and careful judgment required of him, that a continuation of the experiment is likely to result in injury, disability, or death to the experimental subject.

At this point you may be thinking, "How does this apply to *me*?" In this chapter, we will examine three ethical principles that social workers can use to protect human subjects in research.

Public Law 93–348, called the National Research Act, was signed into law on July 12, 1974, and addresses the protection of human subjects in research. It recognizes that research and practice may occur together and that any element of research should undergo review for the protection of human subjects. The Belmont Report, published in 1979, summarizes the law as proposing three basic ethical principles: respect for individuals, beneficence, and justice.

Respect for Individuals

Respect for individuals involves acknowledging the autonomy of individuals and protecting those with diminished autonomy. Section 5.02l of the Code of Ethics of the National Association of Social Workers (1999) states that "Social workers engaged in evaluation or research should ensure the anonymity or confidentiality of participants and of the data obtained from them. Social workers should inform participants of any limits of confidentiality." With this in mind, we will first discuss the concepts of anonymity, confidentiality, and informed consent. We will then discuss how to protect those whose capacity to make autonomous decisions is limited.

Anonymity

Anonymity is often confused with confidentiality. In research, **anonymity** means that the researcher will not collect any identifying information on the subjects participating in the research study. For instance, you design an exploratory study in which you will collect information on how consumers feel about the services in your agency. One way to do this is to have a comment box in the lobby or waiting room; consumers can write comments on a blank piece of paper and put them the box. This allows the individual to remain anonymous. However, you notice that only consumers with complaints are making use of the comment box. You then decide to do a descriptive study for which you develop a form that allows consumers to rate their satisfaction with various services on a scale from 1 to 4. To maintain the anonymity of the participants, you do not ask for any information that can be used to identify them, such as name, age, or occupation. Everyone checking into your agency is handed the form and asked to complete it before they leave and place it in the comment box. These are examples of a study using both qualitative and quantitative methods that protect the anonymity of the participants.

Confidentiality

Confidentiality is the assurance that a researcher provides to subjects that all information about them, and all answers they provide, will remain in the hands of the investigator and that no person outside the research process will have access to this information. Subjects have a basic right to know that their information is kept confidential; this also ensures that they feel protected from potential repercussions for answering honestly. The researcher, however, may have the ability to identify the responses of a particular individual. You may be asking, "How then do researchers publish their findings if all information remains confidential?" The answer is that all information is reported in the aggregate (i.e., the findings are combined). The researcher compiles the data and presents it in such a way that no individual can be identified.

Let's say that you are conducting a six-week smoking cessation workshop. You want to follow up with your participants in six months to see how many remain free of cigarettes, how many times they relapsed, and how many returned to smoking on a regular basis. In addition to this descriptive (quantitative) data, you will ask them for written comments (qualitative data) on what worked for them, what did not work for them, what was helpful about the workshop, and what was not helpful. The quantitative and qualitative data you collect will be included in a grant proposal to fund additional workshops. In your summary, you would not state that John Smith relapsed twice and found that cinnamon gum helped curb cravings. But you might say, "One participant relapsed twice and found that cinnamon gum helped curb cravings."

Confidentiality can also become an issue in more subtle ways, especially in small communities where the disclosure of too much information can result in the identification of an individual. For instance, you are reporting treatment outcomes of sex offenders to city council members. During your presentation you describe an offender by stating that "A recently released male sex offender with a history of child molestation has recently reoffended. He has only been in treatment for three months, and our statistics show that those in treatment over six months have a better chance of not reoffending." The audience may be able to identify this individual through news articles and even common knowledge about his recent release or arrest. One way you could have reported your research findings anonymously would have been to report the data in aggregate. In this example, you could report percentages, such as "One hundred percent of participants in treatment less than six months have reoffended, while only 54 percent of participants in treatment over six months have reoffended." The Code of Ethics of the National Association of Social Workers (1999) states that "Social workers who report evaluation and research results should protect participants' confidentiality by omitting identifying information unless proper consent has been obtained authorizing disclosure" (section 5.02m).

Informed Consent

Informed consent is the process of educating potential research participants about the basic purpose of the study, informing them that their participation is voluntary, and obtaining their written consent to participate
in the study. Informed consent involves the researcher helping potential
participants to understand exactly what is being asked of them, and what
their participation will entail. Ingelfinger (1972) argues that informed consent can never be entirely complete. On the other hand, Gorovitz (1985)
believes that the individual has dominion over his or her own body and is
responsible for what happens to him or her. In some ways, both are correct.
As a researcher, it is your responsibility to provide as much information as
possible to potential participants so that they can decide whether they wish
to participate. The ethical researcher will take care to sit down with the
participant and explain in detail what will be required and what will happen during the study.

The practice of informed consent is an important part of any study. One
small part of the informed consent process is asking a research participant
to sign a statement that outlines the information provided in the informed
consent process (see example 2.1). It is important to note that informed
consent must be obtained before any data are collected. In addition, if you
are offering an incentive for participation (for example, a gift certificate at
a fast-food restaurant) in your study, then the subject will receive the incentive regardless whether or not he or she completes the study. The Code
of Ethics of the National Association of Social Workers (1999) states that
"Informed consent should include information about the nature, extent,
and duration of the participation requested and disclosure of the risks and
benefits of participation in the research" (section 5.02e). In addition, section 5.01h states that "Social workers should inform participants of their
right to withdraw from evaluation and research at any time without penalty." The informed consent form must provide the following information:

1. The researcher's identity and the nature and aim of the research
2. The subject's role in the project and the expected duration of the
    subject's participation
3. A description of experimental procedures and any possible risks
    to the subject's physical, psychological, or emotional well-being
4. Any benefits to the subject that may reasonably be expected from
    the research
5. Contact information that subjects can use to obtain answers to
    questions about the research and research subjects' rights, and

EXAMPLE 2.1: INFORMED CONSENT FORM

Dear Participant:

My name is _____. I am requesting your help with a research project I am conducting on the effects of challenge courses. Let me emphasize that you do not have to take part in anything that makes you uncomfortable. If you do not wish to take part in this project (or any of the exercises), you do not have to participate. This is true, also, for the attached questionnaire. You are free to refuse to answer any and all of the questions. The survey is voluntary (up to you), and you can withdraw from the study at any time.

If you agree to participate in the challenge course experience, you will be asked to participate in activities that require you to work with others as a group to solve problems and perform tasks. The facilitator/trainer will explain each activity before you begin.

Challenge courses are supervised by trained facilitators who are experienced and able to keep participants safe. The potential benefits for those who participate in the challenge course are increased communication and trust with group members.

This study has been reviewed to determine that participants' rights are safeguarded, and there appears to be minimal risk or discomfort associated with completion of this study. The answers you provide on the study will be kept strictly confidential, and all your responses (completed surveys) will be stored in a locked file cabinet accessible only to the researcher. This means that no one will be able to find out how you answered any of the questions. The results of this study may be presented at a conference or published as a research article in a journal. These records will be kept in Jones Hall, 100 University Drive, Anytown, Anystate, 10011. Please feel free to ask for help if something does not make sense to you or if you have any questions. If you experience any discomfort, you may contact Jane Smith, Caring Hands Help Agency, 101-000-1234.

If you decide to volunteer, please be sure to PRINT your name on the form and SIGN it to indicate your willingness to participate. That will be indication that you understand the purpose of the survey and that you are willing to help.

Name (Print): _____

Signature: _____

Date Signed: _____

information on whom to contact in the event of a research-related injury or if counseling is needed due to the sensitive nature of the questions

In addition, the informed consent form must

1. Explain to prospective subjects that they are free to refuse to participate or to refuse to answer any question or to withdraw from the study at any time, and that refusal to participate or withdrawal from the project will involve no penalty or loss of benefits to which the subjects are otherwise entitled;
2. Describe how the confidentiality of the information will be maintained (e.g., surveys, audiotapes, or videotapes will be kept in a locked filing cabinet) and the anonymity of the participants will be protected;
3. Explain that participants must be eighteen years of age or older, or parental/guardian consent must be obtained; and
4. Provide verification statement and signature line for participants ("By signing below, I verify that I have been informed of and understand the nature and purpose of the project, freely consent to participate, and am at least eighteen years of age").

Social workers have a long-standing tradition of being the voice (i.e., advocate) of the person who has the least amount of power in a situation. This should be the guiding principle when you are designing your research study with any person who is considered to have diminished autonomy. These populations include individuals who have diminished rights or capacities, including minors; individuals with diminished capacity due to illness or mental disability; and people with severely restricted liberties, such as individuals who are incarcerated.

The legal guardians of minors and individuals with diminished capacity can weigh the risks and benefits of the research and then decide either with or for them whether or not they will participate in a research study. Section 5.02f of the Code of Ethics, states: "When evaluation or research participants are incapable of giving informed consent, social workers should provide an appropriate explanation to the participants, obtain the participants' assent to the extent they are able, and obtain written consent from an appropriate proxy." In example 2.2, the signature lines were modified for the addition of consent of a parent or guardian (or power of attorney).

EXAMPLE 2.2: MODIFIED SIGNATURE LINES FOR CONSENT OF A LEGAL GUARDIAN

If you decide to volunteer, please be sure to PRINT your name on the form and SIGN it to indicate your willingness to participate. That will be indication that you understand the purpose of the survey and that you are willing to help.

Name (Print): _____

Signature: _____

Name of Legal Guardian (Print): _____

Signature of Legal Guardian: _____

Date Signed: _____

Informed consent is much more complicated for individuals with restricted liberties because the pressure to volunteer may come from the authorities in charge of their liberties. Volunteerism is an element of informed consent that requires the person to be free of coercion and undue influence. On the other hand, the individual may *want* to be involved in the research, and denying that opportunity can also be viewed as a restriction of his or her rights. While there is no easy answer to the dilemma posed by such situations, one should examine whether the benefits of participating outweigh the risks. For instance, let's say you are researching the effectiveness of a six-week anger management group. The possible benefits of participating in the treatment may outweigh the risk that the individual may feel obligated to participate. On the other hand, if you are researching homophobia among males, the risk of harm is much greater, and the benefits nonexistent.

Beneficence

The term **beneficence** refers to being charitable or acting with kindness. In research it is an obligation to do no harm and to maximize any **benefits** (i.e., positive values related to health or well-being) while minimizing possible harm. The issue of beneficence relates to determining whether the benefits (which can be direct or indirect and can seem large or small to the participant) outweigh the risks for the participants of the study. To minimize harm, we must identify the risks of the research on human participants.

The Code of Ethics of the National Association of Social Workers (1999) states that "Social workers engaged in evaluation or research should protect participants from unwarranted physical or mental distress, harm, danger, or deprivation" (section 5.02j). Participants need to be protected from the risks of participating in research. **Risk** refers to the possibility that psychological, physical, legal, social, or economic harm may occur. Risk is sometimes expressed in levels, such as, "no risk," "little risk," "moderate risk," and "high risk." Much has been learned from past research studies that have involved a level of risk to the individual participants. One of these has come to be known as the Tuskegee syphilis experiment (1932–1972), a study conducted by the U.S. Public Health Service on a group of mostly poor African American men with syphilis living in the rural South. They were not told that they had syphilis so that the researchers could examine the etiology (progression) of the disease (Jones, 1981). Even after a cure in the form of penicillin became available, they were not offered treatment, which caused long-term health issues for the men and their families. This high level of physical risk would be considered unethical today.

In 1961, psychologist Stanley Milgram conducted an infamous study of how authority figures could abuse their power. Milgram designed a series of experiments in which subjects were instructed to administer a series of electric shocks to another subject. Unbeknownst to those administering the shocks, the individuals who were supposedly being shocked were actually working with the researcher. A disturbing number of subjects were willing to administer dangerously high levels of voltage even though the people they thought they were shocking were pleading for them to stop. Several subjects said they did not feel comfortable continuing with the experiment but continued, regardless, when told to do so by the researcher (Milgram, 1963). To some people this research was a worthwhile endeavor, as it provides evidence of the strong influence those in authority can have over others. One would only have to point to such tragedies as the atrocities carried out under the Nazis as justification for Milgram's study. However, others might argue that the potential trauma this study could cause the participants outweighs the benefit of the information it could provide. (Accounts of follow-up studies with research participants in the study who said they were not permanently harmed by the research have been published.)

Another study that has become somewhat infamous in research circles is a study conducted by a professor of psychology at Stanford University. Philip Zimbardo converted part of a basement in one of the buildings at Stanford into a makeshift prison and recruited students for the study. The students were randomly assigned to be either prisoners or guards. Within a few days, the subjects over-identified with the roles they were playing. Subjects who had been assigned the roles of guards became sadistic and mistreated the individuals assigned to be prisoners. The subjects playing the roles of prisoners soon began to identify as prisoners and worked to plot against the guards (Haney, Banks, & Zimbardo, 1973). The risk for psychological, physical, and legal harm was so great that the study, which was originally intended to last two weeks, was abandoned after a few days.

A debate still rages today (Haney & Zimbardo, 1998) as to whether the information that was gained from these studies (benefits) outweighed the potential harm (risks) to participants. Our point is not to enter into this debate but to illustrate that the regulations governing research were established to ensure the safety and rights of those participating in research.

Debriefing is the process of fully informing subjects of the nature of the research when some form of deception has been employed or when information is not disclosed. Rarely is it necessary for a researcher to deceive subjects. However, there may be times when fully disclosing the exact nature of the research will cause the subjects to act in a way that will skew (alter) the results. For instance, in medication research, participants are frequently placed into three groups. One group gets the new drug, one group gets a drug that is already on the market, and one group gets a placebo. It is not until after the experiment has concluded that research participants are debriefed as to which group they participated in. The Code of Ethics of the National Association of Social Workers (1999) states that "Social workers should take appropriate steps to ensure that participants in evaluation and research have access to appropriate supportive services" (section 5.02i).

In debriefing participants, the researcher must describe the nature and aim of the project, explain why participants were misled or provide information that participants were not previously given, and provide the name and phone number of the person to contact in case participants have questions regarding the project. In addition, it is strongly suggested that the researcher have subjects sign a statement (or other form of documentation) stating that the subjects have been debriefed and all questions about the project have been answered.

Justice

The principle of justice finds its application in the moral requirement that fair procedures and outcomes be used in the selection of research subjects. Justice is the fairness of distribution of benefits and risks among all individuals. This principle can be formulated in four ways: to each person an equal share, to each person according to individual need, to each person according to individual effort, and to each person according to merit. Often in research, vulnerable populations such as the homeless, people of color, institutionalized individuals, and those living in poverty bear the burden of risky research endeavors, whereas those with more influence, wealth, and power are selected for research that has potential benefits.

The Tuskegee syphilis experiment is a good example of researchers imposing potential risks on an unknowing vulnerable population. In an agency-based setting, the convenience of already having a population to research can create opportunities for beneficial interventions, such as new programs. For example, an agency offering and using research to evaluate an evening recovery program for residents of a homeless shelter has benefits for participants. When this recovery program is opened to the public, those benefits are available to everyone.

This becomes problematic when the population is burdened with risky interventions, such as "holding" therapy techniques. Therapeutic holding is a commonly used intervention in residential facilities for the containment of aggressive behavior in children. Although often effective, the intervention has inherent physical and emotional safety risks.

Other Ethical Considerations

The Code of Ethics of the National Association of Social Workers (1999) states that "Social workers should report evaluation and research findings accurately. They should not fabricate or falsify results and should take steps to correct any errors later found in published data using standard publication methods" (section 5.02n). This code addresses two ethical issues: reporting findings accurately and not falsifying data. In research this is called laundering data and faking data.

Sometimes data from real-world sources are erroneous, incomplete, or inconsistent. For instance, on a survey a research participant might select "highly unsatisfied," thinking that he or she is selecting "highly satisfied." Data are incomplete when one of the ten questions asked on a survey is left unanswered. Data are inconsistent when one out of one hundred surveys has responses that are so different from the others that the answers are considered abnormal in the findings. To deal with erroneous, incomplete, and inconsistent data, researchers sometimes clean up the data, which is called laundering data. **Laundering data** is a way of statistically manipulating the data collected to reduce errors and make the findings more accurate. One way one can achieve this is by removing the abnormal responses from the data. However, most applications for laundering data require more complicated statistical techniques, such as grouping the data into blocks, reorganizing the data into tables, then regrouping it into blocks after adjustments are made. The opportunity to manipulate the statistics to support a hypothesis or desired outcome can be tempting. The problem arises in how the manipulation is constructed; this can pose ethical problems if the results do not accurately reflect the findings.

Unfortunately, falsifying or faking data, while not often easily identified, can and does occur. **Faking data** is making up desired data or eliminating undesired data in research findings. One example of faking data would be to duplicate or multiply the answers collected in a research study in order to increase the number of responses. If only five people responded, the researcher might repeat their answers ten times and now have fifty responses. The findings are more convincing with a larger sample and can allow for more rigorous statistical analyses (discussed in chapters 10 and 11). Another example is to simply not include responses that do not support the hypothesis. For instance, researchers have collected data on how satisfied clients are with the services at their agency. They throw out some negative responses and keep all the positive responses to increase the percentage of clients reporting satisfaction. Perhaps the most devious type of faking is simply making up findings without conducting the research. This can occur when a person mimics another research study but changes the characteristics and findings.

There are as many reasons for faking data as there are examples, such as wanting findings to support a hypothesis, increasing the chances of publication, providing evidence needed to apply for or continue a funded grant, or even meeting requirements of a class project.

One final ethical issue encountered in research that is often overlooked (especially by students) is plagiarism. The Code of Ethics of the National Association of Social Workers states that "Social workers should take responsibility and credit, including authorship credit, only for work they have actually performed and to which they have contributed" and "Social workers should honestly acknowledge the work of and the contributions made by others" (section 4.08). Being ethical as a social worker means not only conducting research in a humane manner, but also giving credit to others' work. The research process depends on an assumption that people are being honest and forthcoming when they write papers and report findings. If researchers, instructors, and students fail to be honest in their work, the entire process loses credibility and the research process becomes suspect. The issue of plagiarism has become an increasing concern among educators in the past few years. With the invention of the Internet, it has become increasingly easy for students to take advantage of others' work without assigning proper credit to the true authors.

In its simplest form, **plagiarism** means taking credit for work that is not one's own, either in whole or in part. This can take many forms, including copying or repeating research without giving proper credit. Individuals who plagiarize are not always intentionally being deceitful; many simply do not understand that when you use someone else's ideas, words, or work you need to give proper credit. This means citing other people's work in the body of your paper and on the reference page. The same is true when a person paraphrases someone else's thoughts. The rule of thumb is if you utilize another person's work, you need to give him or her credit. If you quote that person, then his or her words are enclosed in quotation marks and proper citation is given. If you utilize the person's thoughts or main ideas but paraphrase what he or she wrote, then you need to cite the person. Providing proper citations is more than a matter of ethical integrity in research—it is a form of courtesy shown to other authors and researchers.

An **institutional review board** (IRB) is a committee mandated by the federal government to oversee the protection of human and animal subjects in research. Any institution of higher learning that receives federal money (including financial aid for students) has an IRB committee that oversees research with human subjects and animals and ensures that all research is conducted in a safe, ethical, and humane manner. Hospitals and other facilities that conduct research with humans or animals also have committees to ensure that research is carried out in a humane manner. A review board can be beneficial to researchers by ensuring compliance with ethical practices and standards that protect the rights of research participants. In fact, the Code of Ethics of the National Association of Social Workers (1999) states that "Social workers engaged in evaluation or research should carefully consider possible consequences and should follow guidelines developed for the protection of evaluation and research participants. Appropriate institutional review boards should be consulted" (section 5.02d).

Federal regulations stipulate that research that is conducted for the purposes of publication or presentation or to contribute to knowledge must gain IRB approval. If you plan to present your research in a journal or at a conference, plan to submit your research to the IRB at your institution. In addition, some universities require students to submit a research protocol and meet the board's requirements when conducting research as part of a class project. It is a good idea to keep in mind the principles established by these boards and to incorporate them into your own research. The first and foremost issue to consider is the safety of your subjects. It is imperative that as a researcher you always consider the issue of what might go wrong. It is a good idea to keep in mind Murphy's Law (if something can go wrong, it probably will).

Applied Learning Activities

Activity #1

You are a case manager at a homeless shelter located in a large city. The shelter has one hundred beds and provides emergency shelter for men, women, and families with children. Residents of the shelter are allowed to stay for up to ninety days. The goals of the shelter are to help consumers obtain employment, secure permanent housing, and access health care and to identify other services needed. Your task as a case manager is to link them to the necessary services.

As an employee of the shelter for the past four years, you have developed a hypothesis that certain case management techniques seem to be more effective than others with the residents of the shelter. These techniques are intensive case management (meeting with residents at least twice per week), developing goal attainment scales with each resident, and requesting that each of your residents keep a detailed log of daily activities.

1. What does the Code of Ethics say about evaluating your practice?

2. What should the overarching ethical principles in designing a study be?

3. Does the potential for harm exist? If so, what will you do to protect human subjects?

4. How will you address the issues of confidentiality and anonymity?

Activity #2

You are a social worker who works at a domestic violence shelter. Your job is to provide services to children of the women who enter the shelter. The shelter has capacity for fifteen children, and your caseload averages about ten to twelve children each month. Your job is to link the children with counseling services, medical care, and other social services as needed. In the past three months, you have noticed that there has been an increase in aggressive behavior among the children in the shelter. You want to develop an intervention utilizing a play therapy technique that you learned in your social work classes and present your findings at a state conference for social workers. You design a study in which the children in the shelter are randomly placed in one of two groups. One group will receive play therapy, and the other group will receive no intervention. You will then compare the behaviors of the two groups of children. Before you implement this study, answer the following questions:

1. What does the Code of Ethics say about obtaining informed consent when children are used as research participants?

2. How will you address the issue of confidentiality for those mothers and their children who want to participate in the study?

3. What do you say to potential participants about their right to withdraw from the study?

4. Does the potential for harm exist? If so, what will you do to protect the subjects?

5. Are there potential benefits to the subject? What are they?

Activity #3

You are a social worker working for an agency that runs group homes for adults who are developmentally delayed. The four group homes have the capacity to house eight adults each. The ages of the adults in these homes range from thirty-one to forty, and they generally interact positively with each other. However, many of the adults engage in inappropriate touching and other sexual behavior. Your agency has decided to begin teaching sex education classes that will include a good touch/bad touch component in an effort to reduce the inappropriate behavior. The agency will phase in the curriculum, teaching it at one group home at a time. You decide to track the results for possible future publication. To do this, you will record the number of incidents of inappropriate behavior prior to the classes and then continue to record the number of incidents during and after the completion of the classes. You will compare these to the number of incidents at the other group homes that are waiting for the classes to be conducted. First, however, consider the following ethical issues:

1. How will you obtain the informed consent of your research participants?

2. In addition to the participants' informed consent, is it necessary to obtain any other signatures?

3. Is it possible to adequately inform your research participants of what you are asking of them?

4. If the answer to the previous question is no, is it ethical to proceed with the classes even if they agree to it?

5. Are there potential risks or harmful effects to the subjects? Are there potential benefits?

Key Points

- The three guiding principles for protecting human rights in research are respect for individuals, beneficence, and justice.

- Three methods for protecting human rights in research are confidentiality, anonymity, and informed consent.

- Confidentiality is the assurance that a researcher provides to subjects that all information about them, and all answers they provide, will remain in the hands of the investigator and that no other person outside the research process will have access to this information.

- Anonymity is the practice of not collecting any information that will identify the subject.

- Informed consent is letting potential subjects know what the basic purpose of the study will be and that their participation is voluntary, and obtaining their written permission to participate in the study.

- Debriefing is the process of fully informing subjects of the nature of the research when some form of deception has been employed.

- Plagiarism is the unauthorized use of another person's work and failure to give him or her credit.

- Institutional review boards oversee the rights of human subjects involved in research.

Additional Resources

Broad, W. (1980). Would-be academician pirates papers. *Science, 208,* 1438–1440.

The now infamous case described in this article is an example of unethical research practices. Elias A. K. Alsabti's license to practice medicine in Massachusetts was revoked because of articles he submitted for publication that were discovered to be plagiarized. The Board of Registration in Medicine found that this demonstrated a deficit in the moral character necessary for a physician to practice medicine. Later, the Supreme Court of Massachusetts upheld the revocation of his medical license.

Haney, C., Banks, W., & Zimbardo, P. (1973). Interpersonal dynamics in a simulated prison. *International Journal of Criminology and Penology, 1,* 69–97.

This article provides a detailed description of the Stanford prison experiment.

Haney, C., & Zimbardo, P. (1998). The past and future of United States prison policy: Twenty-five years after the Stanford prison experiment. *American Psychologist, 53(7),* 709–727.

The authors reflect on the experiment at Stanford University twenty-five years later. They examine the current state of correctional policy in the United States and provide some insights as to how social psychology might guide prison policy makers.

Jones, J. (1981). *Bad blood: The Tuskegee syphilis experiment.* New York: Free Press.

This book chronicles the study and the resulting legislation that made it mandatory for researchers to fully inform all subjects of their rights.

Milgram, S. (1974). *Obedience to authority: An experimental view.* New York: Harper and Row.

Milgram presents an expanded analysis of his now infamous studies on obedience to authority. In this text, Milgram discusses the conditions of the experiment and how subjects reacted to changes in the structure of the experiment.

Zimbardo, P. (1973). On the ethics of intervention in human psychological research: With special reference to the Stanford prison experiment. *Cognition, 2,* 243–256.

Zimbardo presents a "post-mortem" analysis of the Stanford prison experiment, which provoked a discussion about changing public policy regarding prisons and prison-like institutions (such as psychiatric hospitals). In this article, Zimbardo reacts to some critics who state that subjects were harmed by the experiment and claims that subjects suffered no lasting effects from the experiment.

CHAPTER THREE

Literature Review

THIS CHAPTER WILL INTRODUCE YOU TO the concept of the literature review. It will explain what a literature review is and how it is used to help the research process, the basic terminology found in research articles, and a six-step process for conducting a literature review. This chapter will also explore the role of the literature review in shaping the overall type of research you choose to conduct, and how a review of the existing literature can guide your development of a research question or hypothesis.

What Is a Literature Review?

Let us begin our exploration of a literature review with a definition of the term. A **literature review** is simply a search of the published research that allows you to synthesize what is known about the topic you are studying. To clarify, when we say "published research," we are talking about rigorous forms of research such as studies that appear in academic journals such as *Social Work and Research* and the *Journal of Poverty* as opposed to articles found in non-academic magazines such as *People* and *Time*.

Literature reviews are used to explore past research findings to direct and improve future research. Taking the time to search through articles and published research can be a tremendous time saver in the long run. It prevents you from reinventing a study that has already been conducted. A literature review can also provide a list of important variables, or the things being measured, or for which data is collected, that will guide your study. By researching what is known and what is not known, you can design a study to build on the knowledge and experience of others or to explore or expand knowledge where little or none exists.

A literature review can also help situate a study within a theoretical perspective. A **theoretical perspective** might best be viewed as a model that makes assumptions about something, attempts to integrate various kinds of information, gives meaning to what we see and experience, focuses on relationships and connections, and has inherent benefits and consequences.

Previous research can assist researchers in numerous ways. First, earlier studies can be used to develop a list of variables to use in a study. Moreover, by reviewing these articles, you can tell if a variable has been studied often and if these studies agree on the importance of the variable. This way you will know if you are addressing a neglected topic or trying to solve a long-running debate about the effects of a specific variable. Second, reading published articles can help students define tricky concepts, learn how to develop surveys, and see which groups of people have been overlooked in research.

A question that often arises is "How do I know when I have enough articles?" The answer is that there is no real way to know. There is always the possibility that another new study will be published in some obscure journal of which you are unaware. On the other hand, as you become more familiar with the literature, you will begin to recognize authors who have written on and researched a topic extensively. After conducting a thorough search of a subject, you will intuitively have a feel for the literature and a sense that you have a grasp of what is available. You do not have to read all the published works on a subject, as your intent is simply to gain an understanding of what is known. On the other hand, it is possible to not review enough articles. Nobody would take a study on a well-researched topic seriously if it only had five to ten citations.

Exactly how large a literature review needs to be for a quantitative study is a matter for discussion. One has to use judgment in deciding whether there is enough research to support a quantitative study. It is not so much an issue of the number of articles but more an issue of considering what research designs were employed and what knowledge was created as a result of those studies. The important thing to remember is that a literature review is not a one-time event. It is conducted several times throughout a study. During a qualitative study it would be conducted initially (to determine what has been published on a particular phenomenon) and again at the end of the study to help make sense of what has been found. In a quantitative study, the literature review is conducted initially to determine what is known and to guide the design of the research and can be added to during data collection. The literature review is conducted again at the end of the study to help interpret results, and to determine if any new literature has been published since the initial literature review.

Step 1: Conducting Your Search for Research Articles

Key Words

Begin by going to your campus library or an Internet browser to access databases. More will be said about relevant databases later in this chapter. Before beginning, you need to select some terms to narrow your search. These are known as **key words.** Key words are words selected as search terms in any database search. These words may be found in the abstract of the article and again as identifiers for the article.

Let us assume that you are a case manager working at a group home for children and you notice that a significant number of the children in the group home are displaying high levels of aggression toward other children. You want to design a study that will help you discover any common factors among the children that may be related to their aggression. For your search on children and aggressive behavior, you make a list of key words that includes the terms "childhood aggression," "physical aggression," and "aggressive behavior." These terms will define and narrow your search.

When conducting a search of the literature, you may conduct an initial search by entering key words in a database such as Social Work Abstracts and find few or no published articles on a subject. You then conduct a second search in another database such as PsycInfo because each discipline has a database that maintains descriptions of studies in its subfields. However, this search may reveal similar results. This would indicate, at least initially, the need to begin conceptualizing a qualitative study. However, if the same search reveals several studies, then clearly a quantitative study is in order.

Searching for Sources

The next step in this process is to decide where to search. A literature search is somewhat like a treasure hunt. When one reference has been found, this can lead to others, and so on, in an ever-expanding quest. For example, you may begin your search at your university or college library. By accessing the library database and typing in the words "childhood aggression" you may find the library contains over 10,000 articles, books, monographs, and other items containing that exact term. While browsing through the list, you find a book titled *Trajectories of Physical Aggression from Toddlerhood to Middle Childhood: Predictors, Correlates and Outcomes* that may be worth an initial investigation. The next step would be to review the book's bibliography or list of references. This list would then lead you to similar journal articles and studies that have been conducted on childhood aggression. This list, in addition to your original list, could guide you in your search for journal articles.

To list all the social service–related databases that exist would be impossible (new ones are created and old ones are deleted regularly). A reference librarian at your campus library will be happy to help you review the databases available at your campus. Many social work students limit their searches to social work databases such as Social Work Abstracts. This database is an excellent resource; however, we caution you to not limit your search to those databases that are specifically related to social work. There are many other useful databases such as PsycInfo, Cinahl (a nursing database), Sociological Abstracts, and Dissertation Abstracts International (a database that publishes graduate students' research for a cost). Any database for social sciences might be helpful. Spending some time in your campus library will help you gain familiarity with these and other databases.

Library databases state whether an article is available online, and if not, whether the article is located at your library. You can retrieve full-text articles by selecting the link provided. Then the article can be saved or printed, if desired. Most university libraries provide an interlibrary loan service. This service is usually free or of minimal cost to students and allows you to obtain articles and books for a short period of time. This service greatly expands the resources of the library. If an article is not available, you can order it through an interlibrary loan service. A copy of the article is either e-mailed to you or sent to your library for you to pick up.

Step 2: Choosing Your Articles

As you begin to compile a list of literature to review, it is important to have some general guidelines when you are deciding whether to use an article. Choose articles that are as closely related as possible to your subject. This will save you time, and by choosing articles that are specific to what you are examining, you will be able to focus your search. Choose articles (whenever possible) that are no more than ten years old. There may be times when you need to cite a work that is more than ten years old. This may be an article that is considered a landmark study; this will be evidenced by the number of other people who have referenced this work. Or it may be that some topics were thoroughly investigated during an earlier time period and have not been studied much in the last decade. While it is acceptable to use older articles for these reasons, do not rely solely on dated studies. Your credibility could be jeopardized because it will look like your knowledge of the subject is not up to date.

Choose articles from reputable peer-reviewed journals (a research librarian, instructors, and colleagues can help you if you are uncertain which journals have a better reputation than others). A peer-reviewed journal is one that sends article submissions to experts in the field before accepting them for publication. These experts read the articles and evaluate them for content, accuracy, and methodological concerns. The reviewers are not provided any information on the authors, which helps eliminate bias. This is referred to as a *blind review*. This process is unique because the decision to publish a study does not fall on a single editor. Instead, the editors of the journal send out articles for reviewers to read so that they can make comments. Based on those comments, a determination is made whether to print the article as it is, ask for revisions, or reject the article.

Part of the reviewer's job is to consider the methodology employed and to look for flaws in the research. **Methodology** describes the research methods, procedures, and techniques used to collect and analyze information. However, the fact that a study has been subjected to a **peer review** and has made its way into print does not mean that it is stellar research. You, as a consumer, have to learn to discern between good research that has inherent limitations and just plain bad research. You can do this by becoming educated, learning to think critically about what you are reading, and questioning for yourself whether the methodology makes sense.

There is no doubt that the Internet is a technological boon to society. Today, we have more information available to us instantaneously than at any time in our past. Many journals and authors now post their articles on the World Wide Web. Some are free, and some require a subscription. However, the Internet needs to be viewed with some caution—especially when it is used for research. The fact that something is posted on the Internet does not mean that it is factual information. Misinformation often makes its way online. Because of this, we recommend that you use Web sites that host peer-reviewed journals. In addition, most authors who post their research cite which journal has published the article.

Step 3: Reviewing Your Articles

To find relevant information in a research article, you need to understand the sections of an article and some terminology used in research. There are generally six main sections to an article: the abstract, introduction, review of literature, description of methods used, results/findings, and discussion (see figure 3.1). You can also use this outline as a guide as you write your own research proposal.

Main Parts of an Article

ABSTRACT

The **abstract** is a brief summary of the article. Generally, an abstract is no more than 250 words; it tells the reader the purpose of the study (questions or hypothesis) and provides a brief description of the research method and design.

INTRODUCTION

The introduction of an article explains the question, problem statement, or hypothesis that motivated the study. Moreover, the introduction should

FIGURE 3.1: FORMAT OF A RESEARCH ARTICLE

Abstract

Purpose of the study (questions or hypotheses)
Brief description of the research method and design (e.g., sampling, intervention, analyses)
No more than 250 words

Introduction

What is the problem statement?
What is the hypothesis?
What are the independent and dependent variables?

Review of Literature

Briefly state what the literature has said about this issue.

Methods

Describe the sample/subjects. Who are they? What are their characteristics? Where are they from? How many are there?
Was an intervention, such as a treatment, education, or service, used?
How did they collect data? Did they use standardized (questionnaire, survey, records) or non-standardized methods (observation, interviews, comments)?

Findings or Results

What were the results or findings of the study?
Did the results answer the questions or problem statement of the study?
Did the results accept or reject the hypotheses?

Discussion

What were the authors' conclusions?

tell the reader the main topic of the study, when the study was conducted, and why the topic is important. In chapter 1 we discussed how you start out with a basic research question. For instance, you might be wondering about your agency's services ("I wonder what my clients think about the services at this agency") or a new treatment ("I wonder if this intervention will work with my clients") or people's opinions ("I wonder if college students are more open-minded than adults who have not attended college about GLBT issues"). Remember that in a qualitative study, a researcher is looking for new information or more in-depth information. In a quantitative study, a researcher is looking to add to, confirm, or disprove existing knowledge.

Depending on the type of study, the researcher might use a **problem statement,** an open-ended statement that tells you what the study is intended to do but does not predict what the results might be—even if the researcher has an idea of what to expect. A problem statement might be "This study will determine the effects of progressive muscle relaxation, as opposed to guided imagery, on body temperature."

In contrast, the hypothesis predicts the relationship between variables. A hypothesis can predict no outcome, a positive outcome, a negative outcome, or more than one outcome. For example, a hypothesis might look like the following: "Being sexually abused during childhood will not affect the promiscuity of adults" (no outcome), "People who are sexually abused during childhood will be more promiscuous as adults" (positive outcome), "People who are sexually abused during childhood will be less promiscuous as adults" (negative outcome), or "Girls who are sexually abused during childhood will be more promiscuous as adults, whereas boys who are sexually abused during childhood will be less promiscuous as adults" (bidirectional outcome). This speculation would be based on the various ways of knowing—that is, on the researcher's own experience, the expertise of others, history of the issue, and a review of the literature on related research.

Social workers study an endless amount of variables. Some examples of commonly used ones are sex, age, education, income, self-esteem, drug use, and domestic violence. When we are attempting to understand the relationship between variables, it is important to label variables. Variables are commonly labeled independent variables and dependent variables. An **independent variable** (IV) is the factor (stimulus) that supplies the intervention or is said to be manipulated by the researcher. A **dependent variable** (DV) is predicted by or depends upon other variables (usually independent variables). In social work practice, the dependent variable is often called the outcome. For instance, look at the question "Did the smoking cessation classes help people quit smoking?" For this research question, the smoking cessation class is the intervention being introduced (IV) and the participants' smoking behavior is what is being measured (DV).

While every explanatory study needs at least one independent variable, all researchers should assume that reality is governed by a combination of different independent variables. For instance, a person's attitude toward homeless people can be governed by his or her race, sex, income, and perceptions of job opportunities; whether he or she lives in a rural or urban community; and his or her personal experience with poverty. These are all independent variables that may predict attitudes toward homeless people. There are other types of variables used in the data analysis that are discussed later in this text. For now, you are looking for how the information the researchers want to collect is being defined so that it can be measured.

REVIEW OF LITERATURE

The review of literature is a discussion of what information the authors located or did not locate in relation to the research questions before they started the study. In essence, this is the result of their own literature review, which is presented in a narrative form following the abstract and introduction. Was there a wealth of information? Was there limited information? What was missing in the literature? Was there research that contradicted other studies?

METHODS

The methods section describes the sample, any intervention that was used, and how the data were collected. The sample of the study is basically the participants who provided the evidence. Sometimes an entire population is researched, as when all the clients in an agency have provided information on the services they received. However, most of the time we usually can't study everyone in our target population for practical reasons of time and cost, so we are faced with drawing a smaller sample for our study and then generalizing, or projecting, the sample results with some degree of confidence back to the target population at large.

There is an entire chapter on various types of sampling and how to conduct sampling located later in this text. For now, we will focus on collecting only the characteristics of the sample: who, what, where, and how. For instance, *who* are the participants? Are they college students, substance abuse clients, exotic dancers, residents in a shelter, or mothers of twins? *What* are their characteristics? In other words, what are their ages, sex, marital status, sexual orientation, and other identifying characteristics? *Where* are they from? Are they from a rural university, from an inpatient treatment facility, from several cities across the Midwest, from one home-less shelter, or from a large city? Finally, *how many* were in the sample study?

If an intervention was used, what was it? For instance, was it a relax-ation method, a parent education class, or a service (e.g., transportation, child care, house cleaning)? Data collection refers to how the data were retrieved from the participants. Did the researchers use methods such as videotaping or audio-taping or keep journals or other field notes, in which the researcher records experiences, perceptions, feelings, statements from participants, and other information? Or did they use methods such as sur-veys or other questionnaires? Did they look at existing information such as records? Were there multiple methods of data collection, such as a sur-vey and a follow-up interview?

RESULTS OR FINDINGS

In the results or findings section you will find an analysis or compilation of the findings of the research. Did the study address the problem state-ment or hypothesis stated in the introduction? A qualitative study might look at themes or at new information that was found. If applicable, did the study reject (disprove) or accept (support) the stated hypothesis? The find-ing for the hypothesis "Clients using progressive muscle relaxation will have a significant increase in body temperature over clients using guided imagery" might be "There was an average difference in body temperature of five degrees between clients using progressive muscle relaxation and those using guided imagery for the fifty sample subjects who participated in the interventions. This difference is statistically significant," and the related conclusion might be "Therefore, it can be concluded that clients using progressive muscle relaxation will have a greater increase in average body temperature than clients using guided imagery." The results support the hypothesis!

DISCUSSION

In the discussion section, you will find a discussion of what the authors think are the pieces of knowledge learned from the research study. The findings will be tied back into what the literature already informs us about the issue studied and what this new knowledge adds to, confirms, or rejects about that knowledge. Did the research inform us about a practice or a policy? Does the author think that more research is needed, and why?

Critique of the Article

Once you have collected all the information from the article, it is impor-tant to critique what is presented. By critiquing the articles you review, you are building a foundation for your own research. For instance, does the article leave out any important variables? Do you agree or disagree with the way the variables are defined and measured? Why? Was the sample large enough to reflect the practices of people outside the study? What were the strengths and weaknesses of the study?

Step 4: Organizing Your Search Results

After getting copies of numerous studies, you will quickly discover that researchers do not always agree on the most important elements of an event or phenomenon. For instance, some studies may say that a person's sex predicts anorexia, while other studies argue that socialization, such as parenting, media, or peers, has a larger impact on people's eating behaviors. Your job is to organize these competing claims into a coherent list of different variables that may affect your research topic.

Index Cards

There is no single way to decide how to evaluate the articles, books, and notes you will accumulate. One method that is time honored and has proved effective is to use a stack of blank index cards. Begin by writing some basic information for each article or book on each card. This should include the author's name, the title, date of publication, publisher (or journal), and page numbers. This information will be invaluable later when you compile your reference page and will be helpful should you need to find particular items again. On the other side of the card, record your notes about the publication. Notes about sample size, methodology, and strengths or weaknesses of the research design can help you decide later on which articles to focus on and which to ignore. This method allows you to save on the cost of printing the articles and to organize the information for when you write the literature review summary without creating a table or spreadsheet. In addition, you can alphabetize the authors' last names by sorting your cards.

Computer Software

Another approach to organizing your information is to use your computer. This requires you to save and/or print out your articles as you select them. Then you can enter the information into a table in a word processor (like Word) or a spreadsheet (like Excel), or you can use software such as EndNote that stores and organizes bibliographies. These methods allow you to sort entries alphabetically and to cut and paste or import the information.

Groupings

You may wish to use your printed articles or your note cards to organize them into categories of studies with similar findings and then construct a table that will display the patterns you find. This should assist you in identifying the variables that have been repeatedly studied and those that have been relatively ignored. Likewise, these groups will show if the impact of a variable is confirmed by other studies or if there are conflicting findings or incomplete conclusions about the impact of a variable.

Table 3.1 is an example of a table that might be produced for our literature review on childhood aggression. Notice that the last names of the authors dictate the order in which the studies are listed. Alphabetizing publications by authors' last name is a common practice. The example is not meant to be a complete table, nor to be exhaustive. It is simply a demonstration of how you may choose to organize data. Feel free to set up your tables in a way that make sense to you. Note that some of the studies in the table (see the articles by Arsenio and Nangle, Erdley, Carpenter, and Newman) are not research studies but are essays that discuss, compile, or analyze research done by others. Also, one study dated 1961 (by Bandura, Ross, and Ross) is included because it is a landmark study that led the way researchers worked to understand the effect of adult modeling on children's behavior.

Example 3.1 is a sample literature review based on the information in table 3.1. Notice how the sample summarizes what is known rather than discussing each study individually; each citation can contain multiple studies. A **citation** gives credit to the authors for what you are reporting; these are reported by last name, then date. Also, notice that when we are citing a study with more than two authors for the second time, we use the term "et al.," which is Latin for "and others."

Step 5: Developing a Problem Statement or Hypothesis

The last step is to use the literature to begin to develop some type of a problem statement or a testable hypothesis. But first you must decide whether you will be conducting a qualitative or quantitative study. Your literature review can help you to determine whether you will be conducting a qualitative study or a quantitative study. The role of the literature review

TABLE 3.1: ORGANIZING REFERENCE INFORMATION

AUTHOR'S NAME	DATE	WHAT WAS EXAMINED	RESULTS
Arsenio	2004	Presentations concerned with childhood aggression	Long-term patterns of childhood aggression are as stable as patterns of intelligence
Bandura, Ross, and Ross	1961	Children's imitations of aggressive behavior	Children who witnessed adults hitting a doll were also aggressive toward the doll
Brook and Whiteman	1992	Is childhood aggression related to adolescent delinquency and drug use?	Anger/aggression in childhood may be a predictor of drug use and delinquency in adolescence
Brown and Parsons	1998	Are there subtypes of aggression?	Reactive (normal) and proactive (problematic) aggression are two types of aggression.
Eron and Huesmann	1984	Does gender role predict aggressive behavior?	Boys were found to be more aggressive than girls.
Evans, Heriot, and Friedman	2002	Are there temperamental characteristics that contribute to a pattern of hostility in children?	A pattern of irritability and negativity can account for hostile behavior in children.
Fuller, Chemack, Cruise, Kirsch, Fitzgerald, and Zucker	2003	Does intergenerational aggression and alcohol use predict aggression in children?	Aggression in grandparents predicted aggression and alcoholism in parents, which predicted aggression in children (third generation).
Geen and Thomas	1986	The relationship between media images and violence	A significant relationship between violence in media and aggression was found.

TABLE 3.1: (CONTINUED)

AUTHOR'S NAME	DATE	WHAT WAS EXAMINED	RESULTS
Greenburg	1983	The effects of aggression over time	Aggression in childhood is a predictor of adult aggressive behavior.
Herrenkohl and Russo	2001	What is the relationship between child maltreatment and early childhood aggressive behavior?	The results suggested a relationship between severe physical discipline and childhood aggression.
Nangle, Erdley, Carpenter, and Newman	2002	Research on social skills training for childhood aggression	Six major developmental areas were identified: age, gender, race, social cognition, peer group influence, and interventions.
Rubin	1998	What causes childhood aggression?	Rejection and violence by parents were traits linked to aggression in children. Watching violence on television was also linked to increased violence in children.
Wood, Wong, and Chacher	1991	Is violence in the media related to childhood aggression?	Viewing aggression on television and other media sources extended into aggression in other areas of the child's life.

depends, largely, on what type of study is being conducted. Conversely, the type of study that will be conducted is dependent upon the literature review. Let us explore this seemingly circular logic. Knowledge emerges from qualitative research as an end product. Researchers first collect the data and begin to make tentative descriptions and develop common themes out of the information. Then, we go back to the literature and begin to search for similar information that will help us to make sense of our findings. With quantitative research, on the other hand, we utilize existing

---

EXAMPLE 3.1: LITERATURE REVIEW

A review of the literature suggests that there are correlations between variables that account for childhood aggression. Some authors found that aggression in children can be a sign of several maladaptive factors within the family, such as drug use (Brook & Whiteman, 1992; Fuller, Chemack, Cruise, Kirsch, Fitzgerald, & Zucker, 2003) and violence (Bandura, Ross, & Ross, 1961; Fuller et al., 2003; Herrenkohl & Russo, 2001; Rubin, 1998). Other studies assert a relationship between children viewing violent television programs and aggressive behavior (Geen & Thomas, 1986; Rubin, 1998; Wood, Wong, & Chachere, 1991). Still others found that aggressive behavior is a gender issue (Nangle, Erdley, Carpenter, & Newman, 2002) and more prevalent in male children (Eron & Huesmann, 1984). Finally, studies suggest that individual or situational characteristics, such as a long-term pattern of aggressive behaviors (Arsenio, 2004), whether the aggression is reactive (normal) or proactive (problematic) (Brown & Parsons, 1998), and a pattern of irritability and negativity in the child (Evans, Heriot, & Friedman, 2002), may be related to acts of childhood aggression.

Based on the findings of above studies, children who spend time watching violent television programs and playing violent video games may demonstrate a higher level of aggression than other children. One theoretical model that emerges is the theory that children imitate what they see, known as social learning theory (Bandura et al., 1961).

---

knowledge and theoretical perspectives to guide the development of our research question or hypothesis. In some cases theories emerge from or are revised following the quantitative process.

Developing a Problem Statement

As we discussed above, problem statements are open-ended inquiries that do not predict what the results of the research study might be. Let us imagine for a moment that in the fall of 2001 you were a case manager working with the mentally ill in an outpatient clinic. You noticed that many of the consumers on your caseload suddenly began to miss appointments after the terrorist attacks of September 11, 2001. As a practitioner, you wanted to understand this relationship but were unsure what to do. A search of the literature revealed that there were virtually no articles dealing with the effects of terrorist attacks on the mentally ill. You decided to conduct an exploratory study in which you would interview three or four of your consumers to gain an in-depth understanding of what they were experiencing. Your research question was: "What effect did the 9/11 terrorist attack have on mentally ill clients?" You then created the following problem statement: "Little is known about the effects of the 9/11 terrorist attack on mentally ill clients."

Developing a Hypothesis

As discussed in chapter 1, a hypothesis is generally considered a testable statement. This means we can confirm or reject our hypothesis. After looking at the studies reviewed in table 3.1, perhaps you can develop a research hypothesis that will begin to guide and form your study. Based on what you have read in the sample literature, you learned that several things may be related to children's aggression: the child's sex, amount of violent television that the child views, family dynamics, and the child's individual characteristics or a situational event he or she is experiencing. Drawing from these findings, you might develop a research hypothesis. You develop a research hypothesis that states, "Male children will demonstrate more aggressive behavior than female children after watching violent television programs." You can develop a study from this hypothesis.

Your goal is to develop a testable hypothesis, that is, one for which there are variables on which you can gather empirical data. There are two basic problems to watch for when you are developing a hypothesis. First, a researcher can accidentally leave out a basis for comparison. Suppose, for instance, that you formulate the following hypothesis: "Children watching violent television programs will demonstrate more aggression." This statement begs the question "More aggression than whom?" Another form of non-testable hypothesis is one that is really more of the researcher's value judgment, or his or her opinion, such as "Children should not be allowed to view violent television programs because they may become violent." This is a value statement and is not testable.

Hopefully at this point you are beginning to see the connection between the literature review and conducting research. Consulting the existing knowledge (conducting a literature review) early in the process will allow you to save time and energy by helping you gain an understanding of what is already known about a topic.

Step 6: Compiling Your Reference Page

The last part of your literature review involves making a reference page. The **reference page** is the alphabetical list of studies that you chose to include in your review and is formatted according to the writing style you are using. For instance, most social work journals require articles to be submitted in APA (American Psychological Association) style. There are books and style guides published on the various writing styles, for instance, APA, Chicago, and MLA. Example 3.2 shows the reference page for the literature review in example 3.1 and is formatted in APA style. As a note of caution, be aware that APA and other writing styles change over time. Therefore, remember always to consult the current style guide.

Applied Learning Activities

Activity #1
Use step 1 to conduct a literature search. Select an article and use the outline in figure 3.1 to review it.

Activity #2
Conduct a literature search and write a brief literature review based on one or more of the following research questions. Select five references and organize the descriptions of the studies in a table, summarize the findings in a report, and create a reference page.

1. What is the relationship between socioeconomic status and child maltreatment?

2. What is the relationship between intensive case management services and inpatient hospitalization admissions?

3. What is the relationship between domestic violence and substance abuse?

Key Points

- A literature review is a search of published research that allows you to review what is known about the topic you are studying.

- A literature review helps shape a research design by giving the researcher an overview of previous studies on a topic.

- To conduct a search of the literature, you must identify key words to enter into a search database, such as Social Work Abstracts or PsycInfo.

EXAMPLE 3.2: REFERENCE PAGE

Arsenio, W. (2004). The stability of young children's physical aggression: Relations with child care, gender, and aggression subtypes. *Monographs of the Society for Research in Child Development, 69*(4), 130–144.

Bandura, A., Ross, R., & Ross, S. (1961). Transmission of aggression through imitation of aggressive models. *Journal of Abnormal and Social Psychology, 63*, 575–582.

Brook, J., & Whiteman, M. (1992). Childhood aggression, adolescent delinquency, and drug abuse: A longitudinal study. *Journal of Genetic Psychology, 153*(4), 369–384.

Brown, K., & Parsons, R. (1998). Accurate identification of childhood aggression: A key to successful intervention. *Professional School Counseling, 2*(2), 135–141.

Eron, L., & Huesmann, L. (1984). The control of aggressive behavior by changes in attitudes, and conditions of learning. In R. Blanchard & D. Blanchard (Eds.), *Advances in the study of aggression* (Vol. 1, pp. 139–171). Orlando, FL: Academic Press.

Evans, I., Heriot, S., & Friedman, A. (2002). A behavioral pattern of irritability, hostility and inhibited empathy in children. *Clinical Child Psychology and Psychiatry, 7*(2), 211–225.

Fuller, B., Chemack, S., Cruise, K., Kirsch, E., Fitzgerald, H., & Zucker, R. (2003). Predictors of aggression across three generations among sons of alcoholics: Relationships involving grandparental and parental alcoholism, child aggression, marital aggression, and parenting practices. *Journal of Studies on Alcohol, 64*(4), 472–484.

Geen, R., & Tomas, S. (1986). The immediate effects of media violence on behavior. *Journal of Social Issues, 42*(3), 7–27.

Greenburg, J. (1983). Parental behavior, TV habits, IQ predict aggression. *Science News, 124*(10), 148–151.

Herrenkohl, R., & Russo, J. (2001). Abusive early child rearing and early childhood aggression. *Child Maltreatment, 6*(1), 3–17.

Nangle, D., Erdley, C., Carpenter, E., & Newman, J. (2002). Social skills training as a treatment for aggressive children and adolescents: A developmental-clinical integration. *Aggression and Violent Behavior, 7*(2), 169–200.

Rubin, D. (1998). What makes a child violent? *Parenting, 12*(6), 96–102.

Wood, W., Wong, F., & Chachere, J. (1991). Effects of media violence on viewers' aggression in unconstrained social interaction. *Psychological Bulletin, 109*, 379–383.

Additional Resources

American Psychological Association. (2001). *Publication manual of the American Psychological Association* (5th ed.). Washington DC: American Psychological Association.
> This is the official style manual of the American Psychological Association. The APA style has been adopted as the official writing style for social work and other professions.

American Psychological Association. (2005). *APA-style helper 5.0.* Washington DC: American Psychological Association.
> This software provides a template for APA documents. The user simply types in responses to prompts such as "title."

American Psychological Association. (2005). *Concise rules of APA style.* Washington DC: American Psychological Association.
> While the style manual is the definitive reference for all questions about APA style (including questions about referencing, quotes, etc.), the concise rules guide offers tips on avoiding common grammatical errors, choosing an appropriate format for statistics, and the like.

APA Web site: http://www.apastyle.org/
> This is a useful Web site for ordering materials (such as the APA style manual) and finding answers to specific questions.

CHAPTER FOUR

Variables and Measures

THIS CHAPTER DISCUSSES HOW TO DEVELOP your variables, how to conceptualize and operationalize your variables, and how to measure your variables. We will first discuss how to operationalize concepts so that they can be measured for evidence. Measurements will be discussed, including how to measure variables using four levels of measure. This chapter will also introduce two new terms: reliability and validity.

Variables in Research Design

Variables are fluid and sometimes difficult to define and measure. For example, researchers may come up with many different ways of defining verbal abuse, such as yelling, cursing, and belittling. How you choose to specifically define particular variables is called conceptualizing variables, and how you measure a concept (variable) is called operationalizing variables. How you define and measure your variables depends on what it is you want to know or, more specifically, what your research problem statement, question, or hypothesis is.

Conceptualizing a variable refers to how we translate an idea or abstract theory into a variable that can be used to test a hypothesis or make sense of observations. Therefore, conceptualizing a variable is another way of saying how experts are defining a concept. For example, most literature defines child maltreatment as abuse or neglect. Then these broad categories are further defined into more descriptive categories. The category of abuse can be divided into physical abuse, sexual abuse, and emotional abuse. The category of neglect can be further divided into medical neglect, physical neglect, and emotional neglect. By using more descriptive categories, we are able to capture more specific information about the type of abuse an individual has encountered.

In research, it boils down to how we measure our variables or choose to operationalize them. **Operationalizing** a variable refers to how we define a concept so that it can be measured. How you operationalize a variable may depend on what information you want to collect and how you collect it. Do you only want to know if an individual has experienced childhood maltreatment, or do you want more precise information such as what kinds of maltreatment? We will come back to this later in this chapter when we discuss measurements.

Viewing and Using Variables

It is important to keep in mind that variables are fluid and that the meaning attached to a variable can differ from person to person. In other words, they evolve in how people view them and use them. The following two examples illustrate cases in which the variables of sex and race may be viewed differently by different people.

In some studies, sex is identified as either female or male, and gender identified as either masculine or feminine. Sex is usually associated with a person's biology (chromosomes and hormones), and gender is a culturally constructed concept of what is female and what is male. Jack was born in 1957. Jack married his wife, Elaine, at age nineteen and had a son at the age of twenty. Now, at the age of fifty, Jack has officially changed his name to Jane. Jane has had a sex change operation, wears dresses and a wig, and receives hormone shots. Jane is still married to Elaine and now considers this a lesbian relationship. According to Jane's official birth certificate and marriage license, Jane is still a male, while physically and socially Jane is a female. How would you as a researcher record Jane's sex? Would this be different from how you would record her gender?

Race and ethnicity can also create similar concerns. Race is commonly used as a measure for biologically based human characteristics known as phenotypes. Categories used for race are sometimes based on skin color (white, black) or other characteristics that have been labeled Hispanic and Asian, whereas ethnicity is a culturally constructed concept connected with the history, culture, and national origin that form group identities such as Irish, Jewish, or African American. What if someone has black parents but is raised in a white family? What if you can trace your family back to Ireland but do not know anything about that culture? A pressing issue is how to claim race when your father is black and your mother is Asian, as is the case for the famous golfer Tiger Woods. A person who is biracial is two non-specified races, but what if your father is biracial (black/white) and your mother is Native American? Does that mean you are tri-racial?

Types of Variables

Variables can be placed into three general groups: independent variables, dependent variables, and control variables.

As stated in chapter 3, the independent variable (identified as IV) is often thought of as the variable that is controlled or manipulated by the researcher. At other times, it is described as the variable that may have an impact on a change in the dependent variable. The dependent variable (identified as DV) is the variable that is changed by another variable, or is said to depend on the independent variables. For example, if we know how many alcoholic drinks a person consumes in an hour (the independent variable), we can predict his or her blood alcohol level (the dependent variable). In social work practice, the dependent variable is the variable that is being measured to determine if change has occurred. For instance, look at the question "Did the smoking cessation classes help people quit smoking?" For this research question, the smoking cessation classes (independent variable) are the intervention being introduced, and the participants' smoking behavior (dependent variable) is what is being measured.

A predictive variable is a type of independent variable, and a criterion variable is a type of dependent variable. Prediction is a special kind of relationship where one thing precedes the other and we use information about the first to forecast or predict the second. In predictive studies, variables are sequenced or are arranged in a distinct time line. In predictive studies the predictor is the first variable (the one we have information about and are using) and the criterion is the second variable (the one being predicted). Also, you could have more than one predictor and/or criterion variable. This depends on your research question or problem statement. Let's look at some predictors of child maltreatment:

- Age (IV) is a predictor of abuse (DV): younger boys are abused more than older boys and older girls are abused more than younger girls.
- Income (IV) is a predictor of child maltreatment (DV).
- Stress (IV) is a predictor of child maltreatment (DV).
- Social isolation (IV) is a predictor of child maltreatment (DV).

A **control variable** is a variable that researchers control for in a research study. When researchers **control for** a variable, this means that they subtract the effect of that variable on the dependant variable by holding the variable constant. Researchers often use control variables as a type of theoretical insurance. That is, they may not think that the control variable will influence the dependent variables, but they include the variable just to be safe. Many control variables are demographics. **Demographics** are the physical characteristics of a population, such as age, sex, marital status, family size, education, geographic location, and occupation. For example, assume for a moment that based on the literature, you believe a person's sex affects his or her self-esteem. Your support group for parents without partners has both male and female members. Therefore, you want to control for sex when you conduct your study of the support group by including sex in your study. In other words, you want to ensure that the support group helps consumers regardless of their sex.

By including sex, you can use statistical methods to look at the response differences between males and females, or to subtract the influence of sex from the data (depending on what type of analysis you use). Another way to control for sex in your support group study would be to assign males to one group and females to another group. You could then compare their scores.

Going back to the child maltreatment literature, you can see from the following list that marital status (IV) and race (IV) were not found to be predictors of child maltreatment (DV) when income was controlled for. Similarly, the parent's sex (IV) was not found to be a predictor of abuse (DV) when time spent with the child was controlled for.

- Single parents seem to be more abusive (DV); however, the effect disappears when income is controlled for.
- African Americans are believed to abuse (DV) more often than whites; however, this effect disappears when income is controlled for.
- Mothers abuse (DV) children more often (60%) than fathers; however, this effect disappears when time spent with children is controlled for.

As you can see, the effect of a predictor can sometimes be explained by another variable. For instance, both race and marital status no longer appear to be predictors for abuse when income is controlled for. This illustrates the problem of omitting key variables in your study, which can distort the findings.

A **confounding variable** is a type of control variable that obscures the effect of another variable. In such cases, the effects of a variable's impact cannot be determined because of other influences confounding the relationship. For example, a relationship between traditional male gender role expectations and wife abuse may be confounded by a history of paternal abuse. That is, the power of traditional gender role expectations may be stronger for people who have been abused by their fathers. Several studies that look at the effect of a person's race on his or her comfort with homosexuality find that African Americans are more homophobic than whites. However, this association is misleading. When the studies add access to higher education as a variable, the impact of race disappears. That is, African Americans have attitudes about homosexuality that are similar to those of whites when they have similar educational levels.

As a result of the effect confounding variables can have on a study, researchers need to include many types of variables in their studies. A broad list of variables should include independent variables and control variables that are relevant to the study. To include all possibilities, the researcher consults the literature to identify what has already been studied. Let us examine the variables used in two separate studies. These studies used substantiated child maltreatment case files to look at the differences between families with twin children and families without twin children (DV). The variables used in the first study were:

- type of maltreatment
- number of children in the home
- annual income
- use of fertility drugs to conceive
- whether or not the children were born prematurely
- whether or not there were birth defects when the children were born
- number of adults in the home
- age of the children in the home
- square footage of the residence
- parental psychological problems
- social supports available

The variables used in the second study were:

- type of maltreatment
- number of children in the home
- annual income

Which study would you use? What makes your choice the better option?

What Is a Measure?

A **measure** is a tool or instrument that is used to gather data. For instance, a measurement tool could be a survey (e.g., population survey), a test (e.g., IQ test), a scale that has several questions (e.g., depression scale), or a poll (e.g., opinion poll). A measure has two parts—the item (stimulus) and the response. The item is generally a statement, question, or observation that requires some type of measurable response. A measurement tool is sometimes trying to measure a concept such as alcoholism, depression, self-esteem, and marital satisfaction. Because a concept can have multiple definitions, it must be operationalized for the measure.

Defining and Operationalizing Measures

Now let us begin looking at how we develop the items of the measure. For this, it is important to discuss how concepts are defined and operationalized. Remember, the term *operationalize* refers to how we define a concept so that it can be measured. Let us look at some examples. Alcoholism is defined as excessive use or compulsive use of alcohol in many standard dictionaries. How do we know excessive use or compulsive use when we observe drinking behavior? Whose standard do we use? If you did research on the prevalence of alcoholism at your university or college, you might find multiple conflicting statistics, depending on how you operationalized this concept. For example, in one study you may operationalize alcoholism using criteria established in the American Psychiatric Association's *Diagnostic and Statistical Manual of Mental Disorders*. In another study you may simply ask whether individuals believe they are alcoholics, and for still another study, you might investigate how many individuals have been diagnosed with alcoholism by a mental health professional. As you can guess, each of these studies would lead to different findings on the prevalence of alcoholism at your university or college.

An example of an instrument for measuring alcoholism that is commonly used is the Michigan Alcoholism Screening Test (MAST). The MAST was developed by Melvin L. Seltzer (1971) to detect alcoholism. This particular scale has twenty-four questions (concepts defining alcoholism) with scores assigned for each response option (how concepts are operationalized). The total of all twenty-four scores can indicate non-alcoholism (score of 3 or less), suggestion of alcoholism (score of 4), or alcoholism (score of 5 or more). Question 8 of the instrument asks: "Have you ever attended a meeting of Alcoholics Anonymous?" If the response is yes, it is assigned five points and indicates alcoholism according to this instrument's definition. Therefore, individuals who attended an AA meeting for reasons other than their own alcohol use, such as to support a friend, would meet the criteria for alcoholism based on how this measure was operationalized.

With this in mind, you can easily see how research can be corrupted by how a concept is operationalized. We can manipulate how we operationalize concepts such as abuse, poverty, crime, and homosexuality to fit our desired outcome or mislead readers. For example, city law enforcement might operationalize incidents of crime as all arrests or every conviction, including simple misdemeanors such as shoplifting. The findings might be used to support the need for more resources or to justify the current resources. In another study, the travel and tourism office of the same city might operationalize incidence of crime as only felony crimes against individuals. This would be used to establish a lower rate of crime for the city in an effort to attract more tourists.

Poverty provides a good example of the difficulty that can arise when we try to operationalize a concept. The battle over how to define poverty has raged for years. The issue comes down to concerns over "relative" versus "absolute" poverty. Measures of relative poverty focus on deprivation from a subjective and comparative point of view—"How poor do I feel?" or "How poor am I compared to others around me?"—whereas measures of absolute poverty focus on the amount of income an individual or family has to purchase the goods that sustain healthy life. While this definition might sound straightforward, listing all the material things people need can get very complicated. Therefore, different definitions of poverty can produce vast differences in how we operationalize poverty. The bottom line is that how we define this concept has a bearing on who will receive services.

Levels of Measure

Four levels are used to measure variables: nominal, ordinal, interval, and ratio. The first two levels of variables are called *discrete variables,* or *categorical variables.* Both nominal-level and ordinal-level variables are discrete because they are made up of distinct separate units or categories. The last two levels of a measure are called *continuous variables* because they are made up of a large (sometimes infinite) number of units. Both interval-level and ratio-level variables fall into this category. With each subsequent level of measure, we gain the ability to more precisely measure what we are studying. Keep in mind that we want to be as precise as possible in our measurement.

Discrete Levels of Measure

The first level of measurement we will examine is the nominal-level variable. **Nominal-level variables** are mutually exclusive (that is, responses fit into one category and cannot be in another) and are exhaustive (no other options are available). One type of nominal-level variable is a **dichotomous variable**, for which there are only two responses to choose from (e.g., yes or no, treatment group or nontreatment group). We can measure sex as a nominal-level variable (a person is either male, female, transsexual, or hermaphrodite). We can measure attitudes at a nominal level ("Do you like research? Yes or no?"). We can measure religious affiliation as Catholic, Protestant, Jewish, Muslim, or other. One way to determine if the measure is nominal is to decide whether you can add or subtract from the measure. For instance, you cannot subtract a Catholic from a Muslim and get another religion. This highlights a problem with nominal-level variables—they are limiting. Let us say, for example, that eight people state on a survey that they are Catholic. This gives us no information about the extent of their involvement in their faith, such as church attendance, tithing, and praying. So we move up a level to ordinal-level data to gain greater detail.

With **ordinal-level variables**, in addition to being mutually exclusive and exhaustive, responses are rank ordered. For example, for the question "How much do you like research?" ordinal-level responses could range from "not at all" to "somewhat" to "very much." Notice how this provides more information than purely nominal-level responses (yes or no) for "Do you like research?" Nominal-level variables can tell us whether someone feels positively or negatively about something, but not to what degree. By using rank ordering, we are beginning to establish different levels or degrees of responses. The limitation of ordinal data, however, is that it is not precise. For instance, the difference between "somewhat" liking research and liking research "very much" can be big or small. The next level of measurement begins to achieve greater precision.

Continuous Levels of Measure

The next level of measurement is the interval-level variable. With **interval-level variables,** items are rank ordered and each step is mutually exclusive and exhaustive, and there are equal gradations between each step. This means that the difference between the responses can be determined through addition or subtraction. An example is IQ. One person's IQ can be 110, and another person's 140, an increase in IQ of exactly thirty points. Another example is the range between -10 and -20 degrees Fahrenheit, which is the same as that between 50 and 60 degrees, or exactly ten degrees.

The fourth level of measurement is the ratio-level variable; this is the most precise level of measurement. **Ratio-level variables** have all the attributes of the other three levels (items are mutually exclusive and exhaustive, they are rank ordered, and there are equal gradations between steps). The main difference between interval and ratio measurement is that interval-level variables have no absolute or fixed zero point, whereas ratio-level variables have an absolute zero point. Items measured at this level might include such things as income (you could conceivably have no income) or number of children. Notice that both income and number of children would meet all the criteria: they are mutually exclusive categories that are rank ordered and have equal gradations and an absolute zero.

Keep in mind that variables are fluid because they can be viewed and used in various ways. In table 4.1, the researcher has taken what is a ratio-level variable ("How many days in the last week have you experienced episodes of crying?") because it has an absolute zero (0–7 days) and is treating it like an ordinal variable by dividing it into categories. When this variable is treated as interval level, the results can provide more information, such as how many or what percentage reported one or two days per

TABLE 4.1: EXAMPLE FOR EACH LEVEL OF MEASUREMENT

ITEM (STIMULUS)	RESPONSE OPTIONS	LEVEL OF MEASUREMENT
Have you ever been treated for depression?	Yes No	Nominal
In the past month, I have thought about ending my life.	Not at all Sometimes Frequently	Ordinal
How many days in the last week have you experienced episodes of crying?	None 1–2 days 3–4 days 5–6 days Daily	Interval
How many times have you attempted suicide?	(Respondents enter a number.)	Ratio

week as opposed to three or four per week, five or six days per week, daily, or none.

In the following examples, indicate what level of measurement is being used:

- A student is polling other students on campus about their position on abortion. Students have the option of defining their position on the issue as "support abortion" or "do not support abortion."
- A substance abuse counselor wants to know how satisfied consumers are with the on-site Alcoholics Anonymous meetings. She administers a survey that asks respondents to indicate if they are "very satisfied," "somewhat satisfied," or "not satisfied."
- The supervisor of an after-school program needs to know in what grade each student is currently enrolled.

Standardized Measures

There are multiple standardized measurement instruments in circulation today. A **standardized measure** is one that has been given to enough people that we can compare one person's scores to those of other test takers. For example, you have probably taken the ACT or a similar exam. This test has been normed or standardized so that your scores could be compared with those of other test takers. A similar example would be tests of intelligence quotient (IQ tests). Most people who take this test score in the range of average intelligence (around 100). Some compilations of measures are described at the end of this chapter.

Standardized measures have limitations. To illustrate some important limitations, let us return to the example of the Michigan Alcoholism Screening Test. The MAST was normed on multiple groups: 116 hospitalized alcoholics, 99 people arrested for drunk driving, 98 people under review for revocation of their driver's licenses because of excess accidents and moving violations, and 103 controls (individuals who functioned as part of a control group). The groups were largely made up of white males between the ages of twenty-five and forty-four years. What are potential problems that might arise if the MAST is administered in the following situations?

- You are working with members of a gang who are in high school. Drinking alcohol appears to be an important part of their culture.

- You are working with parents referred by Child Protective Services for alcohol abuse. The majority of these parents are women.
- You are working with Hispanic immigrants referred through the court system for charges of driving while intoxicated.

Standardized measures such as the MAST are used universally, regardless of the population for which they have been normed. Researchers should be informed of how standardized measures are normed so that they can avoid placing individuals into stereotypical categories that do not take into consideration issues of diversity such as culture, sex, age, and nationality.

Reliability and Validity in Measurement

Two of the factors that contribute to the credibility of a research study are the measurement's reliability and validity.

Reliability is the word used to describe the stability and consistency of a measurement. For instance, a tape measure is a highly reliable measuring instrument because it does not change over time (i.e., it is stable), and it measures everything according to the same standards (i.e., it is consistent). There are four major categories of reliability for most instruments: test-retest, equivalent form, internal consistency, and interobserver reliability.

Test-retest reliability has to do with the consistency of your measure from one time to the next. When a researcher administers the same measurement tool multiple times to the same group following the same research procedures, does he or she obtain consistent results (assuming that there has been no change in what is being measured)? If so, the measure has test-retest reliability.

Equivalent form reliability is concerned with consistency between two versions of a measure. If a researcher wanted to develop a new measurement tool for anxiety, he or she could administer the new measurement tool alongside a more traditional measurement tool to the same group. If consistent results were found, it could be argued that the new measurement tool had reliability for measuring the concept of anxiety. Another option is to create two new instruments that measure the same concept. This requires a long list of variables so that the concept can be divided between the two instruments. Again, both instruments would be administered at the same time to the same group, and then the researcher would compare the scores from both instruments to determine if they were equivalent.

Internal consistency is the consistency among the responses to the items in a measure. It is the extent to which responses to items measuring the same concept are associated with each other. This form of reliability is examined when a single measurement instrument is administered to a group of people on one occasion. Tests of internal consistency estimate reliability by grouping items in an instrument that measure the same concept. For example, you could write two sets of three questions each that measure the same concept (e.g., social isolation) and if the responses to those two groups of three questions were consistent, you would know that your instrument is reliably measuring that concept. For instance, if we were measuring the concept of social isolation, we might ask respondents if the statements "I feel lonely at times" and "I never feel lonely" accurately describe their experiences, and we would expect these items to have opposite answers.

Another practice used to determine internal consistency is called split-half reliability, which involves randomly dividing the items related to a concept into two groups. Then the scores of the two groups are compared to determine if they are measuring the same concept. In this way, you are not developing two surveys, as required by the equivalent form method. The more items that are included and the stronger the consistency between the two groups of scores, the greater the reliability is.

Interobserver reliability must be measured when more than one observer uses the same instrument to rate the same person, place, or event. If different observers or interviewers use the same instrument to score the same thing, their scores should match. The more similar the ratings, the more reliable the findings are. For instance, four observers are using an observational assessment tool to measure the quality of interactions between a mother and her child on a playground. The rating scale of the tool ranges from 0 to 10, and two observers rate the mother as a 4, while another observer rates the mother as a 2, and the final observer rates the mother as a 6. These score are fairly similar to each other. This measure would be less reliable than if the ratings were more widely spread, for instance, scores of 2, 3, 6, and 10.

An alternative version of this type of reliability is called **intraobserver reliability**. This means that there is one observer rating a person, place, or event two or more times. As with interobserver reliability, the findings are compared to ensure that the measurement is consistently getting similar scores each time.

Validity is a term that is used to describe how much a measurement tool (such as a scale, survey, poll, or test) measures what it is meant to measure. It is the match between how a concept is conceptualized (defined) and how it is operationalized (measured). For example, if we are using a scale that measures depression, we would expect the scale to ask questions about changes in the person's eating and sleeping habits (either eating or sleeping more or less), number of suicidal ideations, and the like. If these were the questions that were asked, we might say the scale had validity. Conversely, the measurement would not focus on other psychological traits such as anxiety, poor body image, or attention deficits. A few years ago, a national fast-food chain bragged that it had the best french fries in the world. This assertion was based on their claim to have sold the most french fries globally. How is the validity of this claim flawed? In this example, the focus was on the number of fries as opposed to the quality of taste. Think for a moment about the issue of availability. This fast-food chain has a global presence; the more stores there are, the more fries they sell. But this does not mean that the claim that the chain's french fries are better is valid.

The fact that a measurement instrument is reliable (it is consistently measuring the same thing over and over) does not mean that it is valid. For example, let us say that you want to measure your participants' level of depression. You select a measure that has been normed and is standardized. However, the instrument you select is a scale that measures how a person feels about him- or herself (a measure of self-esteem). Even though you are consistently measuring your participants' self-esteem, you may not be measuring their level of depression. This is an issue of validity.

Let us return again to the MAST instrument. The validity of the measure was established in the following ways:

- The MAST was able to classify respondents as alcoholic or non-alcoholic.
- Only 15 out of 526 people originally classified as non-alcoholic by the MAST were found to be alcoholic.
- The MAST correctly identified 92 percent of the 99 respondents hospitalized for severe alcohol problems.

Consider the following questions:

1. The MAST classified respondents as either non-alcoholic or alcoholic. How do we know these classifications are correct? (Think about what you have learned about operationalizing and defining measures.)
2. Should the study report how many people who were classified as alcoholic were actually non-alcoholic?

3. Does administering a survey to hospitalized alcoholics influence the findings?

So how do we establish validity? There are several types of validity: face validity, content validity, criterion-related validity, concurrent validity, and construct validity.

Face Validity

Face validity refers to whether a measure seems to make sense (be valid) at a glance. When a student asks another student to look over a paper to see if his or her answers appear to be correct, the student is requesting a review of the face value of the paper. However, when the paper is evaluated by the standards of the instructor and the overall performance of the other students on their papers (the norm), the comments the student receives from the instructor may differ from those he received from the student who looked only at the face value of the paper. Therefore, caution must be taken when one is determining the validity of research based on the face value of what is presented. In fact, many researchers do not consider face validity a useful form of validity, and face validity should never be the only form of validity used to validate a measure.

The following are some issues that you can look for when you are examining the face value of a measurement tool.

1. Forced generalities. These are questions that force a respondent to make generalizations. An example would be "Do you trust people in your community?" A yes answer implies blanket trust in everyone in the community.

2. Inapplicable items. Some items do not apply to all people or their situations. For instance, the question "Are you close to your father?" implies that everyone has a father.

3. Double-barreled questions. A variable that asks two questions but only allows for one reply is a double-barreled question—for example, "On a scale from 1 to 5, how would you rate your satisfaction with your supervisor and colleagues?" In this situation, respondents may be happy with their supervisor, but not with their colleagues.

4. Unclear items. An unclear item may lead to responses that are unintended because the question was misunderstood. An example would be asking: "Do you visit your advisor regularly?" The interpretation of "regularly" is different for each respondent.

5. Leading questions. A leading question is one that tries to lead a respondent to a particular response, for instance, "With the rising popularity of violent video games, do you think there should be mandatory ratings for children?"

6. Overdemanding recall questions. "Have you been sent to the principal's office in the last week?" is a question that demands less recall than "How many times have you been sent to the principal's office in your lifetime?"

Content Validity

Content validity refers to how well the items in a measurement represent the concept that is being measured. For example, going back to the issue of conceptualizing child maltreatment, by reviewing the child maltreatment literature, a researcher developing a tool to measure child maltreatment would find that the measure would need to include the commonly identified types of both abuse and neglect.

As with face validity, there can be difficulties in relying solely on content validity. Experts may disagree concerning the range of content provided in a measure. For example, a scale measuring obsessive compulsive disorder (OCD) that asked, "Do you have great difficulty discarding things even when they have no practical value?" would pose problems if experts do not agree that this item is representative of the concept of OCD. In this instance, while hording behavior *can* be related to OCD, many people without OCD hang on to items that they never use.

Criterion-Related Validity

Criterion-related validity refers to a measure's ability to make accurate predictions and is also referred to as predictive validity The name *predictive* comes from the fact that this form of validity is derived from how well the measure predicts an outside criterion. For instance, how well SAT scores predict college grades is an indication of the SAT's criterion validity. As another example, a scale measuring students' satisfaction with their educational experience at a university could be compared to how many incoming students stay at that university (graduation rate). In this case, student satisfaction predicts the criterion (graduation). This type of validity is difficult to establish because researchers may not be able to gain access to the criterion, such as the specific course grades or graduation rates of the sample.

Concurrent Validity

Concurrent validity refers to how well a measure correlates with some other measure of the same variable that is believed to be valid. For instance, if a researcher designed a survey to measure depression, he or she could compare it to another measure of depression to see if they predict the same outcome. For example, if an instrument measuring the concept of job satisfaction gives results that are similar to those given by a job satisfaction instrument that has already been validated, the new measurement has concurrent validity. Therefore, when concurrent validity is being measured, the two measures are taken at the same time. This is different from measuring predictive validity, where one measure (e.g., a measure of job satisfaction) is meant to predict responses to a measure that is administered at a later time (e.g., a measure of job retention).

Construct Validity

Construct validity refers to the extent to which the items of an instrument accurately sample a construct. A **construct** is the concept or the characteristic that an instrument is designed to measure. Whereas measures of content validity ask whether an instrument measures the full range of possibilities within a concept (e.g., alcoholism), construct validity is the degree to which an instrument actually reflects the construct being measured. In other words, with content validity we are determining whether the instrument includes the items (content) that can accurately operationalize a concept, and with construct validity we are determining whether the overall instrument was constructed to measure a single concept such as alcoholism, and not OCD or social isolation. This type of validation is commonly used in social research when there is no existing criterion for validation purposes. There are two types of construct validity: convergent validity and discriminate validity.

Convergent validity refers to how well the measures of a construct (e.g., depression or alcoholism) that you expect to be related to each other are, indeed, found to correspond to each other (measure the same construct). Conversely, **discriminate validity** refers to the degree to which the measures of a construct that you would not expect to be related are indeed measuring different constructs.

Applied Learning Activities

Activity #1

Identify the independent variable and the dependent variable:

1. Amount of time studying and scores on a final exam

2. The number of divorces a mother has had and her children's fear of intimacy in adult relationships

3. A person's sex and fear of intimacy in adult relationships

4. Number of hours a child spends playing violent video games and the child's aggression scores on a child behavior scale

5. Scores on SATs and grade point average in the freshman year of college

6. Use of Ritalin or Cylert and amphetamine usage during adolescence

Activity #2

Sandy is a social worker at a nursing home. Sandy notices that residents of the nursing home who are more physically active seem to be less depressed, have more energy, and generally seem to be healthier than the more sedentary residents. Sandy reviews the literature and finds a relationship between physical activity and depression in the elderly. Based on her literature review, Sandy develops the following research hypothesis: Residents of the nursing home who exercise a minimum of twenty minutes a day, three times a week, will have lower levels of depression than those who don't. Sandy develops the following research design to test her hypothesis:

- She recruits volunteers from the residents to participate in an exercise class. The class meets three times a week for thirty minutes. A total of twenty residents volunteer to participate in the exercise class.

- She asks residents who don't wish to participate in the exercise class to act as a comparison group by taking a pre- and posttest. She is able to obtain a comparison group of nineteen residents who will take the pre- and posttests (but are not willing to participate in the exercise classes).

- She gives members of both groups a standardized depression inventory at the beginning of the study (pretest).

- After four weeks, a total of fifteen people complete the exercise classes and take the posttest. Sixteen of the original nineteen members of the comparison group complete the posttest. Sandy compares the scores of the two groups.

1. What are the strengths of Sandy's design?

2. What are the weaknesses of this study?

3. How can you determine measurement validity?

4. How can we determine if the measure is reliable?

Key Points

- Variables can be categorized into three groups: independent variables, dependent variables, and control variables.

- The dependent variable is predicted by another variable, or is said to depend on the independent variable.

- The independent variable is often thought of as a variable that is manipulated by the researcher.

- Conceptualizing a variable refers to how we translate an idea or abstract theory into variables that can be used to test hypotheses or make sense of observations.

- A control variable is any variable that the researcher wants to hold constant (control for).

- A confounding variable obscures the effect of another variable.

- A measure is a tool or instrument that is used to gather data.

- There are four levels of variables: nominal-level variables, ordinal-level variables, interval-level variables, and ratio-level variables.

- The term *operationalize* refers to how we define a concept so that it can be measured.

- Reliability refers to the ability of a measure to remain stable and consistent over time.

- Validity is a term that describes how much the instrument measures what it is meant to measure.

- There are several types of validity: face validity, content validity, criterion-related validity, concurrent validity, and construct validity.

Additional Resources

Fischer, J., & Cochran, K. (2007). *Measures for clinical practice: A sourcebook* (4th ed.). New York: Oxford University Press.

This is a two-volume set of books that compiles multiple measures devoted to couples, families, and children. A description of the purpose, norms, scoring, reliability, validity, primary reference, and availability is provided for each measure.

Mental Measurements Yearbooks
The University of Nebraska Press and Rutgers University Press both produce a yearbook of mental measurements.

Robinson, J., Shaver, P., & Wrightsman, L. (Eds.). (1999). *Measures of political attitudes.* San Diego, CA: Academic Press.
This book offers a compilation of measurement scales on issues such as racial attitudes, trust in the government, and political participation.

CHAPTER FIVE

Sampling

SO FAR, THIS BOOK HAS MOSTLY ADDRESSED the planning stages of research. Now we will move into the stage of choosing what variables to observe and gathering data. In this chapter, we will investigate the issue of sampling. This chapter will look at different sample options and examine which ones are more or less likely to offer an adequate representation of a population. We will discuss sample size, two types of sampling—probability sampling and non-probability sampling—and several techniques for sample selection.

What Is Sampling?

One of the goals of research is to draw conclusions from a sample of observed cases in a population. In research, a **population** is a set of entities from which a sample can be drawn to either describe a subsection of that population or generalize information to the larger population. Within a population there are individual members, called **elements.** In most studies it is impossible to study all pertinent cases in a population, so we must choose a sample of the elements within the population. For example, it is not possible to study every case of binge drinking on every U.S. college campus or even on a single campus. When we select a subset from a population, this group is referred to as a sample. Sampling allows the researcher to make the best use of time, money, and other resources.

A **sample** is a group of elements selected from a larger population in the hope that studying this smaller group will reveal important things about the group and may represent the larger population. Sampling, then, is the process of selecting elements from which observations will be made.

People do this every day; students take their first social work class and imagine what the rest of their social work classes will be like. Or you might meet a victim of domestic violence and make generalizations about other instances of domestic violence or domestic violence victims. While people sample daily, they rarely think about good and bad sample experiences and can therefore come to inaccurate conclusions.

Social and behavioral sciences research is often conducted on individuals or groups (e.g., hospitals, schools, and families). A **sampling frame** is a list of all elements or other units containing the elements in a population. For example, we are going to survey all the students living in a dorm about the quality of food on campus, but we can only obtain a list of the rooms (not the residents) in the dorm. Therefore, we will be drawing our sample from the dorm rooms, which are called enumeration units, as opposed to the individual students in each dorm room, who are the elements. An **enumeration unit** contains one or more units to be listed in the sampling frame.

There are times when the researcher samples different elements within a sampling frame. For instance, we could sample the dorm rooms about the quality of food at the university and then sample individual students on campus about the quality of the food. Both the dorm rooms and the individual students would be called sampling units. A **sampling unit** is a population selected for inclusion within a sampling frame. The dorm rooms are selected in the first stage of sampling and become the primary sampling units (they are also the elements in the study). The general student population becomes the secondary sampling units because they are not necessarily elements of the study, as some students do not reside on campus.

Random Selection and Random Assignment

Researchers can derive a sample using **random selection**, a means of selecting a sample from a larger population in which each member of the population has an equal chance of being selected for a study, or **random assignment,** the selection and placement of individuals from the pool of all potential participants to either the experimental group or the control group.

For example, let's say you want to know if studying in a group results in a better grade in research classes than studying individually. There are four sections of a research class offered this semester. Ideally, you would want to survey all the students in these classes, but for the purpose of this example, you randomly select half of them from the class rosters (for instance, every other person on the roster lists). This is random selection. Then, you randomly assign members into one of two groups (perhaps by drawing names out of a hat). One group (the experimental group) studies together and the members of the other group (the control group) study on their own. This is random assignment.

Sample Size—How Many Is Enough?

As researchers, we need to be confident that our sample is representative of the population from which it was drawn. **Representativeness** is assumed when characteristics of the sample are similar to those of the population from which the sample was drawn. There are several ways that we can ensure representativeness. One of the easiest ways is to have a large enough sample. We know that a very small sample can be misleading. For example, interviewing three survivors of Hurricane Katrina about their intent to return and rebuild their home might reveal that all three do not plan to return to their hometown; however, a larger sample may reveal that while some report no intention of returning, many more plan to return and rebuild. Unfortunately, there are no hard-and-fast formulas to use to determine the appropriate sample size. There are, however, some guide-lines that you can use. One technique that is widely utilized (and has gained widespread acceptance) is simply counting the number of variables in your study and then selecting a certain number of cases for each vari-able. Different researchers have different opinions on what that number of cases should be, but most people agree that between ten and twenty cases per variable is adequate. Thus if you had ten variables, you would need a sample size of between one hundred and two hundred subjects. Therefore, for many researchers the challenge is not having a large enough number of variables in the study, but recruiting enough subjects to participate.

External Validity and Internal Validity

One goal of many research studies is to apply findings beyond the group from which they were drawn. For example, you study the activities of gang members in one city to try to understand gang activity in all cities. This makes sampling an important process in conducting research. **External validity** (sometimes referred to as *generalizability*) is the extent to which a study's findings are applicable or relevant to a group outside the study (often the population from which the sample was drawn). The more that a study can be generalized to a larger population, the more external validity the study has. **Internal validity**, in its simplest form, refers to how confident the researcher can be about the independent variable truly causing a change in the dependent variable (as opposed to outside influences).

External Validity

External validity cannot be quantified in terms of a specific set of guidelines. However, it can be evaluated in light of several characteristics. One characteristic is whether the study is explained in enough detail that other researchers could duplicate the study if they wished. The more a study can be replicated, the more external validity it assumes. Two other characteristics of external validity are related to how the sampling was conducted: how the respondents of the measure were chosen and the size of the sample.

Internal Validity

Internal validity is different from the validity of a measure. Internal validity is a measure of the worth of the overall research design. It exists when a conclusion that A leads to or results in B is correct. When designing your research study, you need to keep in mind the following seven threats to internal validity:

1. Extraneous and widespread events that coincide in time with your study. For example, you are working with students in an after-school program to teach seventh graders social empathy skills during the fall of 2001. How do you know that the repercussions of the attacks of 9/11 did not account for some of their increased social empathy?

2. Maturation or the passage of time. The passage of time during a study (especially for studies lasting months or years) can have an effect. For example, we know that people commit less crime as they become sick or weak. Therefore, if you were researching crime among older adults, factors associated with age alone may account for a lower incidence of crime in older respondents.

3. Enhanced test-taking skills. After taking a test the first time, respondents' performance on subsequent tests often improves. For example, let us imagine that we are conducting a workshop for consumers in a homeless shelter on effective job-interviewing

techniques. We give participants a pretest and then provide a workshop on techniques for effective job interviewing. After the workshop, we give the participants the same test again (posttest). If they scored significantly better on the posttest, we might be tempted to argue that it was the workshop that made the difference. However, we can't be certain that taking the pretest didn't prepare them to do better on the posttest.

4. Instrumentation. If different measures are used for the pretest and posttest, how do we know that the posttest is not easier than the pretest? For example, an easier posttest might inflate the difference in scores and thus affect the findings of the study. In other words, the results may be inaccurately reporting that the intervention was effective. Problems involving instrumentation can also develop when a researcher uses a measure that is not measuring what it is intended to measure or that is not normed for the population to whom it was given.

5. Selection bias. Selection bias refers to the differences between groups that are being compared that occur when group members choose which group (the treatment group or nontreatment group) to be in. The differences between the members of the two groups might explain away any change that occurred after the intervention. For example, participants who self-select to be in a treatment group dealing with attitudes toward feminism may already be more politically liberal. It is important to make sure selection bias is eliminated as much as possible through randomization.

6. Experimental mortality. This refers to subjects dropping out of a study. This is one of the most common threats to internal validity and can affect sample size (you may not have enough respondents left at the end of the study to have a meaningful finding) and generalizability (your study no longer represents the characteristics of the population your sample came from).

7. Ambiguity about the direction of causal inference. To establish causation, the independent variable must precede (cause) the change in the dependent variable. For example, studies looking at substance abuse and mental health issues have established that there is a relationship between the two variables. What is not clear is which variable precedes the other.

One of the best ways to control for threats to internal validity is to use a group to compare the study group to, which strengthens the study. By having a non-study group to compare against the study group, the researcher can make a stronger argument that any change in the study group is due to the intervention, not to outside influences.

Probability Sampling

In **probability sampling,** each and every member of the population has a non-zero chance of being selected for the study (being included in the sample). That means every single type of person or thing has a greater-than-zero likelihood of being in a study. Probability sampling allows the researcher to make relatively few observations and generalize from those observations to the wider population. **Probability sampling theory** requires the researcher to select a set of elements from a population in such a way that those elements accurately portray the parameters of the total population.

Probability Sampling Techniques

There are four types of sampling techniques used in probability sampling: simple random sampling, systematic random sampling, stratified random sampling, and cluster sampling.

In **simple random sampling,** each person in the population is assigned a number, and then a sample is generated randomly from this population. This technique requires the compilation of a list of everyone in the population, such as all residents in a nursing home. The process for selecting the sample can be as simple as drawing numbers from a hat that will be matched to the names on the list. When drawing a sample from a population, one can return or not return subjects to the sampling space after each draw. Returning a number to the hat after it is drawn is called *sampling with replacement* and is a preferred method. When one is using sampling with replacement, each selection from the population is independent of the selections already made. For example, if your population at the nursing home had twenty-five individuals (elements) to select from and you were to randomly select individual number 4, that individual would become part of your sample. Then you go back to your original twenty-five elements and draw again, leaving the number 4 as an option. If you draw number 4 again, you return it to the hat and continue to draw until you get a different number to add to your sample. Drawing a sample without returning elements to the hat is called *sampling without replacement.*

For **systematic random sampling,** every *n*th number is selected at random (for example, every third person or every tenth person). In essence, this is identical to simple random sampling but uses a more organized technique to produce the sample. Here simple random sampling is always used to select the first number. For example, if you want to draw a systematic sample of 1,000 individuals from a student roster containing 100,000 names, you would divide 100,000 by 1,000 to get 100, meaning you would select every 100th name on the list. You would start with a randomly selected number between 1 and 100. For example, if you started with the number 47, you would then select the 147th name, the 247th name, the 347th name, and so on.

Stratified random sampling is a method for obtaining a greater degree of representativeness. Remember, probability sampling theory requires the researcher to select a set of elements from a population in such a way that those elements accurately portray the parameters of the total population from which the elements are selected. To do this, you divide your population into subgroups, or strata (for instance, by sex), then you draw the sample from each stratum, using a probabilistic procedure.

Cluster sampling (sometimes referred to as multi-stage sampling) is a method for drawing a sample from a population in two or more stages. This is used when the researcher cannot get a complete list of everyone in the population but can get complete lists within clusters of the population (such as the population of a city from a phonebook). Generally, the researcher wishes to get clusters that are as diverse as possible, whereas in stratified random sampling, the goal is to find subjects who are as similar to one another as possible. Cluster sampling is accomplished through two basic steps: listing and sampling. Listing entails constructing a list of a subset of the population. Sampling occurs within your chosen clusters. The disadvantage is that each stage of the process increases sampling error. In fact, the margin of error is larger in cluster sampling than in simple random or stratified random sampling. However, one can compensate for this error by increasing the sample size.

Perhaps you are examining child maltreatment reports by grade level in your thirteen-county region. You get a list of the schools for each county (primary cluster list) and identify a random sample of approximately 30 percent from each county (secondary cluster list). See table 5.1 for an example. You will then collect child maltreatment reports by grade level in each

TABLE 5.1: EXAMPLE OF CLUSTER CODING BY COUNTY

COUNTY	NUMBER OF ELEMENTARY SCHOOLS IN EACH COUNTY (PRIMARY LIST)	IDENTIFIED SCHOOLS (SECONDARY LIST)
Fargo	6	Jefferson Elementary Jackson Elementary
Bishop	3	Washington Elementary
Johnson	7	Lincoln Elementary Carter Elementary
Sewer	5	Clinton Elementary Bush Elementary
Lake	8	Adams Elementary Buchanan Elementary
Lincoln	10	Johnson Elementary Kennedy Elementary Lincoln Elementary
Norman	2	Roosevelt Elementary
Tulane	6	Reagan Elementary Grant Elementary
Orange	5	Taft Elementary Garfield Elementary
Camargo	5	Fillmore Elementary Harding Elementary
Fisher	9	Hoover Elementary Hayes Elementary Tyler Elementary
Newman	5	Harrison Elementary Wilson Elementary
Angel	5	Nixon Elementary Reagan Elementary

identified school. A sample of clusters will best represent all clusters if a large enough number is selected and if all clusters are very much alike.

Sampling Error

A **sampling error** is an error that occurs because only part of the population is directly contacted. With any sample, differences are likely to exist between the characteristics of the sampled population and the larger group from which the sample was chosen. Sampling error can be reduced in two ways. First, the larger the sample is, the smaller the sampling error. For instance, a sample size of 10 percent of the population will have less sampling error than a sample size of 5 percent of the population because more of the original population is represented within your sample. Second, a homogenous population produces samples with smaller sampling errors than does a heterogenous population. Stratified random sampling is based on this second method. Rather than selecting your sample from the total population, you ensure that appropriate numbers of elements are drawn from homogenous subsets of the population. This means you break the sample into smaller sections with similar qualities such as age, sex, race, and occupation. For example, you want to measure client satisfaction with the services in a large social service agency. You suspect that race is a factor in consumer satisfaction. So, you separate your participants according to race and then randomly select an appropriate number from each racial category (proportionate to the number of individuals in the category). For example, if you had one hundred whites and fifty African Americans, you might randomly select twenty whites and ten African Americans (one-fifth of each group) to sample. Again, stratified random sampling is used most often when a simple random sample cannot guarantee enough representation from small subgroups that are important to your study.

Non-probability Sampling

Social work is often conducted in settings where it is not possible to use random selection of subjects or random assignment to an experimental or comparison group. This occurs for a variety of reasons. Often a list of possible respondents for a particular study does not exist. Also, a researcher is often only able to find subjects who are willing to volunteer for one group (such as the treatment group) as opposed to being randomly assigned. Sometimes finding participants willing to join either group can be a problem. So, a second form of sampling is available—non-probability sampling. Any technique for selecting a sample in which every individual does not have a greater-than-zero chance of being selected is a **non-probability sampling** technique. There are four sampling techniques used in non-probability sampling: convenience, purposive, quota, and snowball sampling.

Convenience sampling is sampling in which one relies on available subjects. That is, you get information from any source of data you can. This is one of the most frequently used sampling techniques in social work research. Some examples of researchers who use this would be a case-worker who studies her own agency, a college professor who studies students at his college, or a researcher who observes people in her own church. This type of sampling limits the generalizability of the research to the population from which the sample is drawn. Another drawback to this method is it can be subject to sampling error because of researcher bias (selecting the sample that gives the best outcome).

Purposive sampling (also called judgmental sampling) is simply selecting a sample based on one's knowledge of a population or drawing a sample with some predetermined characteristics in mind. For example, perhaps you are a caseworker at an agency that assists consumers in obtaining assistance with utility bills. You need to do a study for a grant that would help quantify the characteristics of your participants (such as whether they rent or own their homes, whether they are employed, their level of education, their income level). Because your study must be completed soon and it is the middle of a cold winter, you decide to select the individuals who are requesting assistance for electric bills. You feel that individuals who seek assistance for electric bills reflect the majority of your clientele, as opposed to clients who seek assistance with telephone payments.

Quota sampling is a means of selecting a stratified non-random sample in which a researcher divides a population into categories and selects a certain number (a quota) of subjects from each category. Individual subjects from each category are not selected randomly; they are usually chosen on the basis of convenience and ease. Imagine that you are studying the treatment of individuals in a mental health setting. You want to see if professionals with different professional training treat clients in different ways. So your sample includes the first psychiatrists, psychologists, and social workers you are able to find.

In **snowball sampling,** the researcher starts with one or more members of the group being studied to gain access to other members of the same group, through a referral system, for the purpose of building the sample.

Snowball sampling is most appropriate when members of a population are difficult to locate. For example, if you are studying women who have disabled children and you are having difficulty locating these mothers, you may find that once you have established a relationship with one mother, she may be willing to introduce you to other women who have disabled children. Snowball sampling is also often used when the group being studied is engaged in an activity that is illegal or considered to be deviant. For example, to study members of a gang, you need referrals to members of the gang. The strength of this type of sampling is that it creates access that allows you to increase the sample. However, because friends and other associates are usually very similar, there may be little variation in the study.

Limitations of Non-probability Sampling

Although non-probability sampling may be more convenient, it is less likely to be representative of your population than probability sampling techniques. Remember that non-probability sampling techniques do not require that every member have a greater-than-zero chance of being selected. Your study is affected if the ones not included in your sample differ in some way from the rest of the population. Therefore, a random sample will have more generalizability than a convenience sample or any sample where subjects are self-selecting. For example, it might be misleading to apply the findings of a researcher who only studies gangs in Southern California to other areas of the United States because of differences in population size and characteristics, gang-related laws, law enforcement capabilities, and gang prevention programs. One question to ask is "How much does the sample reflect the population from which it was drawn?" For obvious reasons, a larger sample size would have more generalizability than a smaller one because the study is taking into account more of the actual population.

So when is non-probability sampling most useful? Some examples are pilot studies in which you are doing a trial run, agency-based research, and qualitative investigations in which you're not striving for generalizability but rather to reproduce and understand real life.

Applied Learning Activities

Activity #1
Susan is a hospital social worker. She is interested in investigating how effective support groups are for patients who have been diagnosed with a

terminal illness. Susan recruits volunteers who are currently members of a support group by posting signs around the hospital. Susan asks a friend of hers at another hospital (which does not have a support group) to recruit volunteers to serve as a comparison group. Susan and her friend ask each of the groups to complete a standardized instrument as pre- and posttests (with a period of eight weeks in between the tests).

1. What type of sampling is Susan using—probability or non-probability? What is the reason for your answer?

2. Which sampling design are Susan and her friend using?

3. What are the strengths and weaknesses of Susan's sampling design? What design would you choose? How would you carry it out?

Activity #2

Raul is a social worker at a mental health agency. Raul recruits a total of sixty volunteers for a study that will examine the effects of teaching assertiveness skills to people who are diagnosed with mood disorders. Raul places the names of all the volunteers for the study into a hat and draws out each name. As he draws the names, he assigns them either to the group that will learn assertiveness skills or to a waiting list (for the next group to start). The wait-list group will serve as the control group for the study.

1. What type of sampling is Raul using—probability or non-probability? What is the reason for your answer?

2. Which sampling design is Raul using?

3. What are the strengths and weaknesses of Raul's sampling design? What design would you choose? How would you carry it out?

Activity #3

Maria is a social worker at a shelter for battered women. Maria works with the children of women who come into the shelter. Maria has observed that male children with younger brothers or sisters tend to be more aggressive when playing than female children with younger brothers or sisters. Maria designs a study to measure the number of times a child hits, slaps, shoves, kicks, or punches other children. She will also record the age and sex of the child as part of her study. Maria recruits ten boys and ten girls (all with younger siblings) to be in a play group for one hour a day. She then observes their interactions.

1. What type of sampling is Maria using—probability or non-probability? What is the reason for your answer?

2. Which sampling design is Maria using?

3. What are the strengths and weaknesses of Maria's sampling design? What design would you choose? How would you carry it out?

Key Points

- Sampling is the process of selecting a group of subjects from a larger population in the hope that studying this smaller group (the sample) will reveal important things about the larger group (the population) from which it was drawn.

- Probability sampling is a method of sampling in which everyone in the population has an equal chance of being randomly selected for the study and randomly assigned to either the experimental group or the comparison group.

- There are four techniques for conducting probability sampling: simple random sampling, systematic random sampling, stratified random sampling, and cluster sampling.

- Non-probability sampling is a method for selecting a sample where every member does not necessarily have a greater-than-zero chance of being selected.

- There are four techniques for conducting non-probability sampling: convenience, purposive, quota, and snowball sampling.

- Internal validity refers to how confident the researcher can be about the independent variable truly causing a change in the dependent variable. There are seven threats to internal validity: extraneous events, passage of time, testing effect, instrumentation problems, selection bias, mortality of sample, and lack of casual direction.

- External validity (referred to as *generalizability*) it is the extent to which a study's findings are applicable or relevant to a group outside the study. Characteristics of external validity include the ability to be duplicated by other researchers, how the respondents of the measure were chosen, and the size of the sample.

Additional Resources

Ardilly, P., & Tillé, Y. (2006). *Sampling methods: Exercises and solutions.* New York: Springer.

This book lists 116 different exercises of sampling methods—each explained in detail. Each exercise is preceded by an explanation of the underlying theory that supports it. This is an excellent book for anyone seeking a more in-depth understanding of sampling methodology.

Rao, S. (2000). *Sampling methodologies with applications.* New York: Chapman and Hall.

This book describes in detail all commonly used sampling procedures. Along with an explanation of procedures, it includes practical exercises and examples. An additional advantage is that it keeps mathematics to a minimum, which makes the book suitable for undergraduate students.

Tryfos, P. (1996). *Sampling methods for applied research: Text and cases.* New York: J. Wiley.

This text provides cases and illustrations to help the reader understand the concepts of sampling and sampling techniques.

CHAPTER SIX

Qualitative Research Designs

As we discussed in Chapter 1, research studies use either qualitative or quantitative methods, or a combination of both methods. The type of research you choose is governed mostly by the research questions that are posed. For example, a social worker may meet someone who is a child welfare worker and begin to ask questions such as "How did you become a child welfare worker?" or "What is it like for you to investigate a child abuse case?" These exploratory questions may lend themselves to a qualitative study because little is known about the experiences of child welfare workers. In this chapter we will examine the fundamentals of qualitative research. We will discuss what qualitative research means and how it is conducted, and some basic strategies for conducting a qualitative research study.

How Is Qualitative Research Used?

Qualitative research is used if little or nothing is known about a subject. In order to develop a greater understanding of an issue, we need to use methods that allow us to investigate a phenomenon through the use of researcher observation and assessment. All research methods are equally useful and very necessary; however, they utilize different strategies and ask different research questions to gain knowledge. Two strategies used by qualitative researchers are describing the information collected (descriptive inquiry) and speculating on the information collected (speculative inquiry).

Descriptive Inquiry

Descriptive inquiry is the strategy used in qualitative research to develop a greater understanding of issues by describing individual experiences. For instance, some research examines issues related to lifestyle, such as Sinetar's *Ordinary People as Monks and Mystics: Lifestyles for Self-Discovery* (1986), which describes the quest of many people to find spiritual meaning in a materialistic universe. Other qualitative research may build existing knowledge, such as Barton's *Stripped: Inside the Lives of Exotic Dancers* (2006), in which the author uses the participants' experiences to engage long-standing debates over the meanings of femininity and sexuality. These studies distinguish themselves by examining symbolic understandings through the words of the informants. These studies might typify respondents' attitudes, but patterns in the samples are often addressed. In both of these cases, the researchers are exploring the *individual* level of understanding (how each individual describes his or her experiences) as well as the *collective* level of understanding (what is common and not common about the experiences).

Social workers frequently use the strategy of descriptive inquiry in agency practice. For instance, in documentation it is valuable to record the client's statements ("I am always tired and I cry easily") as evidence to support an impression (the client is depressed). Client assessments are the recorded descriptions of clients' statements as well as social workers' observations and impressions. Soliciting feedback such as clients' verbal and written comments is another important source of descriptive inquiry. Two ways to get verbal comments from clients are to interview them individually or to hold a focus group. A **focus group** is an open discussion in which individuals share their opinions about or emotional responses to a particular subject. For instance, a focus group can be used to gain information on what residents think about the current living conditions at a shelter. This information can be used to get a better understanding of their experiences or to meet the individual needs of residents, for example, by installing a sliding shower head for a resident who is very tall or very short. Researchers at a shelter might collect written information by asking residents to journal their thoughts, feelings, and experiences or by implementing a system that allows consumers to offer written comments, like a comment box.

It is not uncommon for agencies to use data collected from assessments and from consumers' feedback to describe the issues related to the population they serve in reports to boards of directors and in presentations to the public. These reports and presentations create a greater understanding of clients' experiences and empathy for them among others who have never had the experiences themselves. It can also provide knowledge that is useful in supporting a request for a program or resources from grant-funding sources to improve the lives of clients.

Qualitative researchers want to discover more about the interactions between people and their environment. They want to gain an in-depth understanding of what a person is feeling, thinking, and experiencing. For example, people who want to fully understand the perspectives of someone addicted to gambling can learn a great deal by reading an addict's comments on the many lures of the games. It is not important to be able to make generalizations to all people—just to know what this person is experiencing.

Speculative Inquiry

In qualitative studies, data analysis is a process of **speculative inquiry,** in which the collected information is used to generate common themes. For instance, we might ask, "What has this been like for you?" As we ask several different participants the same question, we can begin to review their answers to see if any common themes are emerging; that is, we can see if people are saying similar things about the same topic. This inductive method of going from the individual to the collective can lead us to generate new hypotheses and theories based on the knowledge we have gained.

The process of speculative inquiry is a form of **inductive research,** which is the gathering of information based upon observations and quotes that is organized into common themes. As more information is acquired, we increase our understanding and can develop research questions about the phenomenon at hand. **Deductive research** is the process of reasoning that moves from a general hypothesis or theory to specific results through the use of quantitative methods.

Qualitative Research Methods

A discussion of qualitative research needs to begin with the various types of qualitative designs. Essentially, there are five main research designs in qualitative research: ethnography, grounded theory, phenomenological study, case study, and biography. Biography is based on a single person's life reflections and is not widely used in social and behavioral sciences research. For that reason we will confine our discussion to the four other designs. While phenomenology uses descriptive inquiry as a strategy for understanding and grounded theory uses speculative inquiry, ethnography and case study use both descriptive and speculative inquiry strategies. At times, it may seem that some of the designs overlap and duplicate others. We will try to make these distinctions as clear as possible.

Phenomenological Design

Phenomenology is a type of research design that seeks to understand the lived experience of the individuals who are being studied (their perceptions, thoughts, ideas, and experiences). Phenomenological research, in some ways, embodies the field of qualitative research because it is concerned with gaining an in-depth understanding of the experience of the individual under study. Phenomenological research uses descriptive inquiry. Sometimes researchers become research participants themselves to gain firsthand knowledge. When researchers employ this technique, they make no attempt to be detached; rather they actually immerse themselves in the experience. They then rely on their own interpretation of the experience (i.e., they use introspection) to make sense of what they experienced. This is called participatory research.

Perhaps you are working in an agency where many of your clients are referred for welfare assistance and you want to be able to explain what they can expect when they apply. You could conduct a study in which you make an appointment at the local public assistance office and go through the process of applying for public assistance. At each step of the process, you would keep careful notes of your experiences, feelings, and reactions. You would encounter others going through the process and could gather information from their comments. You then could use this experience to share with clients what it was like for you to experience the application process for welfare assistance. This would be an example of a descriptive inquiry as part of a phenomenological study.

Grounded Theory Design

Grounded theory is a type of research design that utilizes a recursive form of question and analysis. The researcher begins with a set of questions often referred to as **grand tour questions.** These are large, overarching questions that identify the broad intent of a research study and are based on the existing knowledge (i.e., experience, knowledge from others, tradition, and prior research). The questions or requests are open ended, for example, "Describe for me what it was like for you," or "What was it like for you?" In the interviews, the researcher collects the information from the participants. A review of the information often leads to more specific questions, resulting in a speculative inquiry.

In social work practice this is done to identify primary issues or problems. For example, often a family will seek help only after bearing the burden of a problem for a long period of time. By this time, many more problems and issues have emerged and it is difficult to identify the primary or precipitating issues. Therefore, you start out by asking a broad open-ended question such as "What brings you here today?" You listen to a plethora of concerns and then ask for something more specific, for example, "What would you say are your top three concerns?" This leads to more specific questions, such as "What have you done in the past to get relief?" and "Have you experienced this problem before?" After collecting enough answers from family members and adding your own observations and practice experience, you can now develop common themes to use to identify the primary or precipitating problems (going from specific to general).

Ethnographic Design

Ethnography is a research design that is centered on cultural behavior. Ethnographic research seeks to record the cultural aspects of a group (these may include such aspects as language, dress, social norms, and behaviors). It is concerned with the organization of society and the study of humans. Ethnography uses both descriptive and speculative inquiry to evolve understanding.

This design might be useful in work with subcultures such as teen gangs. A social worker working with gang members would want to find out as much as possible about the culture of various gangs. For instance, what are the colors, the gang signs, and the common clothing; how do members get initiated into the gangs; and how can they get out? What gangs are rivals, and which gangs use violence? These are important cultural questions that can be explored to help the social worker studying gang-related practices. Many cultural practices are shaped and reshaped through trial and error, which makes it difficult for members to identify, describe, or define what they do. Rules are sometimes more implicit than explicit. Thus ethnography relies as much on observations as on interviews.

Case Study

A **case study** is a detailed analysis of a single person or event (or sometimes a limited number of people or events). Case studies are interesting because of the uniqueness of the case being studied. This creates a limitation because the case is not representative of other cases. The data you collect from a former foster child living in a rural area whose foster parents paid no attention to her might be similar to data for other foster children in the same situation but might not accurately reflect the experiences of foster children from urban areas or more attentive families. Another problem with case studies has to do with objectivity. The person who is presenting the case usually has some preconceived bias (opinion based on knowledge from his or her own experiences, knowledge of the experiences of others, or tradition). Otherwise, why chose to study this case? However, it is acceptable in case studies for a bias to play a role in the interpretation of events and the selection of the facts to include in the case.

Let's say that you are a mother of twins and that you want to do a case study of one mother with twins and her weekly routine. While collecting information (observations and comments), you use your own experience to interpret what is happening. For instance, while one twin is talking to the mother, the other is getting a forbidden cookie. This may be interpreted as the mother not being able to be in two places at once. However, as a mother of twins, you have experienced similar scenarios that have led you to believe that the twins might be working together to reach a goal. The following are some types of case studies.

ILLUSTRATIVE CASE STUDIES

Illustrative case studies describe a domain; they use one or two instances to analyze a situation. This helps interpret other data, especially when researchers have reason to believe that readers know too little about the study parameters. These case studies serve to make the unfamiliar familiar and give readers a common language to use to discuss the topic. The chosen site for inclusion should typify important variations and contain a small number of cases to sustain readers' interest. The use of illustrative case studies may involve some pitfalls. Such studies require presentation of in-depth information on each case, but the researcher may lack time on-site for in-depth examination. In addition, it may be difficult to hold the interest of those being interviewed in order to gain the in-depth information desired. The most serious problem involves the selection of instances. Cases must adequately represent the situation or program under study. For instance, a researcher wanting to illustrate the role of a foster parent would not want to select only new parents to observe or interview, as the participants in the study would not provide enough in-depth information on what this role entails.

EXPLORATORY CASE STUDIES

Exploratory (or pilot) case studies can be conducted before the implementation of a large-scale investigation. For instance, where considerable uncertainty exists about a program's mission, goals, and services, an exploratory case study can help researchers identify questions, select measurement samples, and develop measurement tools. The greatest pitfall in the exploratory study involves premature conclusions: the findings may seem convincing enough but are inappropriate for release as conclusions. For instance, an exploratory study soliciting workers' opinions regarding clients' failure to show up for appointments might lead to conclusions that clients are not motivated, that the client-worker relationship was never formed, or that the worker was overburdened with cases and could not devote the time necessary to the client. However, if the study solicited clients' opinions, the results might show that lack of transportation, lack of available child care, and lack of money to purchase gas or child care are predominate factors in no-show rates. Other pitfalls include researchers' tendencies to extend the study beyond the exploratory phase, and inadequate representation of diversity within the study.

CRITICAL INSTANCE CASE STUDIES

Critical instance case studies examine one or a few sites for one of two purposes. For instance, a researcher might want to observe the roles of social workers and patients in an emergency room. A very common application involves the examination of a situation of unique interest in which the researchers have little or no interest in generalizability. In the case of the emergency room observations, the purpose might be to examine the interactions between social workers and families when a patient has died. A second, rarer application entails calling into question a generalized or universal assertion and testing it by examining one instance. Again, in the emergency room scenario, this could involve testing a specific crisis intervention technique used by social workers with families when a patient has died. This method is particularly useful for answering cause-and-effect questions about the instance of concern (e.g., Does the crisis intervention technique reduce the effects of the crisis as intended?). Inadequate identification of the evaluation question is the most serious pitfall in this type of study. Correct application of the critical instance case study involves recognizing the underlying concerns. In the emergency room scenario, using a crisis intervention technique with the family of a young man who died in a car accident would be a correct application, whereas grief counseling would be a better technique for a family that has prepared for the death of their grandmother from a long-term illness.

PROGRAM EFFECTS CASE STUDIES

Program effects case studies can determine the impact of programs and make inferences about reasons for success or failure. Data rely on observations and/or structured materials that are often gathered through mixed-method research designs. In this type of case study, the researcher uses multiple sites in order to investigate why things happen and what the cause of the problem is. This case study uses predetermined themes, and findings are usually thematic and describe site differences. Pitfalls include failure to collect enough data, failure to examine enough sites to provide a diverse representation, the use of insufficiently trained evaluators, and difficulties in giving evaluators enough data collection latitude to obtain insight without risking bias. One solution would be to conduct the case studies in a set of sites chosen for representativeness and then verify the findings from the case study through targeted examination of administrative data, prior reports, or a survey. This type of case study utilizes methods derived from program evaluation that are discussed in chapter 8.

PROSPECTIVE CASE STUDIES

In a prospective case study design, the researcher formulates a set of theory-based questions in relation to the social or cultural issue under review and then examines these questions at a predetermined follow-up time by using pattern matching or a similar technique to examine observed outcomes in light of the questions that were formulated at the beginning of the study. This type of study usually involves taking a cohort of subjects and watching them over a long period. For instance, you hypothesize that the longer a foster child stays in a foster home, the fewer behavioral problems he or she will exhibit. Therefore, you observe the behaviors of a foster child in care over several months. This type of case study is predominately done using quantitative methods.

CUMULATIVE CASE STUDIES

This case study method brings together the findings from case studies done at different times. In contrast to the program effect case study, the cumulative case study aggregates information from several sites collected at different and even quite extended periods of time. The techniques for ensuring sufficient comparability and quality and for aggregating the information are what constitute the "cumulative" part of the methodology. The cumulative case study can have a retrospective focus, in which information across studies done in the past is collected. For instance, this can be useful for examining types of interventions used with a particular behavioral problem in order to identify best-practice outcomes. Or a cumulative case study can have a prospective outlook and a series of investigations for different times in the future can be designed.

NARRATIVE CASE STUDIES

Case studies that present findings in a narrative format are called narrative case studies. This involves presenting the case study as events are unfolding. For instance, a narrative case study can relay the events that occur when an individual discovers he or she was adopted by reporting the comments that are made during the discovery process. This can include comments as each new family member (e.g., mother, brother, sister) is discovered. While the findings cannot be generalized, they can be used to identify issues confronting the individual during the discovery process, and this knowledge might be beneficial to other individuals going through the same thing or to professionals working with these individuals.

Data Collection

Once you have created a working research question and selected a design, the next step is to begin developing the data collection method. Two of the most common ways data can be collected are through observation and through interviews.

Observations

Observations are used to describe the behavior of individuals or groups in their natural settings. Researchers must choose whether to identify themselves as researchers and explain the purpose of their observation. For instance, in one study, a researcher lived in a slum district of Boston to observe first- and second-generation immigrants from Italy, and in another study a researcher lived and traveled with jazz musicians to figure out how people become marijuana users. This is called *overt observational research*. The problem with this approach is that unless the observation is unobtrusive, there may be some subject reactivity. In other words, subjects tend to modify their behavior when they know they are being watched. They portray their ideal selves rather than their true selves. The issue of reactivity is especially problematic if those being watched are engaged in a behavior that is illegal or considered unacceptable by others (e.g., cheating on a test, stealing from a parent, or breaking the confidentiality of a client). This effect often decreases with time, as after awhile the subjects forget they are being observed. This is called *habituation*.

In *covert observational research,* the researchers do not identify themselves as researchers. Either they mix in with the subjects or they observe from a distance. Some famous covert research studies have involved a researcher becoming a maid without revealing her true identity to her employers and a researcher who checked into a psychiatric facility incognito. The advantages of this approach are that it is not necessary to get the subjects' cooperation, and the subjects' behavior will not be contaminated by the presence of the researcher. Some researchers have ethical misgivings about the deceit involved in this approach. It is important to consider whether harm can occur to those being observed before covert research is conducted.

The degree to which the researcher involves him- or herself in the study makes a difference in the quality and amount of data he or she will be able to collect. There are four observation roles a researcher can assume:

1. The *complete participant* is a member of the group being studied and conceals his or her role as a researcher from the group to avoid disrupting normal activity. The disadvantages are that the researcher may lack objectivity, the group members may feel distrustful of the researcher when the research role is revealed, and the ethics of the situation are questionable, since the group members are being deceived.

2. In the *participant as observer* role the researcher is a member of the group being studied, and the group is aware of the research activity. The advantage is that the researcher is a member of the group. This role also has disadvantages, in that there is a trade-off between the depth of the data revealed to the researcher and the level of confidentiality provided to the group for the information they provide.

3. In the *observer as participant* role, the researcher participates in the group activities to the extent allowed by its members, yet the main role of the researcher is to collect data, and the group being studied is aware of the researcher's observation activities. In this role, the researcher is an observer who is not a member of the group; he or she is interested in participating only as a means of conducting better observation and thus generating a more complete understanding of the group's activities. This peripheral membership role enables the researcher to observe and interact closely enough with members to establish an insider's identity without participating in those activities constituting the core of group membership.

4. The researcher assumes a *complete observer* role when he or she is completely hidden from view while observing or is in plain sight in a public setting, yet those being studied are unaware that they are being observed. In either case, the observation in this stance is unobtrusive and unknown to participants.

Of these four stances, the most ethical approach to observation is the role of the observer as participant, as the researcher's observation activities are known to the group being studied and the researcher's emphasis is on collecting data, rather than participating in the activity being observed. However, all research roles can be ethically assumed if there is assurance that the potential benefits outweigh the risks for the participants of a study.

Researchers may decide which observational role they assume based on what type of observation is required to gain the information desired. For instance, in *descriptive observation,* researchers assume that they know nothing, and they observe anything and everything; the disadvantage is that this leads to the collection of information that may or may not be relevant to the study. The second type of observation, *focused observation,* is information that is culled from observation and supported by interviews, in which the participants' insights guide the researcher's decisions about what to observe. The third type of observation is *selective observation,* in which the researcher focuses on different types of activities to delineate the differences between those activities.

The following are tips for conducting observational research:

- Be unobtrusive in your dress and actions.
- Become familiar with the setting before beginning to collect data.
- Keep your observations short at first to keep from becoming overwhelmed.
- Be honest, but not too technical or detailed in explaining to participants what you are doing.
- Use memory tools to remember information, for example, remembering key words or the first and last remarks in conversations, especially if you are recording data after observing participants.
- Actively observe the details you want to record later, such as the interactions occurring in the setting, including who talks to whom, whose opinions are respected, and how decisions are made. Also observe where participants stand or sit, particularly those with power versus those with less power, or men versus women.
- Keep a running observation record.
- Be tolerant, adaptable, and flexible.

Interviews

The main task in interviewing is to understand the meaning of what the interviewees say. Interviews are particularly useful for getting the story behind participants' experiences; therefore, the interviewer can pursue in-depth information around the topic. In mixed-method research, interviews may be useful as follow-up to questionnaires or other quantitative data collection methods to further investigate their responses. In the personal interview, the interviewer works directly with the respondent and is considered a part of the measurement instrument.

The *conversational interview* has no predetermined questions; this allows the interviewer to remain as open and adaptable as possible to the interviewee's nature and priorities. During the interview, the interviewer "goes with the flow." With the *interview guide* approach, interviewers have some basic questions that are intended to ensure that the information in the same general areas is collected from each interviewee; this provides more focus than the conversational approach but still allows the research-ers a degree of freedom and adaptability in getting information from the interviewee. The *open-ended interview* asks the same open-ended questions of all interviewees; this approach facilitates fast interviews that can be easily analyzed and compared. Finally, the *fixed-response interview* asks the same questions and requires interviewees to choose answers from among the same set of responses. This format is useful for those not experienced in interviewing.

The interviewer has to be well trained in responding to any contingency. The following are tips for interviewing:

- Be familiar with the topic.
- Choose a setting with the least distraction.
- Explain the purpose of the interview.
- Address terms of confidentiality.
- Outline the procedure of the interview.
- Indicate how long the interview usually takes.
- Provide the interviewer's contact information.
- Allow the interviewee to ask questions or express doubts about the interview.
- Prepare a method for recording data, such as audio-recording or note taking.
- Use simple, easy, and short questions.
- Speak slowly and clearly.
- Be tolerant, sensitive, and patient when the interviewee expresses provocative and unconventional opinions.

- Avoid digressions from the topic.
- Clarify the responses to test the reliability and validity of what the interviewee says.

Finally, get the respondents comfortable in the interview as soon as possible by asking for some facts before asking about controversial matters. Intersperse fact-based questions throughout the interview. Ask one question at a time, and ask questions about the present before questions about the past or future. Attempt to remain as neutral as possible and provide transitions between major topics or when the respondent has digressed from the topic on which you wish to focus. The last questions might be formulated to allow respondents to provide any other information they want to add and their impressions of the interview.

An Example Qualitative Study

Health-care workers have noticed a substantial increase in twin births over the past two years. As a social worker in this field, you are interested in preparing parents to deal with issues unique to rearing twins. To do this, you decide to do research to identify common experiences among mothers of twin children. You discover from a brief literature review that very few social work–related studies have been published on this issue. So, you begin by selecting a qualitative design. You may decide to select a grounded theory approach that will allow you to start with some questions that address basic assumptions and then expand your questions over time. You begin by developing an outline for completing the study.

Research Outline

You have already chosen the purpose and design of the study; now you can complete an outline for your study. This is basically a proposal that addresses the purpose of the study, how you will gain access to subjects, selection of participants (who and how many), protection of subjects' rights, your research questions, and the collection and analysis of information. As you can see from example 6.1, an outline is a carefully laid-out plan for the various parts of the study with a time line for completing the study. Thinking through your project is critical; researchers who do so have a better rate of completing their studies successfully and within time constraints.

EXAMPLE 6.1: MOTHERS OF MULTIPLES RESEARCH OUTLINE

PURPOSE OF STUDY: To identify common experiences for mothers of twin children

RESEARCH DESIGN: Grounded theory design

GAINING ACCESS: Letter to Mothers of Multiples support group and phone call to president of group

SELECTION CRITERIA OF PARTICIPANTS: Sampling will be by convenience. Participants must:
- be mothers of twins
- have a single-birth child
- have twin children between the ages of three and six
- be able to complete all aspects of study by (date here)

SELECTION AND DESCRIPTION OF SITES:

Individual interviews will be conducted at each participant's home or a public library (participant's choice for comfort). Focus group will be held at either the university or a participant's home, depending on majority preference.

SAMPLE SIZE: 4–10

GRAND TOUR RESEARCH QUESTION: "What differences have you experienced in your life since having multiple-birth children as opposed to a single birth child?"

TIME LINE:
- Recruitment completed by:
- Interviews completed by:
- Focus group completed by:
- Paper completed by:

HUMAN SUBJECTS PROTECTION: See informed consent form—approved by (Instructor's name here).

DATA COLLECTION: Individual interviews will be audio-taped. Participants will edit results of study (to increase credibility).

DATA ANALYSIS: Content comparison for common themes

THEORETICAL FRAMEWORK: Inductive

DEMOGRAPHICS TO COLLECT: Mothers' age, race, education, marital status, age at the time of the twins' birth, and employment; whether or not mothers receive public assistance; number of children in the home; weight of twins at birth; whether or not fertility drugs were used to conceive; whether or not mothers want more children; whether or not mothers attend support groups; type of twins (identical or fraternal)

Interview Questions

The grand tour question in this study is intended to identify common experiences of mothers parenting twins. Thus your grand tour question will be "What differences have you experienced in your life since having multiple-birth children as opposed to a single-birth child?" In this sample study, you make four assumptions. That is, you expect that personal experiences, financial experiences, family experiences, and social experiences will be issues discussed by the participants. Therefore, you will ask questions on these topics during the interviews to jump-start the conversation and keep the momentum going, for example:

- "In what ways has being a mother of multiples affected you personally?" (personal experience)
- "In what ways has being a mother of multiples affected your finances?" (financial experience)
- "In what ways has being a mother of multiples affected your family life?" (family experience)
- "In what ways has being a mother of multiples affected your social life?" (social experience)

These initial questions are used to generate additional questions and emergent lines of conversation. This is called a **semi-structured interview,** in that you have research questions to start the interview process but will solicit additional information based on the responses to your initial questions, whereas a **structured interview** is limited to the research questions the researcher brings to the interview.

Gaining Access

The issue of gaining access to subjects is particularly important when one is conducting qualitative studies. When the sample size is small, having the opportunity to interview your subjects in depth is of vital importance. This usually means spending several hours talking with each person. As a researcher, it is important for you to spend time thinking about how you may gain access to a particular population. There are several methods, and you as the researcher have to decide which is the best for you. For example:

- You may identify several places where mothers of twins congregate such as support groups or parenting classes specific to mothers with multiple-birth children (a convenience sample).

- You could get contact information for women who delivered twins from your community fertility clinic (a purposive sample of women who conceived through fertility treatment).
- You might be able to identify someone who is a mother of twins. Once you have established a relationship of trust with her, she may be willing to introduce you to other women who are also mothers of twins (a snowball sample).

The bottom line is that the researcher needs to go where the action is (the research site). In this study, you locate a Mothers of Multiples support group and decide to send a letter to the president of the group to recruit volunteers (see example 6.2).

Selection Criteria

The next step is to decide how many people to interview. Qualitative research is not as concerned with sample size as quantitative research, but

---

EXAMPLE 6.2: MOTHERS OF MULTIPLES RECRUITMENT LETTER

Dear Mothers of Multiples,
   I am a student in the school of social work at [name of university]. I am conducting a research project to help describe the experience of mothers raising twins. I am looking for mothers to volunteer to participate in this study and who are available to complete the study process by [date]. The study consists of three parts:

- a personal interview lasting no more than one hour and consisting of five initial questions, conducted in your home, or at a quiet public place, such as a library (without children)
- a brief questionnaire asking demographic information (such as your age, age of children, income, race, employment, marital status, education)
- a group meeting with the other mothers in the study to go over the findings for clarification, additions, and accuracy (about one hour, location to be determined)

   I am looking for mothers who have twin children between the ages of three and six years old and have at least one single-birth child in their family. This is so I can capture any differences between the experience of raising multiple-birth children and singletons. I need prospective volunteers to contact me by [date]. Please feel free to spread the word to other mothers who might be interested.

this does not mean that sample size is not important. As a researcher, you will need to include enough people in your sample to gain an in-depth understanding of what parenting is like for mothers of twins. In addition, while the experiences of one or two mothers are unique and valuable, in a grounded theory design you must find common experiences among several women to increase the credibility of your findings. For instance, a mother tells you her twins have opposite personalities. Until you hear it from other mothers of twins, it is only one person's experience. This finding is appropriate for a phenomenological design; however, in a grounded theory design, your goal is to capture the shared experiences of mothers of twins. Therefore, you are hoping to recruit four to ten participants for your study.

In your study, you have chosen four specific criteria for selecting participants. First, you believe that the parenting experience may be perceived differently by mothers and fathers. Therefore, you are only interested in understanding the experience of parenting from a mother's point of view. Second, you want mothers who have a single-birth child in the home because you want to ensure that the experiences discussed are unique to parents of twins, and not just the experiences of parents in general. For instance, losing sleep and having less personal time are inconveniences most every parent experiences. How would someone know if having twins has caused her to have even *less* sleep and *less* personal time unless she can compare it to her experience of parenting a single-birth child? Third, you want mothers of twins who are at the same developmental age. By selecting mothers with twin children between the ages of three and six, you are increasing the likelihood that the children of your respondents will have had some similar developmental experiences. Finally, you will select only mothers who are available to complete the interviews within the established time frame. This will reduce the likelihood that participants will drop out of the study. For instance, you may contact a volunteer to schedule an interview but find that because she was unaware of the study's time line, she has planned a vacation for the time during which you will be interviewing your subjects. As a final note, keep in mind that limited availability and strict access requirements are always issues that can shrink a projected sample size.

Ethical Considerations

It is important to keep in mind our discussion of ethics and the ethical considerations raised in chapter 2. In research with people, it is important to safeguard their anonymity and their confidentiality. While the individuals in your grounded theory study may not be anonymous, they can have the assurance that their personal information will remain confidential.

It is also important that research participants understand their rights as subjects in the study. We strongly suggest that you develop an informed consent form and have it approved by the school's institutional review board and have your participants sign the form. Example 6.3 can be used for grounded theory research.

Recording Information

Once you have identified the research questions to be asked and found subjects to participate in your study, the next step is to decide how you

---

EXAMPLE 6.3: MOTHERS OF MULTIPLES INFORMED CONSENT FORM

You are being asked to participate in a research project. This research project is part of the requirements for an undergraduate social work degree at [name of university]. You will be asked to participate in an interview, and as part of this interview you will be asked questions about your experience being a mother of twin children. Your participation will require approximately sixty minutes of your time.

The principal investigator in this research project is [your name], who is currently a student at the [name of university]. **All research projects that are carried out by the investigator are governed by requirements of the university and the federal government.**

There are no reasonable foreseeable risks or discomforts that can occur to you while you participate in this research. You may discontinue your participation at any time.

As part of this research, audio-taping will be utilized to record your statements. By signing this statement, you give the researcher permission to record your conversation. The tapes will be transcribed and then destroyed. Your name will not be used, and in no way will you be identified. Any reference to you will be deleted from the transcript and replaced with a fictitious name.

Your participation is completely voluntary. You will receive no special consideration, reward, or compensation for participating.

Your Name   or   Your Instructor's Name

xxx xxx-xxxx   xxx-xxx-xxxx

_____   _____

Name (Please Print)   Date

will record the information. Some researchers prefer to audio-tape their interviews and then transcribe the tapes later. Others prefer to use video-tapes to record their subjects' responses. Still others record information in notes or collect information from journals and written comments. Regardless of the format that you decide to use, it is important to remember to protect the confidentiality of the participants in your research.

Analysis

For some researchers, the analysis is the most difficult portion of the entire qualitative research process. The researcher can end up with pages of notes, and the classification and categorization of so much evidence can lead to confusion, overload, and uncertainty. Therefore, after you have finished collecting information, you will compile the information in a word-processing program (see example 6.4). This provides you with a paper copy of the subjects' spoken words and allows you, the researcher, to begin to analyze what has been said.

You can increase the credibility of the findings by verifying the information you collect. You can clarify individual answers during the interview by repeating what you heard to ensure accuracy. In your twins study, the mothers agree to review the narratives collected from their interviews to ensure their accuracy. This is especially helpful when you have taken notes as opposed to using an electronic recording device that captures exact wording.

Literature Review

In the qualitative research design, the literature review is used to shape the study based not so much on what others have found but rather on what others have not explored. Therefore, literature reviews can occur before and after information is collected. A review of the literature before a study enables the researcher to determine what general knowledge is available and is not available. In the example study, you discover from a brief literature review that very few social work–related studies have been published on the issue of parenting twins (see example 6.5). This prompted you to do a qualitative study. After you conduct the study, you go back to the literature to research the common themes that were found. In this way, you are adding to any existing knowledge.

Writing the Report

The qualitative researcher is concerned with providing a detailed and accurate description of the subject's experience rather than an objective

EXAMPLE 6.4: MOTHERS OF MULTIPLES INTERVIEWS

PARTICIPANT 1: People stop us all the time. I find myself getting almost ugly with people sometimes. You just can't walk into the store; like at Wal-Mart, people will ask, "Are they twins?" And they try to reach out and touch them. I am trying to teach them not to be too friendly with strangers, and it makes that job really hard. "I am glad it is you and not me"—I hear that a lot. It's not just because I have twins, but because I have four kids. Some people will say, "Oh my God, are they all yours?" Others will say, "You're not going to have any more, are you?" I can't believe people have the nerve to say that. What gives people the right to say whatever they feel? I can't believe it. Some people will come up because they have twins in their own family. When my husband is with me he will say, "You don't have to be ugly." Everyone has a comment. I have gotten to the point where I learn not to look at people so I don't encourage contact. One lady walked by and said to her mother, "Come look at the kids!" and called her mother over, and then she said, "That's what I am afraid is going to happen to me." One woman said, "Oh my God, bless your heart." And I said, "Yes, He really has." So, I am having trouble with that; it has been a big adjustment for me.

PARTICIPANT 2: The real big difference is the attention you attract in public. That has been just such a basic thing; it's just everywhere you go, you have to stop and talk. Not everybody, but it seems like it, almost. You can't go anywhere quickly, just because how tedious it is to get everyone in and out, and you have to stop and talk along the way. Everybody says, "Oh, you have your hands full." That's probably the thing I have heard the most. And then, uh, people comment about, uh, they make comments about the four boys, all the time. We get the "double trouble" that you hate, you know. You get that comment all the time. And, uh, "We don't see how you do it." Personal questions: "Are you going to have any more children" and "When are you gonna have a girl?" You know. People ask a lot, right off the bat, "Are they twins?" They're identical. People often ask their names. People ask so much more with twins, I find there is really a fascination with multiple births by just the general public, even though it's more common now than it used to be with fertility drugs and stuff. Still, it is a real fascination with it, umm, I never realized that. People often stop to chit-chat, just all sorts of things; people might even stop you in a store and call somebody over to see the twins.

EXAMPLE 6.4: (CONTINUED)

PARTICIPANT 3: It's a parade. You're a spectacle. I have had several people come up and say, "Are they twins?" So, I decided to put them in the same outfit and different colors. When my husband and I are together, we can buy groceries in forty-five minutes. But it takes an hour and a half easy when the twins are with us. Because people stop and say, "Aren't they the cutest kids" and "I always wanted twins," and it goes on and on. When my husband goes with us, he usually takes one of the twins and I take the other. You hear a lot of "I always wanted twins." You hear a lot of family stories. But the thing that irritates me is "Better you than me," and the one that kills me is "Do you have a favorite?" and I always say, "Uh-huh, the one that is not crying." They want to know things like "How much did they weigh?" They think they have the right to know the whole personal history. "Are they identical?" "Are they boys?" And then they ask, "Were you on fertility drugs?" And I say, "And your name is?" People don't normally ask others if they are on drugs, but I get that all the time. But people mostly ask, "Are they twins?" And being president of the Mothers of Multiples Club, when I see someone with twins, I will say, "Oh, how old are the kids?" and that will tell me right away whether or not they are twins.

PARTICIPANT 4: A lot of people comment about the twins at the mall. There is more attention attracted to twins than to single babies. We do have a lot more people stopping us. I am glad for the twins club because it is not that big of a deal. They are all in the same boat.

---

and dispassionate overview of the findings (as would be expected in a quantitative report). You may spend a great deal of time and energy telling a narrative that will help the reader understand the subject's experiences. In your grounded theory study, you would try to find general themes in all the interviews and use quotes to illustrate those themes in your report. The report is organized to summarize common themes regarding each assumption as well as additional themes that were not presumed. For example, one of the recurring themes in the narrative of each subject in your grounded theory study is the issue of the public's reactions to twins. This may lead you to formulate a new hypothesis that being a mother of twins requires one to have more interactions with others in public than being a mother of single-birth children does. Example 6.6 is an example of a summary of the assumptions concerning social experiences discussed by the mothers of twins.

EXAMPLE 6.5: MOTHERS OF MULTIPLES LITERATURE REVIEW

The U.S. Department of Health and Human Services reports that for 1996 there were 1,000,750 live births of twins, a 150 percent increase over the last ten years (Martin et al., 1997). This rapid increase in multiple births is largely due to the use of fertility drugs and better medical interventions (Kiely et al., 1992). Multiple-birth children are more prone to health-related risks, such as being born premature, and associated health-related problems can create a large increase in medical costs for the family. This stressor and others associated with parenting fragile multiple-birth newborns are diverse and unmet by health-care professionals. This may be due to a lack of awareness of what needs exist for these families.

    Walton et al. (1994) report that parents of multiple-birth children feel that health caregivers are not aware of the stresses they experience and are unsure how to advise them. Some specific stressors for parents of multiple-birth children noted by Malmstrom and Biale (1990) are sleep deprivation, economic hardships, lack of time for parents to be alone, and lack of in-home help. In addition, Papiernik (1990) calculates the cost of multiple births due to extensive perinatal care and higher rate of handicaps to be ten times greater for twins than for single-birth children. The bottom line is that physicians, social workers, and other caregivers need to understand the special needs of multiple-birth families in order to provide psychosocial services (Bryan, 1997).

If your research outline includes a collection of demographic information in addition to the narrative data, you will want to compile this data. This information may be useful when you are writing the report. Table 6.1 shows the demographics that were collected for our sample study.

Applied Learning Activities

Activity #1

    You are a social worker at a homeless shelter. Your consumer population has changed recently, and you are seeing more women with children at the shelter than previously. You are interested in understanding what issues are common among these families so that you can provide some general services targeting this population. Few studies have been published about the experiences of homeless mothers. You have asked to do all the case management for these women.

EXAMPLE 6.6: MOTHERS OF MULTIPLES REPORT

Social experiences were a predominant theme. All four women reported a lack of privacy in public due to stranger curiosity. The comments and questions most encountered were "Are they twins?" "You're not having more are you?" and "I'm glad it's you and not me." One mother summed up her frustration concerning public curiosity with this statement: "They want to know things like how much did they weigh. They think they have the right to know the whole personal history."

Another common experience for all four mothers was the additional time it takes in public when they have their twins with them. "You can't go anywhere quickly, just because how tedious it is to get everyone in and out, and you have to stop and talk along the way." "We do have a lot more people stopping us." "People stop us all the time." "When my husband and I are together, we can buy groceries in forty-five minutes. But it takes an hour and a half easy when the twins are with us."

The literature reports that families with multiple-birth children suffer economic hardships, medical problems, and multiple stressors. What the literature fails to identify are the *specific* stressors and hardships facing these families. In this study, specific information has been captured to help ferret out the unique social struggles experienced by these four women.

One recommendation for practice is to educate families about the social impact of twins in public. With the overexposure of quintuplets and sextuplets in the media, the mothers of twins in this study felt their privacy was invaded in public but felt neglected in supportive donations such as seen with families of quintuplets.

1. What questions would you ask?

2. What research design would you use?

3. How would you select participants?

4. How would you record their information?

5. How would you protect their confidentiality?

Activity #2

You are a social worker for a juvenile correction facility. You have noticed that there is an unspoken rank and file among the residents (for instance, certain kids are allowed to cut in the lunch line while others are not) as well as a code of behavior that staff has observed. You are interested

TABLE 6.1: MOTHERS OF MULTIPLES DEMOGRAPHICS

	MOTHER #1	MOTHER #2	MOTHER #3	MOTHER #4
AGE	33	39	27	36
RACE	White	White	White	White
EDUCATION	3 years college	Bachelor's	High school diploma	Master's
MARITAL STATUS	Married	Married	Married	Married
PUBLIC ASSISTANCE	None	None	WIC	None
EMPLOYMENT	Full time	None	Part time (at home)	None
FAMILY INCOME	$62,000	$120,000	$36,500	$75,000
NUMBER OF CHILDREN IN THE HOME	3	4	4	4
AGE/SEX OF CHILDREN	34mo/male 34mo/male 19mo/male	6yr/female 5yr/male 34mo/male 34mo/male	8yr/female 5yr/male 32mo/male 32mo/male	5yr/male 3yr/male 14mo/male 14mo/male
WEIGHT OF TWINS AT BIRTH	4lbs, 0 oz 4lbs, 10 oz	7lbs, 6 oz 8lbs, 1 oz	6lbs, 13 oz 6lbs, 4oz	5lbs, $\frac{1}{2}$ oz 5lbs, 14 $\frac{1}{2}$ oz
MOTHER'S AGE WHEN TWINS WERE BORN	29	36	25	35
FERTILITY DRUGS USED WHEN TWINS WERE CONCEIVED	Yes	No	No	No
WANT MORE CHILDREN	No	No	No	Maybe
SUPPORT GROUPS USED	AMOM	AMOM	AMOM Church	AMOM Church PTA
TYPE OF TWINS	Identical	Identical	Identical	Identical

in understanding the culture of this facility through the eyes of the residents. You will observe the residents you have in your caseload (this is your sample) and interview them during their regular weekly individual meetings with you.

1. What questions would you ask?

2. What research design would you choose?

3. What researcher role would you use?

4. How would you record their information?

5. How would you protect their confidentiality?

Activity #3

You are a social worker for a women's domestic violence shelter. You are interested in studying the lived experiences of the women in the shelter to understand any perceptions, thoughts, ideas and experiences that they may have in common. You will utilize the nightly support group setting for the women (this is your sample) to explore and compare their experiences.

1. What questions would you ask?

2. What researcher role would you assume?

3. What issues would you encounter in attempting to gain access to subjects?

4. How would you record their information?

5. How would you protect their confidentiality?

Key Points

- The four most common qualitative research designs are ethnography, grounded theory, phenomenology, and case study.

- Ethnographic research designs are centered on cultural behavior. This research design seeks to record the cultural aspects of a group.

- Grounded theory is a type of research design that utilizes a recursive form of question and analysis. The researcher begins with a set of questions that lead to further questions. From the individual information collected, common themes are identified.

- Phenomenological research designs seek to understand the lived experience of those who are being studied.

- A case study is a detailed analysis of a single or limited number of people or events. A case study can be illustrative, exploratory, a critical instance, program effects, prospective, cumulative, or narrative.

Additional Resources

Berg, B. (2006). *Qualitative research methods for the social sciences* (6th ed.). Boston: Allyn and Bacon.
This text provides a good discussion of focus groups. While the focus is not social work, the author provides detailed information on conducting qualitative research.

Creswell, J. (1998). *Qualitative inquiry and research design: Choosing among five traditions.* Thousand Oaks, CA: Sage.
Creswell does an excellent job of presenting the five main traditions of qualitative inquiry and giving the reader a solid example of how each is carried out.

Denzin, N., & Lincoln, Y. (1998). *Strategies of qualitative inquiry.* Thousand Oaks, CA: Sage.
This is a classic text on the techniques for conducting qualitative inquiry.

Erlandson, D., Harris, E., Skipper, B., & Allen, S. (1993). *Doing naturalistic inquiry: A guide to methods.* Thousand Oaks, CA: Sage.
This text provides practical and hands-on advice for beginning qualitative researchers.

Padgett, D. (2004). *The qualitative research experience.* Belmont, CA: Wadsworth.
One of the strengths of this book is that it provides both practical advice and excellent examples for each type of qualitative method.

Schwandt, T. (1997). *Qualitative inquiry: A dictionary of terms.* Thousand Oaks, CA: Sage.
A handy companion to many of the texts above, this book provides

thorough and understandable definitions of the terminology used in qualitative research.

Yin, R. (2009). *Case study research: Design and methods* (4th ed.). Thousand Oaks, CA: Sage.

This text provides more in-depth information on designing case studies.

CHAPTER SEVEN

Quantitative Research Designs

THIS CHAPTER WILL FOCUS ON THE process of conducting quantitative research, or using research designs that attempt to explain the relationship between two or more variables. In this chapter we will look at developing a testable hypothesis, the differences between correlation and causation, cross-sectional and longitudinal designs, and group research designs.

Getting Started

We know that all social work research should be subjected to the "so what" rule (So what does this have to do with social work or what is the value to social work?). Provided you can adequately answer this question, you then proceed to the second issue—ethical considerations. In chapter 2, we reviewed ethical considerations, and you may recall there was one overarching principle—all research must be careful to ensure that no harm is done to human subjects. This extends to protecting subjects' anonymity and their confidentiality. Once these considerations have been satisfied, you are ready to proceed with the literature review.

When researchers start their literature review, they must address several questions. These questions are:

1. What is known about this subject? What research has been conducted to date? What has been discovered thus far?
2. What level of knowledge exists? Are we at a level that suggests exploratory studies are needed (because little is known about something)? Or has enough information been acquired that we

can draw some tentative conclusions (i.e., conduct descriptive research)?

3. Have enough studies been published that we can begin to postulate research questions about the relationships between variables (i.e., conduct explanatory research)? Moreover, do the studies agree or disagree on how one variable influences another variable or even which variables are important?

Let us assume that after conducting our preliminary literature review and answering these questions, we have discovered that enough information exists for us to design a quantitative research study. Based upon our search of the existing literature, we have been able to develop some tentative research questions. These questions are designed to address a gap in the existing knowledge.

Developing a Testable Hypothesis

You may remember from chapter 1 that hypotheses are generally defined as testable statements that predict a relationship between at least two variables. In later chapters we will discuss how to test our hypotheses and examine some statistical methods for determining whether our hypotheses are indeed supported (i.e., whether they can be accepted or rejected). In the meantime, let us discuss the issue of establishing research hypotheses for a quantitative study.

When researchers are developing a research hypothesis, they turn to the existing literature. Quantitative research is deductive; that is, it is driven by the findings of other studies (either qualitative or quantitative) and what is already known. You, as a researcher, should not be developing hypothesis statements based on a guess or opinion; rather, you should be guided by what other researchers have found. For instance, some studies found that people who accept racial stereotyping are less inclined to support increased funding of welfare. With that in mind, you can develop a hypothesis about the relationship between these variables with different sample characteristics (e.g., "Does this apply to all races?"). Then you will read more research to build more hypotheses.

Since human behavior is usually driven by numerous factors, each explanatory study can have several independent variables. For example, a married couple may get a divorce because of boredom with each other, fights over money, arguments over how to deal with children or in-laws, or infidelity. If researchers want to examine each of these variables, they should write a hypothesis for each independent variable, for instance, "Couples who bicker over finances are more likely to divorce" and "Divorce occurs more frequently when one of the spouses has a sexual encounter outside the marriage."

What Is Descriptive Research?

The concept of description has a much different meaning in a quantitative design than when it is employed in a qualitative design. Description is used in qualitative or inductive research to help the reader understand the lived experience of people experiencing a phenomenon. Description is used to convey the feeling of being there and to help the reader understand the experience from the person's own perspective. In qualitative research, one of several **non-standardized methods,** or informal methods of collecting data, such as the use of broad and open-ended question (recorded for accuracy) or a journal or field notes, may be used to do this.

Descriptive research is used to obtain information concerning the current status of a phenomenon in order to describe variables or conditions in a situation. The quantitative methods that can be used range from correlational studies that describe the relationship between variables and surveys, which are used to describe the status quo (both discussed later in this chapter), to evaluative studies (discussed in chapter 8), which can evaluate specific characteristics of a program within an agency. Quantitative research methods handle descriptive data by systematically recording information that describes characteristics about the population or phenomenon being studied. This may involve the use of standardized methods of data collection, such as surveys in which data are recorded in a quantifiable fashion or are collected from case records.

Correlation versus Causation

When you are conducting quantitative research, you are attempting to determine whether any relationship exists between variables, and if so, what kind. The relationship can be causal (one variable is causing a change in the other), which tends to be difficult to demonstrate, or it can be a **correlational relationship,** in which two (or more) variables are linked. A change in one variable may be associated with some degree of change in the other variable. For example, husbands who embrace traditional gender roles may be more likely to hit their wives than husbands who embrace nontraditional gender roles. Likewise, social work students whose parents are politically active usually find their policy classes more pertinent than do their peers whose parents are not politically active. However, to say that one variable is correlated with another does not mean one caused the change in the other. When a study finds associations or correlations between its variables, one cannot automatically conclude that the independent variables produced the change in the dependent variable. A **causal relationship** requires three conditions to be met: (1) the independent variable must come before the dependent variable (known as temporal ordering), (2) the independent and dependent variables must be correlated, and (3) the correlation between the independent and dependent variables cannot be explained by the impact of another variable. Absence of one of these conditions destroys the chance of causation. Thus, to demonstrate causality, one must show that traditional gender roles affect abuse by themselves and that there are no hidden (confounding) variables. For instance, we must rule out the possibility that other factors such as having an abusive father, working in a male-dominated occupation, and taking classes on domestic violence may also have an effect on spousal abuse. In addition, we must prove temporal ordering—that is, were traditional gender roles embraced before the men hit their wives? It is possible that husbands hit their wives before they espoused traditional gender roles and that they began to use the statement "Wives, obey your husbands" after the fact as justification. One truism in research is the axiom that "Correlation does not imply causation." The fact that two things are correlated does not mean that one is causing the other.

Data Collection

Once you have created a working research hypothesis, then the next step is to begin developing the data collection method. Two common methods of collecting quantitative data are through archives and other preexisting data and through surveys.

Archival or Retrospective Research

Archival or retrospective research, sometimes referred to as secondary research, relies on preexisting data or records. This research method often involves content analysis, a qualitative analysis of material in which the content of the data is examined and themes are identified. In quantitative research, researchers use archival research to determine what information they want to collect, or what the variables in the study will be.

Perhaps you are a caseworker for Child Protective Services and are interested in conducting a descriptive study of therapeutic foster care placements during the last twelve months. You would create a sample study employing a quantitative descriptive design from case files over the past twelve months. You would begin by identifying some data that you want to collect, such as each child's age, sex, race, reason for placement (defined as type of maltreatment), length of placement, and placement upon discharge from foster care. These and other variables begin to form the basis of your research to describe therapeutic foster care placements during the last twelve months.

Surveys

Surveys pose closed-ended statements or questions to which subjects are asked to respond. They are a relatively inexpensive way to reach a large number of people quickly as well as to describe a small population or an individual. Suppose, for example, that you wanted to find to what extent subscribers are satisfied with a quarterly newsletter published by your agency. You may choose to interview them in person or by phone, using a survey tool. Unfortunately, interviews are often difficult to arrange because people's schedules do not always coincide and their time is limited. Also, interviewers must be trained—a costly and time-consuming process—if they are to obtain reliable information. Even with printing and mailing charges, surveys cost considerably less than interviews administered to the same number of people. Many people are familiar with surveys and are accustomed to completing them. Mailed surveys may be particularly easy to complete, since people are under no pressure to finish all the questions within a certain amount of time, but can fail to provide a good response rate of return.

Constructing surveys for a large sample or population is not easy and requires many skills. The directions and the questions should be written clearly and easy to read, and the survey should be easy to complete and return. Piloting the survey with a small number of people enables researchers to examine reliability and validity issues on the instrument before giving it to a larger sample. Telephone surveys, mail-out and Internet surveys, and face-to-face interviews are the most convenient collection methods. Each has positive and negative aspects that will be discussed in turn.

TELEPHONE SURVEYS

Telephone surveys are relatively easy to conduct and are cost effective. One individual can call many people in a short amount of time and thus collect a large amount of data. For this reason, telephone surveys are quite popular. On the downside, telephone surveys are inherently limited to those individuals who have a telephone, who are at home when the surveyor calls, and who are willing to spend the time to answer questions. For this reason, the people who take a survey may not be representative of the group the survey is intended to describe. For example, a telephone survey was conducted on people's perceptions of the presence of police officers within the community. The person conducting the survey missed those people who either didn't have a phone or were unwilling or unavailable to take the call. It could be argued that those who were willing to respond to the interviewer's questions had strong opinions concerning the presence of police in the community and wanted to be heard.

MAIL-OUT AND INTERNET SURVEYS

Another way to conduct surveys is to use mail-out or Internet surveys. These are also popular because they are relatively simple, and if administered correctly, they can be an effective way to collect data. When you are conducting a mail-out or Internet survey, you should develop a brief cover letter or statement that describes the purpose of the survey, who is conducting the survey, and why it is important to fill out and return it. Make sure that all ethical considerations discussed in chapter 2 are covered, and include information on the approximate amount of time it will take to complete the survey. Finally, make sure to provide a self-addressed and stamped return envelope (for snail mail) so that respondents can simply drop the completed survey in the mail.

INTERVIEWS

Face-to-face (in-person) interviews have several advantages. For instance, the interviewer can clarify questions on the survey, thereby reducing the number of unanswered questions, which are common with mailed surveys. Another advantage is that face-to-face interviews are relatively easy to administer. One individual can stand in one spot (for example, a crowded shopping center on a weekend) and collect information from many individuals. The downside of face-to-face interviews is that they can be labor intensive, and depending on how much information is needed, a large number of people may be needed to get a reasonable sample size.

Cross-Sectional and Longitudinal Designs

A **cross-sectional design** is a research design that looks at a cross-section or subset of a population at one point in time. For example, let us assume that you are conducting a study on the attitudes toward illegal drug use among two groups—one group with members ages sixty-five to seventy, and one group with members between the ages of twenty and twenty-five. You may find that the older group has stronger opinions about drug use and feels that it is detrimental to individuals who engage in it. However, one cannot assume that the younger group will have the same attitudes when they are older.

The cross-sectional method of investigation is useful when the research goal is to compare developmental levels of people at various ages or from various backgrounds. Many children at different ages are studied in groups according to their age, and the results on the same sets of measures are compared for the groups. For example, one can determine the approximate age at which an infant can be expected to roll over, creep, crawl, pull him- or herself up to a standing position, and walk unaided by observing the behavior of groups of children from birth until the age of about fifteen months. If we study a group of one-month-old infants, another group of two-month olds, and so forth, up to the age of fifteen months, we will have a cross-sectional research design.

One must be careful not to infer too much from the results of cross-sectional research designs. For instance, cross-sectional research cannot deal with the issue of temporal ordering. If a researcher finds a correlation between independent and dependent variables in a one-time study, he or she cannot determine which factor precipitated the other. For example, a social worker may find that delinquent teenagers often have delinquent friends. This may be true, but it is impossible to know if the friends' behaviors motivated the teenagers to engage in illicit activities or if the teenagers only chose friends who supported their illicit behaviors.

A **longitudinal design** is a research study that follows one cohort over a period of time (usually several years or even decades). Whereas the cross-sectional design looks at one group at one point in time, the longitudinal design is interested in how the same person or group changes over time. Longitudinal research can address issues and support methods in ways that are not possible with traditional cross-sectional approaches. It is particularly valuable in a number of research areas:

- when the focus is directly on change and the phenomenon being studied is itself inherently longitudinal—for example, the dynamics of poverty, employment instability, social mobility, and changing social attitudes

- when causal processes are being investigated—for example, the effects of unemployment on mental health or of child poverty on later life chances of poverty
- when social change is being studied and the researcher needs to separate age, period, and cohort effects
- when one is establishing the effect of a treatment by following participants involved in an experimental or quasi-experimental design (discussed later) or comparing periods before and after the introduction of public policy, such as a ban on smoking in public buildings

For obvious reasons such as cost, time commitment, and the difficulty of tracking a group over time, these types of studies are rarely undertaken. Some examples of this research are studies looking at people's attitudes toward rape, marijuana use, and the division of labor in families, all of which have changed over the past fifty years

Group Research Designs

Social workers practice with a variety of types of groups in multiple settings. Since research always deals with comparisons of patterns within groups of people or things, researchers must rely on different types of group research designs. There are three major types of group research designs: pre-experimental, quasi-experimental, and experimental designs. Each involves a different type of research, and a researcher's decision as to which to use depends on the purpose and resources available.

Pre-experimental Designs

Pre-experimental research designs can be useful when the research question is fairly simple, and it is impossible to set up experimental conditions. Many social scientists rely on this design because they want to study human habits in the setting in which they occur without using a comparison group. That is, rather than taking a person to a structured environment, researchers study people in the schools, agencies, and places of religious worship where the behavior they are studying actually occurs. In fact, many social scientists believe that this is the best way to study human behavior because these naturalistic approaches allow them to capture information in situations that are closest to real life. But it is importtant to note that a limitation of this research design is that it may pose many threats to internal validity.

This approach is used frequently in social work practice. Let us imagine for a moment that you are offering a class to sixth graders on the effects of alcohol on the body. As a researcher, you can develop the following hypothesis: "Sixth-grade students who attend an alcohol awareness course will increase their knowledge of the effects of alcohol on the body." This is a testable hypothesis; therefore, it is possible to design a study to accept or reject it. Your first task is to develop a lecture that will convey information about alcohol and its effects on the body. Then you explore the factors that may either facilitate or block students' understanding of the material, for instance: "Is the material age appropriate?" "Will the presentation be too lengthy?" "Will there be interruptions?" Next, you develop a short quiz that will measure the information covered in your presentation. You include in the quiz questions on the factors that may affect the students' learning (i.e., confounding variables). For instance, you may ask the students if they understood the material, if they thought the lecture was too short or too long, or if there were interruptions during the lecture that distracted them. Next, you present the material about drinking and how it affects the body over the course of about forty minutes. At the end of the class period, you give the students the quiz to measure what they have learned. This would be a *one-group posttest-only design*. In research notation this would be described as:

$$X \qquad O$$

Here the X represents the service or intervention, and the O represents the observation, or the response of the participant. In this case, the X represents the lecture content on the effects of alcohol, and the O represents the quiz score at the end of the class. It is simply measuring what the students learned post-intervention (i.e., after the intervention). It could be argued that perhaps these students had an exceptional amount of knowledge about the subject before the class started.

Another pre-experimental design is the *one-group pretest-posttest design*. Let us imagine that you administered the quiz before the start of the class to measure their baseline level of knowledge, you then presented the material over the next forty minutes and then you tested them again with the same quiz (this is classical educational methodology). You could then compare the pretest scores with the posttest scores. If their scores improved, it could be logically argued that the improvement was due to what they learned in class. Research notation would diagram this design as:

$$O \quad X \quad O$$

It should be clear at this point that the first O represents the pretest and the X is the class lecture. The second O represents the posttest. The most obvious limitation to this design is the fact that there is no comparison group. Critics could argue that perhaps these students' scores were random or occurred by chance. Thus, it is difficult to determine the true effect of the intervention on students.

Quasi-Experimental Designs

Quasi-experimental designs are designs in which there is a comparison group but it is either not possible or not feasible to use random assignment to assign participants to groups. Random assignment, discussed in chapter 5, increases internal validity and reduces the likelihood of bias because each subject has non-zero probability of being placed in each group. For example, it would not be ethical to recruit a group of volunteers for a study about homelessness and then randomly assign one group to a condition of homelessness for a period of time. You might, however, be able to find a group of individuals who are currently homeless and compare them to a group of people who are living in permanent housing.

Thus without a comparison group of students who did not have the alcohol education class in our example, we would be unsure if the class itself led to the results on the quiz. To deal with this, you might also give the quiz to several other students who did not participate in the class. In other words, you would use a comparison group that had no access to the material to control for these issues. This would be an example of a slightly more sophisticated design known as the *posttest-only with non-equivalent group design.* In research notation it would be:

$$X \quad O$$
$$O \text{ (different group)}$$

Again, X would represent the class lecture and O would represent the posttest. Now, if the students in the class who received the lecture scored much higher on the quiz, you could assert that *maybe* it was due to the lecture. We cannot be certain, however, that there are not inherent differences between the two groups. Confounding variables such as family experience with alcohol abuse, religious beliefs, and sex may have an impact on the level of knowledge each group has concerning the effects of alcohol on the body.

Let us imagine for a moment that you are a case manager working in a community mental health agency with adults. You have been offering a support group for your consumers in which you discuss issues such as daily living skills, money management, and other skills necessary for independent living. The group begins every eight weeks and meets once a week for the two-month period. You have noticed that several of your consumers seem to feel better about themselves after participating in the group. Perhaps you review the literature and find several studies that suggest that support groups are an effective way to increase the self-esteem of your consumers. After completing your literature review, you develop the following hypothesis: "Participants will report an increase in self-esteem following an eight-week support group."

To test this hypothesis, you ask the participants who begin the next eight-week period to complete a self-esteem measurement instrument before the beginning of the first class. As a comparison, you ask an equal number of participants (who are not attending the group, but who are consumers at your agency) to complete the same instrument. Then at the end of the eight weeks, you ask both your support group and the comparison group to complete the self-esteem questionnaire again. In research notation this would be:

$$O \quad X \quad O$$
$$O \qquad O$$

The Os represent the pretest and posttest, and the X represents the support group (the intervention). We could argue that if the experimental group (the group that participated in the support group) had remarkably higher scores on their self-esteem scale after completing the support group (compared to the scores on the pretest), then the difference may be attributed to the support group itself. The scores of the comparison group would strengthen this argument if the comparison group's scores remained similar from the pretest to the posttest (i.e., their scores did not increase or decrease over time).

All research designs have inherent limitations, and the pretest-posttest non-equivalent comparison group design is no exception. Logic would dictate that we could not rule out any alternative explanations for the perceived changes in the experimental group. How do we know, for example, that something else outside the group did not happen to cause the group to feel better about themselves? Perhaps all the members of the group suddenly found new jobs, received promotions, or felt that the climate at their places of work became friendlier toward them. Any number of variables could account for a change in the group outside the influence of the support group itself.

Time series designs are slightly more rigorous than simple quasi-experimental designs such as the pretest-posttest non-equivalent group design outlined above. Imagine again that you are working as a case manager at a community mental health agency. You are working with adults who participate in your support group. This time, instead of recruiting other consumers to serve as a comparison group, let us imagine that all the consumers in your agency are participating in your support group—effectively eliminating the chance to have a comparison group. One solution is the *time series design*. To use this design, you as the researcher would simply give the same self-esteem questionnaire at several points in time before the support group begins. Perhaps you would ask respondents to complete the questionnaire every other day for a week. Then the support group would begin, and after its completion, you would ask them to complete the same questionnaire again every other day for a week. The three pretests could be compared to the posttests. In research notation, this research design would look like this:

$$O \quad O \quad O \quad X \quad O \quad O \quad O$$

Again, the Os represent the self-esteem questionnaire and the X represents the support group. Because there is no comparison group, the researcher uses the self-esteem questionnaires at various points in time as a comparison group by comparing the groups' overall scores over time. If, over the course of a week, the pretests seem to reflect a low level of self-esteem and then the group's level of self-esteem dramatically improves after they complete the support group, you could argue that the intervention may be correlated with the increase in self-esteem. Notice, however, that we are not saying that the intervention *caused* a change in self-esteem; we are simply stating that there is a correlation.

The next design we will examine is the *time series design with non-equivalent comparison group*. This is simply a variation of the time series design discussed above. Perhaps you are able to find a group of consumers who are not willing to participate in your support group but are willing to serve as a comparison group. You may ask both groups to fill out the self-esteem questionnaire a total of three times over the course of seven days before the support group begins and then again three times over seven days after the end of the support group. In research notation, this would look like this:

O   O   O   X   O   O   O
O   O   O   O   O   O

The Os represent the self-esteem questionnaire and the X represents the intervention. We said that the strength of the time series design was that the questionnaire repeated over time served as its own comparison group. When you include the additional component of the comparison group, your design is strengthened. You can now compare the pretest scores with the posttest scores, and these can be evaluated against those of the comparison group. Let us assume for a moment that the comparison group's scores stayed fairly similar over time. Logic would tell us that there is a strong possibility that the support group was effective (assuming that the scores of the experimental group increased after the intervention, of course).

Like all research designs, quasi-experimental designs have both strengths and weaknesses. On one hand, they are methodologically stronger than pre-experimental designs because they use a comparison group with pre- and posttests and/or test the findings at several points in time. However, they cannot rule out alternative explanations for any observed changes in groups. For instance, the members of one group may have much higher IQs than the other group or might be more motivated to participate in the study. These could be alternative explanations for observed changes in groups.

Experimental Designs

The one aspect that differentiates the experimental design from the quasi-experimental designs is the assignment of subjects to groups. In true experimental designs, subjects are randomly assigned to either the experimental group or the control group. Up to this point, we have been discussing the use of a *comparison group*. In quasi-experimental research, the group that receives no treatment (the intervention) is referred to as the comparison group (or sometimes as the nontreatment group). The term *control group* is used only for experimental research.

It is often difficult to randomly assign subjects to one group or the other, for a variety of reasons. For one, there are ethical considerations. Much of what is done in social work research precludes the social worker from assigning subjects to a particular group (that might mean they are not receiving services that could benefit them). Secondly, random assignment of subjects can increase the cost of a study (and many researchers have limited resources). Thirdly, researchers might be studying an event that has already transpired (such as the effects of the 9/11 terrorist attacks), which makes a random assignment impossible. However, for discussion's sake, let us pretend for a moment that you are continuing with your support group study. Let us also assume that we have the luxury of assigning participants to the experimental group and to the control group. Your research design then would be:

R X O
R O

In this design, the Rs represent random assignment of subjects (all subjects have an equal chance of being in either group). As before, the Os represent the self-esteem questionnaire and the X represents the intervention. Since all consumers have an equal chance of being in either group, you can compare the posttest scores of the experimental group with those of the control group, and if they are vastly different, the argument could be made that the intervention must have worked (even without a pretest for the control group). However, adding a pretest for the control group makes our design even stronger. This is the classic research design known as the *pretest-posttest control group design*:

R O X O
R O O

In this design, the Rs represent random assignment of subjects, the Os represent the pretest and posttest questionnaire (the self-esteem instrument), and the X represents the intervention (the support group).

The last research design we will discuss, called *Solomon's four-group design,* is the highest standard in experimental group research designs in that the researcher can feel confident that a change between the pretest and the posttest is truly due to the intervention. In research notation, this is described as:

R O X O
R O O
R X O
R O

As you can see, this complex design combines the pretest-posttest control group design and the posttest-only control group design. The major advantage of the Solomon design is that it can tell us whether changes in the dependent variable are due to some interaction effect between the pretest and the treatment. For example, let's say we wanted to assess the effect of positive information about a group of child welfare workers' community service work (the independent variable) on people's attitudes about child protection workers (the dependent variable). During the pretest, the groups are asked questions regarding their attitudes toward child protection workers. Next, they are exposed to the experimental treatment: newspaper articles reporting on the civic deeds and child rescue efforts of child protection workers. If treatment group 1 scores lower on the posttest than control group 1, it might be due to the independent variable. But it could also be that filling out the pretest questionnaire has sensitized people to the difficulties of being a child protection worker. The people in treatment group 1 have been alerted to the issues and they react more strongly to the experimental treatment than they would have without the pretest. If this is true, then experimental group 2 should show less change than experimental group 1. If the independent variable has an effect separate from its interaction with the treatment, then experimental group 2 should show more change than control group 1. If control group 1 and experimental group 2 show no change but experimental group 1 does show a change, then we know that change is produced only by the interaction of pretesting and treatment.

The Solomon design is often bypassed because it requires twice as many groups. This effectively doubles the time and cost of conducting the experiment. Many researchers decide that the advantages are not worth the added cost and complexity.

Applied Learning Activities

Activity #1

Your agency provides emergency food and used clothing to clients. You are tasked with describing how satisfied the clients at your agency feel about the services that they have received.

1. List the questions that you would ask in order to collect information on clients' satisfaction with these services.

2. How would you collect data using a quantitative method?

3. If you were to use a survey to collect this information, which survey collection methods would you use, and why?

Activity #2

You are interested in describing individuals involved in intimate partner violence. You decide to send a survey to several shelters in several states. You collect data on the following information:

1. Average length of the relationship

2. Number of times the individual has tried to leave the relationship

3. Type of abuse

4. Race of the victim

5. Age of the victim

6. Sex of the victim

7. Average family income

What other information would you collect, and why?

Activity #3

You are a case manager at an outpatient treatment facility. You teach a class on the effects of alcohol, methamphetamines, and other drugs on the body. Clients volunteer to attend your classes, but once they sign up to attend, attendance is expected. Your classes are held once a week, for one hour, and last for eight weeks. You give everyone a test the night before classes begin and again at the end of the eight-week period. You then compare their scores.

1. Would this type of research be considered pre-experimental, quasi-experimental, or experimental? Why?

2. What type of group research design is this?

3. Are there ways that the research design could be made stronger? If so, what could be done to change the research design to make it stronger?

Activity #4

You are a hospital social worker who has been asked to start a support group for people who are attempting to quit smoking. Because the size of the group is limited, you randomly assign people to the group or to a waiting list for the next group, which will start in four weeks. To randomly assign people, you place everyone's name in a bowl and draw names until you have filled the group. Everyone agrees, knowing they have an equal chance of being in the first support group or on a waiting list for the next one. Before the group begins, you ask both the people in the support group and the people on the wait list to fill out a questionnaire about the number of cigarettes they smoke per day. At the end of the four-week support group, you ask both groups to fill out the same survey.

1. Would this type of research be considered pre-experimental, quasi-experimental, or experimental? Why?

2. What type of group research design is this?

3. Identify the independent and dependent variables in this study.

Key Points

- Causal relationships exist when one variable is causing a change in the other, and correlational relationships exist when one variable may be associated with some degree of change in the other variable.

- Cross-sectional research looks at a slice of the population at one point in time.

- Longitudinal studies follow the same cohort of individuals over time. Three commonly used types of surveys are telephone surveys, mail-out and Internet surveys, and interviews.

- There are three main types of group research designs: pre-experimental, quasi-experimental, and experimental designs.

- A comparison group is used in quasi-experimental research. Sometimes called the nontreatment group, it is the group that receives no treatment (intervention).

- A control group is used in experimental research. In studies that use a control group, subjects have been randomly assigned to either the experimental group or the control group.

Additional Resources

Ellis, L. (1994). *Research methods in the social sciences.* Madison, WI: WCB, Brown & Benchmark.
Ellis focuses on research in psychology, sociology, social work, and other human sciences. He utilizes a straightforward approach to explain both research methodology and statistics.

Orcutt, B. (1990). *Science and inquiry in social work practice.* New York: Columbia University Press.
While this text may be a bit advanced for some readers, it presents a strong argument for the use of empirical methods in social work.

York, R. (1997). *Building basic competencies in social work research: An experiential approach.* Boston: A. B. Longman.

York uses assignments and other hands-on approaches to turn students into active learners. York uses more of a holistic approach than other texts, as he introduces concepts in each chapter and then returns to and elaborates upon them throughout the rest of the book.

CHAPTER EIGHT

Evaluative Research Designs

THIS CHAPTER WILL INTRODUCE SOME techniques for evaluating a program. While all research designs can be used to evaluate a program at some level, this chapter presents a research design that looks at process evaluations and outcome evaluations of an agency using qualitative, quantitative, and mixed-method research designs.

Social work ethics demand that we provide high-quality services to our consumers. Section 5.02a of the Code of Ethics of the National Association of Social Workers (1999) states that "Social workers should monitor and evaluate policies, the implementation of programs, and practice interventions." Seeking evidence of the effectiveness of existing programs is one way to determine best practices and fulfill this goal.

In today's economy, as agencies and practitioners confront ever-tightening budgets and increased competition for shrinking funding, it is becoming increasingly necessary for programs to be able to demonstrate not only that their interventions are effective but that they are meeting the goals and objectives they set out to accomplish. Gone are the days when a program could simply request funding dollars with little or no thought to demonstrating effectiveness. Today, funding sources are increasingly demanding that programs be accountable in how they spend their money, how people are helped, and what positive benefits result from the monies spent. Most federal grants and many state and private funding sources are now requiring applicants to have some outside source that will conduct an independent evaluation of the outcomes of the project funded by the grant. To accomplish these tasks, a social worker needs to have at least a basic familiarity with program evaluation.

An evaluation of social service programs can be rewarding research. It is through the process of investigation and analysis that we can answer complicated questions and discover better approaches with consumers. In turn, the discovery of these better approaches can give us hope in meeting the needs of the people we serve.

Program Evaluation

A **program evaluation** is a research design and analysis that evaluates specific characteristics of a program within an agency. There are basically two types of program evaluations: process evaluations and outcome evaluations. Each type has a specific purpose with advantages and limitations and will be discussed individually.

Process Evaluation

A **process evaluation** is generally an internal evaluation process that is initiated in the early stages of a program. An internal evaluation is simply an evaluation that is conducted at the request or desire of the agency. A process evaluation requires the researcher to establish a **baseline**, or a beginning point in research that establishes an initial sense of how a program, group, or individual is currently functioning and allows researchers to track progress over time; changes to the baselines are then monitored over time. It utilizes a qualitative approach as it seeks new information to answer such questions as "What does our program look like?" "Is our program effective?" and "Are consumers satisfied with our services?" It also utilizes a quantitative approach through the use of a measurement instrument, such as a survey that asks: "How satisfied are you with the services you received?" to which respondents are asked to answer on a scale from 1 ("Not at all satisfied") to 5 ("Very satisfied").

A process evaluation can be conducted at multiple times, and many administrators prefer to start the process evaluations early on—generally within the first ninety days of a new program's implementation. The process evaluation can then be repeated at intervals (for example, quarterly, every six months, every nine months, or yearly) to determine if the program is accomplishing its intended goals.

For example, let us imagine for a moment that you are a social worker at a food voucher assistance program. Your agency serves many people who speak little or no English. Your supervisor has written a grant that provides translation services for these consumers. However, rather than wait until the end of the grant period to see if your program is on target, you and your supervisor decide to conduct a process evaluation after services have been offered for ninety days. You select a day (or week) when you will interview consumers and then solicit input from several who have appointments. You ask them to spend a few minutes with you and ask them the following questions:

1.   What has been your experience with the translation services?
2.   What do you like best about the translation services?
3.   What do you like least about the translation services?
4.   How would you like to see the translation services done differently?
5.   Are there any other comments you would like to make about the translation services?

Let us assume that you collected information from only three participants. You may be saying to yourself, "Based on what we've learned in previous chapters, three people is a very small sample, and their answers cannot be generalized to the rest of the population." And you would be correct. You want to collect as much feedback from as many sources as possible. But remember, this is not meant to be explanatory—you are simply trying to determine how the new service is helpful and what could be done to improve services.

Generally, a process evaluation has three main goals: to construct a program description, to monitor a program, and to assess the quality of services being provided. We will look at each of these goals in turn.

Program Description

The first goal, **program description,** is simply an attempt to delineate the setup, routines, and consumer characteristics of a program (see example 8.1). The setup of the program includes the types of services being provided, the location of services, and the mission (i.e., the rationale for these services). Other information that you may want to gather may include the routines of the services provided, such as frequency with which services are offered, times and days services are available, and number and type of workers who offer those services. Finally, you may want to measure the number of consumers you serve and their characteristics: number of consumers, sex, race, age, income level, marital status, number of children, and the like.

Remember that descriptive statistics are ways of organizing, describing, and presenting quantitative data in a manner that is concise, manageable,

EXAMPLE 8.1: SAMPLE PROGRAM DESCRIPTION

The TRUCE Program is a gang prevention program funded through the Helpful Angels and the school district. The consumer population consists of students within the school district between the ages of thirteen and nineteen who are considered at risk by the school district.

Referrals to the TRUCE Program can come from school counselors, principals, parents, teachers, and other concerned family members or professionals. Once a referral is made to the TRUCE Program, the student meets with one of the TRUCE specialists for an initial assessment and orientation into the TRUCE Program. Most students participate in the program because they have been required to do so by the school district, their parents, or the court. Students participate in the program Monday through Friday for one hour after school ends.

The three goals of the program are to help at-risk students resist gang membership, to reduce disruptive behaviors while the students are at school, and to improve grades. To accomplish these goals, TRUCE specialists provide weekly one-hour groups at five sites in the service area.

The overall program objectives are:

1. All students will decrease disruptive behavior in the classroom by 10 percent by the end of the school year as measured by the Behavioral Checklist (to be completed by the teachers).
2. All students will increase their knowledge of how to resist peer pressure to participate in gang activity by 50% by the end of the school year, as evidenced by pretest and posttests scores.
3. All students will increase their GPA by 10 percent from midterm grades to final grades, as evidenced by report cards.

To address classroom disruptions, TRUCE specialists teach classroom social competency techniques. This is done during weekly individual discussions with the student and the student's teacher.

To address how to resist pressure to join a gang, TRUCE specialists use an organized curriculum that teaches refusal skills. They do this by using experiential learning tasks, didactic lecture, and group discussion. Students participate in the curriculum for a half hour four days a week (the fifth day is reserved for meetings with the teacher).

To address student performance with class work, tutors work with students on goal setting for weekly assignments and study techniques that help them prepare for exams. Tutors are available for a half hour Monday through Friday after the student has participated in the refusal skills training or the teacher meeting.

and understandable. They usually deal with individual variables and establish the common patterns found in each individual variable. For instance, describing a population in terms of number and percentage for sex, race, and occupation gives us a picture of some of the characteristics of the consumers served. A program description, then, provides one with an overall picture of the characteristics of the program and participants.

Program Monitoring

Program monitoring, the second goal of process evaluation, is used to examine what happens after people receive services from a program. For example, you may use program monitoring to track utilization of services over time and the effect of services on individual functioning. By monitoring how services are utilized, you can determine which services are most needed by your population and which services can be offered on a seasonal basis. Monitoring items may include frequency of visits, average length of each person's time in the program, number of appointments each person keeps, and number of no-shows. For instance, you find that only two consumers regularly attend a weekly support group during the spring and summer; however, during fall and winter months, there is a large attendance. Based on this evaluation, you only offer the support group in the fall and winter.

You will also want to determine which of the services being provided are beneficial to your service population. Let us imagine that you are a social worker who works at an agency that provides services to teen mothers. Your agency has received a grant that will be used to offer parenting classes to these young mothers. Some of the objectives outlined in the grant are that 70 percent of the mothers who participate in the parenting classes will score higher on a parenting skills posttest than on the pretest. Your job is to conduct a process evaluation at six months to see if the program is on track. Part of the task of this process evaluation would be to examine the pretest and posttest scores for these mothers to see if their knowledge of parenting skills improved. Let us assume that after six months, one hundred teen mothers have completed the parenting classes. You would expect to find that at least seventy (70%) of them did better on the posttest than on the pretest. If this is indeed the case, you would know that the program is on track. If, however, you find that this objective is not being met, you would need to discuss with your supervisor how to proceed. Depending on how close you are to achieving the objective, it may not be cause for alarm. However, if only 50 percent did better on the posttest than the pretest, perhaps some mid-course corrections are in order.

Quality Assurance

The last goal of a process evaluation is quality assurance. **Quality assurance** is a means of determining the level of satisfaction of both services for consumers and programmatic issues for the staff. Programs routinely ask consumers to complete a satisfaction survey as part of a termination-of-services process. Some services, such as assistance paying an electric bill, may be a one-time event. Other services, such as group counseling or a parenting class, last weeks, months, or years. Therefore, when and how often a participant will be surveyed depends on the length of services. Also, how a consumer will be surveyed depends on the structure and funding of a program. For instance, a satisfaction survey that respondents can anonymously deposit in a box may be given to one-time consumers at the end of their appointments. Another program may have grant funding that will allow program administrators to survey consumers by mailing the satisfaction survey to everyone who has participated over the past year. One of the problems with consumer satisfaction surveys is that consumers routinely report they are more satisfied with services than they actually feel (Ingram & Chung, 1997). However, one way to control for this is to include qualitative (open-ended) questions. For instance, you can ask, "What was the best part of your experience with this agency?" and "What was the worst part of your experience with this agency?"

To this point, our quality assurance measures have focused upon the consumer. However, with process evaluations, the staff can also be included in the evaluation. Asking staff such questions as "What are we doing well?" and "What can we do to improve our services?" can provide invaluable information for shaping the direction of a new program. The following are examples of how you might utilize a process evaluation:

1. You can monitor a new or long-standing program or service and present your findings at a staff meeting or a board of directors meeting or to administrators.
2. You can develop, administer, and analyze a satisfaction survey to identify strengths and areas needing improvement within your agency.
3. You can develop a program description by collecting information about the setup, routines, and consumer characteristics of a program at your agency.
4. You can develop program goals and objectives.
5. You can survey staff to look at different practice approaches being used.

Outcome Evaluation

An **outcome evaluation** is a main goal for program evaluation because it is an evaluation that measures the overall effectiveness of a program—that is, it looks at the goals and objectives established by the program to answer the question "Did this program accomplish what it set out to do?" It is an external evaluation, meaning that it is requested or conducted by a regulatory or grant-funding system outside the agency. For example, a grantor might require that services at a homeless shelter be evaluated to provide evidence of whether stated objectives are being met.

Measuring Program Objectives

By nature, objectives need to be observable and measurable. A program evaluator will have a much easier time trying to evaluate the overall accomplishments of a program if the objectives are straightforward and measurable.

Let us imagine for a moment that you have been asked to assist with the outcome evaluation of a program. The program offers group counseling to female adult victims of domestic violence with the objective of increasing their self-esteem. Which of the following two objectives would you rather try to evaluate?

1. Consumers of this program will report that they are feeling better about themselves.
2. Twenty-five consumers will score at least a 40 on the Jones self-esteem instrument by the end of the ten-week program.

The second objective is much easier to evaluate because it has clear criteria (40 on the Jones instrument) with which to judge the changes; therefore, one can see the results. It is our recommendation that all program objectives be submitted to the MOST standard. A **program objective** should be:

· measurable
· observable
· specific
· time-lined

By creating objectives that meet the MOST standard, an evaluator can better determine whether an objective was met. Let us look at each of these items individually.

Measurable objectives are ones that allow an evaluator to collect quantitative evidence of whether the goal was met. For instance, in our example above, an evaluator can look at consumers' Jones self-esteem pretest and posttest scores to determine if an increase, a decrease, or no change occurred. For an objective to be observable, it must be stated in a way that enables participants to easily and correctly respond within the measurement. That is, participants can be observant of their individual behaviors, thoughts, and feelings and therefore can complete a self-esteem survey measuring these. Conversely, one cannot observe another person's self-esteem, but one can measure some behavioral indicators that research has demonstrated to be predictors of good self-esteem, such as maintaining eye contact and holding one's head up while walking.

An objective that is specific states exactly what outcome is expected for how many consumers. For instance, twenty-five consumers must score at least 40 for this objective to be considered to be successfully achieved.

Finally, time-lined objectives give the longitudinal information for the objectives—that is, when and how often do we measure the objective? For instance, in our example, the objective will be measured after the ten-week program is completed. A similar objective might state that the objective will be measured "after every completed ten-week program for one year." In summary, program objectives that adhere to the MOST standard allow a researcher to conduct a thorough and meaningful outcome evaluation.

Writing the Report

When writing, you have to anticipate the concerns and expectations of your reading audience. The overall style and depth of what you will want to include are generally determined by the purpose of your report and the audience for whom you are writing. For example, a brief memo to your supervisor may be sufficient for reporting a description of your consumers. You may want information on the average age, total number of consumers, frequency for sex and race, and average number of visits. However, for formal reports you will need to be more detailed and include certain elements, such as the objectives and their outcomes.

A report for program evaluation addresses program objectives as opposed to research hypotheses. Therefore, an outside evaluator would address the scope of the problem in the introduction, conduct a literature review to determine standards for measurements (i.e., what other outcomes have been determined for each objective), develop or choose measurements for each objective, determine an appropriate sampling size, analyze the results, and present the findings for each objective in a narrative with tables.

Example 8.2 is an outcome evaluation report for a program that provided case management services to low-income mothers in a large metropolitan city. The funding source asked for an initial report of this new program. The report consists of two sections: a consumer description model and a case management model. Objectives concerning consumer description are labeled CD; therefore, CD(1) is the first consumer description objective. Objectives concerning case management are labeled CM; therefore, CM(1) is the first case management objective.

Tables constitute an important part of a written report. A table provides a visual representation that makes information easy to read. Table 8.1

EXAMPLE 8.2: OUTCOME EVALUATION REPORT

CD(1). What percent of pregnant infant wellness participants initiated prenatal care in the first trimester of pregnancy?
 A total of sixteen out of forty-one women (39%) initiated prenatal care in the first trimester of pregnancy.

CD(2). What percent of women who received prenatal infant wellness services gave birth to preterm infants?
 Three of the twenty-five women gave birth to preterm infants (as defined by infants delivered at thirty-seven weeks or less), totaling 12% of the women. In the project area comparison group, seventy-two out of 147 (48.9%) women gave birth to preterm infants.

CM(1a). What percentage of clients were provided referrals to other social service agencies?
 A total of fifty-one out of fifty-eight women (87.9%) were referred to other social service agencies for services. Of the remaining seven (12.1%), five cases were administratively closed and two were missing data.

CM(1b). Of those clients referred, what percentage received services?
 All 87.9 percent of the currently active women referred received one or more services.

CM(1c). What type of services were clients referred to?
 There were fifty-one women receiving one or more of the following thirty-six services.

TABLE 8.1: REFERRAL RATE BY TYPE OF SERVICE

TYPE OF SERVICE	REFERRAL RATE	NUMBER OF CLIENTS
Transportation by Staff	62.7%	32
Well Baby Care	37.3%	19
Emergency Infant Supplies	27.5%	14
Emergency Assistance	27.5%	14
Housing Assistance	25.5%	13
WIC	25.5%	13
Case Management	25.5%	13
Child Day Care	21.6%	11
Emergency Food	21.6%	11
Public Assistance	11.8%	6
Job/Employment Training	11.8%	6
Food Stamps	9.8%	5
Primary Health Care	9.8%	5
Translation Services	7.8%	4

shows an agency's referral rates by type of service. This table was organized by percentage to draw attention to the highest rate of referrals. Keep in mind that any table must be accompanied by a narrative of the results.

Strengths and Weaknesses of Program Evaluation

Each type of program evaluation has both strengths and weaknesses. Some of the strengths of process evaluations are that they are relatively easy to conduct because a process evaluation is very flexible (i.e., it has no rigid structure or time line). Therefore, a process evaluation can be conducted at any time in the fiscal year or funding cycle. In addition, there are no constricting rules as to how to conduct a process evaluation. A process evaluation can be as informal as sitting down with consumers and asking what they like, dislike, and would like to see changed about the program. On the other hand, a process evaluation can be a formalized process that seeks to evaluate the number of consumers served (to date), to gather demographic data about consumers, and to determine overall patterns of usage of the program.

Some problems that can occur with process evaluation have to do with inappropriate timing and inapplicable questions. For instance, inappropriate timing would be evaluating consumer characteristics too early in the implementation of a new program—this would provide little information. Inapplicable questions on a satisfaction survey could mean that consumers may not be able to give an adequate report of what they like and dislike and what they feel needs to change about the program. For instance, asking consumers if they would come back again for services in the future might just be measuring their need for the services instead of their satisfaction.

One of the strengths of outcome evaluation is that it is an unbiased examination of a program's objectives. By unbiased, we mean that the program evaluator is simply examining the stated objectives to determine if those objectives were met. Another positive aspect of the outcome evaluation is that it is not trying to determine what worked or didn't work in the program. This is a positive aspect because the evaluator is not pressured to justify the interventions that were used—rather he or she is simply asked if the stated objectives were fulfilled.

One of the weaknesses of the outcome evaluation is that it provides no indication of whether the program itself is the cause of any change in the consumer. One can never be totally sure that the change in a group, sample, or population is due to the intervention and not due to some outside influence.

Practical Considerations and Common Problems

Program evaluation does not have to be a daunting process, but do keep in mind some of the issues that can plague the novice evaluator. The first issue to consider is that you must be very clear about what program you are evaluating. This may seem so simple and obvious that you would think it does not need to be mentioned, but you would be surprised at how many inexperienced evaluators get bogged down in the process by not being clear about what they are evaluating. One common example is when one attempts to evaluate an entire agency. We strongly encourage you to select one program or service within your agency to focus on. Once you have mastered the skills needed to evaluate a single program or service, you may want to move on to evaluating multiple programs simultaneously.

Once you have established what program you are to be evaluating, it is important to be clear with the administrator or program director as to what type of evaluation you are conducting. Some preparation questions to guide you as you start the evaluation process follow. If it is a process evaluation, ask:

1. How long has the program been running?
2. What would you like to see accomplished in a process evaluation?
3. How will I gain access to consumers? To the staff?
4. What is the goal of this process evaluation—description, program monitoring, quality assurance, or a combination of the three?
5. How soon would you like this completed?
6. How soon would you like a written report?

If it is an outcome evaluation, ask:

1. What are the programs objectives?
2. Are these in some written form that I can have?
3. How soon would you like this completed?
4. How soon would you like a written report?

Another common problem is that because evaluators often want a program to be effective, they take on responsibility for the success or failure of the evaluation. Similarly, this pressure to find positive results can sometimes come from the organization. Not only do individuals dislike hearing complaints about their work, but a negative report can jeopardize funding. Remember that your role is that of an objective auditor and you must report all the findings. Your job is to measure and frankly report what was done against what was proposed. In other words, either the program met its stated objectives or it did not. It is not your role to speculate as to why objectives were met or not met or to soften the critique to cushion the blow to someone's ego. Stating this up front is an important protective factor for the evaluator and can increase others' confidence in the report and the evaluator because it shows that the evaluation was ethically and objectively conducted.

Finally, it is not your responsibility to make recommendations about the findings unless the program administrator asks for these. If he or she does ask for these, recommendations can include what could be improved or done differently; these are included at the end of your report.

Applied Learning Activities

Activity #1

Now it is your turn to practice a program evaluation. Pretend that you are completing a program evaluation at the six-month interval for a program. Below is the description of a fictitious program. Read the program description and then complete the tasks that follow.

Safe Haven is a shelter for adolescent runaways waiting for a court determination and trial. It was established as an alternative to placing adolescents with the general jail population. The goal of the shelter is to keep the residents safe while they wait for their court date. The ages of the residents range from fourteen to seventeen. The Safe Haven staff monitors three safety risks for this population: harm to others, harm to self, and alcohol and drug use. Staff provides specific programming to address these three issues.

First, mandatory group counseling is provided daily from 6:00 to 8:00 P.M., Monday through Friday, so that residents can learn conflict resolution skills to prevent them from harming others. During this group, members listen to a thirty-minute curriculum-based presentation followed by a demonstration. Group members then practice the skills with each other.

Second, all residents are monitored for depression and suicidal ideations to prevent self-harm. Residents meet daily for thirty minutes with a social worker for mandatory individual counseling, Monday through Friday.

Finally, group members participate in a drug and alcohol education class. This is also a curriculum-based educational presentation on refusal skills followed by group practice and process discussions. This mandatory group meets daily from 3:00 to 4:30 P.M., Monday through Friday. Urinalyses are conducted on residents every three days, and a breath analysis every day before bed.

The rest of the day throughout the week, residents are tutored by a teacher who is brought into the shelter. On weekends, residents receive visitors and participate in recreational activities at the shelter under close supervision.

1. Design a program description for this program that includes the types of services being provided and their location; the program's mission; the frequency with which services are offered, as well as time and day; and the number of people you serve (number of residents) and their characteristics (sex, race, age, income, etc.).

2. Develop a minimum of three program objectives. Objectives should be able to meet the MOST standard.

Activity #2

Using the following outcome, develop a table to visually organize your data.

Is there an increase in the percentage of consumers who speak English as a second language who enter prenatal care in their first trimester? Because this program is new, there are no prior statistics to compare with this group. However, in the first five months of this program, there were fifty-eight consumers. Of these, fifteen consumers spoke both Spanish and English and eight consumers spoke Spanish only. Of the fifteen Spanish/English-speaking women, four (27%) entered prenatal care in their first trimester. Of the eight women who only spoke Spanish, one (13%) entered prenatal care in her first trimester. This is a total of 40 percent of the women who spoke English as a second language who entered prenatal care in their first trimester.

Key Points

- There are two reasons that social workers should evaluate their programs. First, social work ethics demands that we "monitor and evaluate policies, the implementation of programs, and practice interventions." Second, funding sources are increasingly demanding that programs be accountable in how they spend their money, how consumers are helped, and what positive benefits result from the monies spent.

- A program evaluation is a research design and analysis that evaluates specific characteristics of a program within an agency.

- There are two types of program evaluations: process evaluations and outcome evaluations.

- A process evaluation (an internal audit) has three main goals: to construct a program description, to provide program monitoring, and to assess the quality of services being provided.

- An outcome evaluation is an external audit that measures the overall effectiveness of a program. This evaluation looks at the goals and objectives established by the program to answer the question "Did this program accomplish what it set out to do?"

Additional Resources

Brinkerhoff, R., Brethower, D., Hluchyj, T., Ridings, J., & Nowakowski, J. (1983). *Program evaluation: A practitioner's guide for trainers and educators (sourcebook and casebook)*. Boston: Kluwer-Nijhoff.
This book can serve as a practical guide for individuals wishing to improve their skills in program evaluation. While somewhat dated, the information in the text remains relevant today.

McDavid, J., & Hawthorn, L. (2005). *Program evaluation and performance measurement: An introduction to practice*. Thousand Oaks, CA: Sage.
This introductory text discusses topics in a detailed fashion, making it a useful guide for individuals in the field who are asked to conduct program evaluations. The book uses a simple and straightforward approach that walks readers through a variety of situations.

Posavac, E., & Carey, R. (2002). *Program evaluation: Methods and case studies*. Englewood Cliffs, NJ: Prentice-Hall.
This book uses case examples and short profiles to walk readers through the steps of the evaluation.

Royse, D., Thyer, B., Padgett, D., & Logan, T. (2001). *Program evaluation: An introduction*. Belmont, CA: Wadsworth/Thomson Learning.
This is a very readable guide to conducting evaluations of a program or an agency. Included is a chapter on writing the report, which is very helpful to the novice.

CHAPTER NINE

Single-Subject Designs

THIS CHAPTER WILL DISCUSS SINGLE-SUBJECT designs and some of the techniques for conducting this type of research. In addition, this chapter will provide a discussion of how to interpret your results in a single-subject design study and explore some of the limitations of this type of research.

What Is a Single-Subject Design?

The single-subject design has many names and may be referred to as small-*n* research design, idiographic design, single-case experimental design, and interrupted time series research design. Although it can be used to evaluate families and groups of more than one person, the single-subject design is a quantitative method of research that is generally used for evaluating an individual's progress over time. Specifically, the single-subject design is a tool that measures whether a relationship exists between an intervention and a specific outcome. For instance, measuring a person's depression over time might give an indication as to whether antidepressant therapy is working. Single-subject designs use the logic of time series designs (you may want to refer back to chapter 7 to refresh your memory). However, rather than using a large group of subjects, the single-subject design measures the changes that occur in an individual.

The single-subject design emerged as a practice tool for evaluating individual progress in the late 1960s and early 1970s. It was partly a reaction to the constrictions of the group research design and partly a result of the works of behavioral psychologists such as B. F. Skinner. Skinner was concerned with behavior modification and believed that rewards and reinforcers could be used to shape or change behaviors. For example, if an instructor wants to promote class participation, then he or she would need to find something that the class would consider desirable (a reward or reinforcer). If the instructor gave out chocolate bars every time someone in the class asked a question or volunteered an answer, class participation would probably be very high. Reinforcing a desired behavior is one underlying concept behind behavioral modification.

Elements of Single-Subject Design Research

There are basic elements to all single-subject design studies. These are selecting the target outcome, selecting the intervention, selecting the measurement tool, collecting baseline data, collecting intervention data, and conducting the analysis (compiling the results).

Selecting the Target Outcome

In order for the single-subject design to be successful, the social worker must first help the participant determine the behavior or feelings to be changed. For instance, the participant may want to improve his or her parenting skills (behavior) or self-esteem (feeling). It is crucial that the social worker and the participant be able to agree on the **target outcome,** or the goal of the intervention (i.e., the way the participant will act or feel in the future). This is similar to defining and specifying your variables in a quantitative experiment.

You will find that some variables are very easy to define. For example, if a consumer comes to you and says she wants help with her abuse of alcohol or other drugs, then the variable might be defined as the number of times the person drinks or uses any mind-altering chemicals each day. But not all variables are so easily defined. What if a consumer comes to you and asks for help with his low self-esteem? This concept is abstract, subjective, and impossible to observe directly; therefore, it is necessary to find a way to measure this variable. As we discussed in chapter 4, one way to measure a construct is to use a standardized measure. For instance, you could select the Self-Esteem Rating Scale. You may then say that the target outcome, to increase self-esteem by the end of the intervention, will be determined by the scores on the Self-Esteem Rating Scale.

Selecting the Intervention

An intervention is the technique used to facilitate a change in research. As in all other quantitative research, it is important to select an intervention based on a literature review. You, as the researcher, would review the literature and select the intervention that is most appropriate for your research participant. This means you do not just guess at the best intervention or do what others are doing, but rather you read empirical studies and find the intervention that has been proved to be a best practice approach. Chances are that you will find a variety of interventions for any particular problem. Your task is to select one that fits your participant. For example, if the target outcome is the alleviation of depression, you may conduct a literature review that suggests a variety of methods for treating depression, including exercise, cognitive behavioral therapy, and medication. However, if your participant is physically challenged, exercise may not be the most appropriate intervention. As another example, let us say that your participant is a thirteen-year-old female with poor self-esteem. Perhaps for this individual you select daily affirmations for the intervention. This intervention requires the participant to look in the mirror each day for five minutes and repeat a series of positive affirmations ("I am beautiful," "I am a good person," etc.).

Selecting the Measure

A measure can be as simple as having participants document every time they smoke a cigarette and bring their numbers each week to a Quit Smoking support group. Standardized measures are often used to collect data in single-subject research because they are convenient and have established reliability and validity. Fischer and Corcoran (2007) present hundreds of different measures in their two volumes of compiled measurement scales for adults, couples, families, and children. For example, you might choose to measure participants' depression by using the Depression Self-Rating Scale. This is an eighteen-item measure that uses simplified language, short statements, and limited response categories, all of which allow the participant to complete the questionnaire quickly. Examples of these items are "I feel like crying" and "I feel very lonely." Responses can be "Most of the time," "Sometimes," or "Never."

Collecting Baseline Data

It is important to remember that no intervention occurs during the baseline phase. The baseline is used to establish a reference point to which any targeted change in the individual following the intervention is compared. During the baseline phase, it is important to collect information over a period of time. It is suggested that you have a minimum of three observations, for instance, three days or events. This allows you to average out the behavior and helps to guard against anomalies. For example, let us assume that you are measuring the baseline for depression. You may ask your participant to complete a standardized depression inventory. If you only have her complete the scale one time, you can't be sure that her answers aren't indicative of a particularly good day (with less depression) or an especially bad day (with higher levels of depression). But if you ask her to complete the same scale over a week, filling out the scale each night before bedtime, for instance, you can assume that an average of the scores for the seven days will be fairly representative of the baseline level of depression.

Collecting Intervention Data

Once the target outcome has been agreed upon, the appropriate intervention has been selected, a method for measuring the target outcome has been chosen, and the baseline data have been collected, you must then collect the intervention data. In our example, you would ask the participant to start the intervention (e.g., exercise, cognitive behavioral counseling, medication) while continuing to complete the depression scale each night for eight weeks. If her depression decreases over the eight weeks, it would be logical to conclude that the intervention worked. As we discussed in chapter 7, it can be tempting to say there is a causal relationship, in other words, that cognitive behavioral counseling caused her depression to decrease. However, we cannot prove that the intervention alone caused the change—the difference in the behavior may also be due to some outside influence totally separate from anything in the intervention. That is, people sometimes get better because they mature or because their environment changes (for example, there may be a change in marital status or employment status).

Reporting Results

There are two ways to report the results of a single-subject design. The first and simplest way is to simply graph the results and examine the graph to see if a change has occurred over time. Figure 9.1 shows the results of a single-subject design that the social worker has charted using Microsoft Excel. The score is the overall weekly mean score, where a score of 6 indicates a high level of depression and a score of 0 indicates no depression. A cursory glance at the figure reveals that the depression decreased between the baseline phase (four weeks) and the intervention phase (eight weeks) of the research. This reviewing of charted data is known as eyeballing data.

FIGURE 9.1: SINGLE-SUBJECT DESIGN: SUCCESSFUL DEPRESSION INTERVENTION

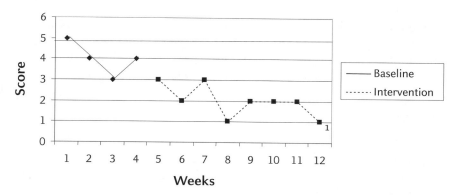

This simply means scanning the results to look for obvious differences between the baseline and intervention phases. But let us assume for a moment that the change in level of depression is not so obviously clear. Figure 9.2 represents a participant's scores where the difference between the baseline and intervention phases is relatively minor (and thus presents a challenge when we inspect the graph to determine whether a significant change occurred). To determine if this smaller change can be considered important, we can simply calculate the average scores and report that there was no difference. Or we can utilize a computer-generated statistical analysis of the data to determine whether our intervention was effective.

FIGURE 9.2: SINGLE-SUBJECT DESIGN: UNSUCCESSFUL DEPRESSION INTERVENTION

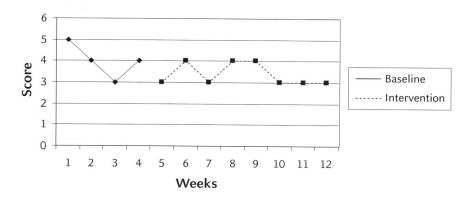

Types of Single-Subject Designs

The designs that we will discuss here are all based on a basic AB design, where A always stands for the baseline score, and B always represents the scores during the intervention. The ABA design expands on this by adding an additional baseline, the ABAB design repeats the baseline and intervention, and the ABC design introduces a new intervention.

The AB Design

The AB design is the most common and least complicated of the measurement designs because there is one baseline measure and one intervention. The following example AB design is used to reduce acting-out behaviors in the classroom.

John is a social work student doing a field experience at an elementary school's resource center on Tuesdays through Fridays. He received a referral for a seven-year-old boy who has been acting out for the past week. The teacher would like the student to work on reducing his acting-out behaviors (the target outcome). The teacher has been identifying these behaviors on a behavioral checklist for the past four days. This checklist allows the user to place checkmarks next to behaviors such as talking without permission; hitting, kicking, or pushing other students; and cursing; in this way, the teacher has operationalized the concept of acting out. As you can see in example 9.1, the baseline scores averaged out to four incidences a day over the four days. John conducts a literature review of effective interventions for child-related behavioral problems. John's chosen intervention is to meet with the student for a half hour every Tuesday through Friday for two weeks for free-play. Together they will color or play a game of the student's choice (e.g., card games, board games), during which time the student can talk about anything that is on his mind, or they can forgo the game and simply talk. During these visits, the student starts talking to John about his parents' divorce and how it has made him sad and angry. John normalizes the child's feelings (i.e., tells the child that what he is feeling is normal) and encourages the child to talk with his parents and the teacher when he feels sad or angry. The teacher continues to chart acting-out behaviors during the two weeks that John provides the intervention. The intervention scores average out to be two incidences per day, a decrease of 50 percent.

While simple to use, this design has limitations. For instance, you do not know how long the effect of the intervention will last, and it is limited

EXAMPLE 9.1: AB DESIGN RESULTS

ELEMENT	RESULTS
Target Outcome	Decrease in acting-out behaviors in the classroom.
Intervention	Play and listen for a half hour each Tuesday through Friday
Measurement Tool	Behavioral checklist
Baseline Data (A)	5, 4, 3, 4 (4 days)
Intervention Data (B)	3, 2, 3, 1, 2, 2, 2, 1 (eight days)
Results	Mean scores: A = 4, B = 2 (decrease in scores by 50%)

to measuring only one intervention. The next designs will address each of these issues.

The ABA Design

If you wanted to be more certain that it was the intervention that was responsible for the change (and not some outside influence), then a slightly more sophisticated design like the ABA design would be appropriate. Here, the second A represents the withdrawal of the intervention and return to baseline. In other words, you would continue to measure the participant after the completion of the intervention. For instance, the child who has been acting out completes the two-week intervention, but the teacher continues to measure any acting-out behaviors, using the behavioral checklist to see if the effect of the intervention continues after the intervention ceases.

Critics of this method state that you can never truly return to a baseline once an intervention has been introduced. In other words, the child has been changed by the intervention and therefore will not have the same scores as prior to the intervention, even if the acting out increases. However, this method can be used to monitor how long the effect of the intervention lasts. In other words, once the student has stopped spending time playing and talking to John, how long will the effect last before the acting-out behaviors return (and possibly worsen)? By monitoring the behaviors after the intervention stops, we can know when to reintroduce the intervention or another intervention.

The ABAB Design

The ABAB design is slightly more sophisticated than the ABA design. In the ABAB design you would begin with the baseline, introduce the intervention, withdraw the intervention and return to baseline, and then reintroduce the intervention. As in the previous example, if acting-out behaviors are monitored after the intervention has ceased and we observe an increase in acting-out behaviors, we can reintroduce the visits with John and monitor the effect over time. One would expect to find a decrease in acting-out behaviors after the reintroduction of the intervention. If this were the case, it would be safe to assume that the intervention was working again. An issue to keep in mind is that while one intervention might work for short periods of time, this design does not allow for different or multiple interventions that may have more lasting effects. In this scenario, the child could become dependent on John's intervention. This is why John advised the child to also talk to his parents and teacher, which could be another intervention that could be measured.

The ABC Design

Up to this point, we have been discussing the use of one intervention. You may be wondering, "What about some complicated target outcomes that require multiple interventions, such as depression?" A review of the literature on depression shows that the most effective treatment is a combination of cognitive-behavioral treatment and medication. For a target outcome that requires more than one intervention, it is recommended that you use an ABC design. An ABC design works the same way as an AB design except that it utilizes multiple interventions (introduced in sequence). Again, using our example of depression, you would measure the baseline phase, then you would introduce the first intervention (cognitive behavioral counseling) and measure it over eight weeks, and then in the weeks that follow you would introduce the second intervention (antidepressants) while continuing the measurement. This design may also be used when one intervention alone is not yielding the results we anticipate. In other words, we start out with an AB design but the level of depression does not decrease as much as was hoped with cognitive behavioral counseling. Therefore, a more intrusive intervention (medication) is introduced to determine if the combination of these interventions will provide relief. One limitation of this design is that you do not know for sure how much the first intervention is creating the change after the second intervention is introduced. In other words, would the change have occurred anyway with more time?

Strengths and Limitations of Single-Subject Designs

One of the strengths of single-subject designs has already been discussed. That is, by measuring the participant's progress toward the target outcome (i.e., the variable), you can determine whether an intervention is successful. However, there is another way to use single-subject research designs. The results of the intervention can be shared with the participant to reinforce progress and treatment decisions. That is, the results themselves become an intervention. For example, the participant with depression has a very bad day during week 6 of treatment and feels that she is making no progress and wants to quit the intervention. By reviewing the results of figure 9.1 with the participant, you can point out her overall progress. This is similar to what individuals do when they are dieting. By weighing themselves weekly and seeing a measurable drop in weight, they reinforce their desire to continue the diet, even when they feel discouraged because they did not lose weight one week. Conversely, if a participant is not progressing as expected, sharing the results may support a decision to introduce a different or more intrusive intervention, such as medication or hospitalization.

Despite the benefits it offers, the single-subject design is limited by the small sample size it uses. This precludes the results from being generalized to others. While this has obvious application for the participant, it does not add to the general knowledge of the public. Also, without a control group, one cannot tell if a research participant would naturally get better without the intervention.

However, the single-subject design is still a very useful tool for practitioners who want evidence-based ways to evaluate their practice. The single-subject design, like all quantitative research, is driven by theory and guided by research and is a useful tool to use in evaluating whether an individual is making progress.

Applied Learning Activity

You are a case manager working with developmentally disabled adults in a residential group home. You have a participant who is a thirty-three-year-old white male. His name is Bruce. Bruce has been diagnosed as mildly mentally retarded with an IQ of around 60. Bruce works in a sheltered workshop, assembling sponges on hair curlers, and enjoys his job. His hobbies include collecting model cars and playing video games, both of which he is very passionate about. He occasionally has angry outbursts. The staff at the workshop have begun to complain about his behavior and have stated that he will be banned from the workshop if he does not get his anger under control. They called you into the office today and related an incident that happened recently during which he suddenly became angry and began to shout at the other workers and throw things around the room. Possible reasons for his behavior were discussed among the staff; however, there is no consensus as to why he is acting this way. The staff wants some assurance from you that he will control his behavior.

Your task is to design a single-subject research study for Bruce. You should:

1. Identify the type of single-subject design you will use and the target outcome.

2. Describe the intervention and the rationale for this intervention.

3. Select the measurement.

4. Describe the process for collecting the baseline data.

5. Describe the process for collecting the intervention data.

6. Finally, discuss any limitations of your study.

Key Points

- A single-subject research design is a method for evaluating individual progress over time.

- The basic elements of all single-subject design research are selecting the target outcome, selecting the intervention, selecting the measurement tool, collecting baseline data, collecting intervention data, and conducting the analysis (compiling the results).

- There are four types of single-subject research designs: AB (one baseline and one intervention), ABA (which adds an additional baseline), ABAB (which repeats the baseline and intervention), and ABC (which introduces a new intervention).

Additional Resources

Barlow, D., Nock, M., & Hersen, M. (2009). *Single case experimental designs: Strategies for studying behavior change* (3rd ed.). Boston: Allyn and Bacon.
The authors have written the majority of texts and articles on single-subject design over the past three decades.

Bloom, M., Fischer, J., & Orme, J. (2005). *Evaluating practice: Guidelines for the accountable professional* (5th ed.). New York: Allyn and Bacon.
The authors provide an in-depth analysis of single-subject design research. In addition, the book comes with a software program that helps the user interpret single-subject designs.

CHAPTER TEN

Introduction to Descriptive Statistics

ONCE YOU HAVE CONDUCTED A LITERATURE REVIEW, stated your research question, identified your variables, selected a research method, and determined how to collect your sample, you will need to decide how your data will be analyzed. Remember that quantitative research allows us to describe variables and to explore relationships between variables. Data that are collected can be described, and the results of quantitative data are presented in numeric form in tables and graphs. In this chapter we will explore how to describe the numerical data we collect for individual variables, and in chapter 11 we will discuss analyses that examine association between variables.

What Is Data Analysis?

Quantitative data analysis is defined as the process of utilizing a variety of statistical procedures to analyze numerical data. Data analysis is usually conducted in steps—first the descriptive analysis of the individual variables is conducted, and then inferential statistics are used to analyze the associations between variables. Data analysis involves counting responses and using other statistical procedures to discover the identifying characteristics of individual variables in a sample and the relationships between two or more variables in the sample. The type of analysis you use depends on the level of your variables and the research method you choose.

The First Step of Data Analysis

There are two steps to analyzing numerical data: using descriptive statistics and then inferential statistics (discussed in chapter 11). **Descriptive**

statistics are ways of organizing, describing, and presenting quantitative (numerical) data in a manner that is concise, manageable, and understandable. They usually deal with each variable individually and establish the common patterns found in each individual variable. Describing a sample in terms of the individual variables (e.g., sex, race, occupation) through measures such as totals and percentages gives us a picture of some of the characteristics of a sample. Descriptive analysis often is helpful for understanding the extent of an event or occurrence, such as the number of rapes on a college campus or the typical salary of child welfare workers. This method is used with both quantitative and qualitative methods. And while numerical descriptions of the sample and/or the common responses can be used in both methods of research, they are not always used in qualitative methods but *must* be used in quantitative methods.

As an example of how descriptive findings are organized, table 10.1 shows results from a descriptive study conducted on test cheating on a college campus. This study draws on the literature by using fourteen independent variables to explain the cheating habits of 118 students in a central Appalachian university. The table reports the results of the five descriptive variables examined for this study. To assess these variables, students were asked to read the prompt "In the last academic year, how often have you engaged in the following actions?" Seven ways to cheat were listed beneath this question. Students were asked to use a four-point frequency scale to respond to each variable. The response "Never" was coded as 1, "Once" as 2, "Two to ten times" as 3, and "More than 10 times" as 4.

Overall, the results show that cheating is at least occasionally practiced by the majority of the students in the sample. Most students have tried all but one of these actions. The majority only abstained from the riskier act of sneaking cheat-sheets into the classroom (66% said they never did), while 57 to 89 percent of students admitted to other cheating techniques. This means that about three out of five students have copied from other students' exams or made their tests available to other students. Moreover, three out of four students have received test questions from someone who completed the test, and an overwhelming nine out of ten students have improperly collaborated on a take-home exam.

Descriptive Analysis

Descriptive statistics help us to make sense of a large amount of data by finding both what is common or typical for a variable and what exceptions exist for a variable. Suppose for a moment that you have conducted a study

TABLE 10.1: DESCRIPTIVE STATISTICS FOR TEST CHEATING

ITEM	NEVER	ONCE	2–10 TIMES	10 OR MORE TIMES	MEAN
Copying from another student during an exam without his or her knowledge	37%	21%	40%	2%	2.059
Copying from another student during an exam with his or her knowledge	40%	23%	35%	2%	1.975
Using un-permit-ted notes during an exam.	66%	18%	15%	1%	1.508
Getting questions or answers from someone who has already taken the test	24%	15%	50%	11%	2.483
Helping someone else cheat on a test.	42%	17%	37%	3%	2.017
Sharing notes from a take home exam	11%	11%	70%	8%	2.746
Making answer sheet available to enable another student to see the answer	43%	20%	33%	4%	1.983

Source: Robinson, E., Ambergey, R., Swank, E., & Faulkner, C. (2004). Test cheating in a rural college: Studying the importance of individual and situational factors. *College Student Journal, 38*(3), 380–395.

that involves one hundred participants and you asked them to complete a survey that consisted of twenty questions. This would result in 2,000 answers—a large amount of material for anyone to read through and attempt to understand. Descriptive statistics allow us to **aggregate** data (compile information in a concise, manageable, and understandable manner) so that the data can be examined relatively quickly. Chances are you have used descriptive statistics for much of your life without knowing it. For instance, most people can describe what their average weight is and within what range their weight generally fluctuates. By calculating the average (also known as the mean) and the range of the variable (weight), we are using one type of descriptive statistics called univariate analysis. **Univariate analysis** involves the examination across cases of one variable at a time. There are three major characteristics of a single variable that we tend to look at: distribution, central tendencies, and dispersion.

Measures of Distribution

Distribution of data is a summary of the frequency of individual values or ranges of values for a variable. The simplest distribution would list every value of a variable and the number of people who had each value. **Frequency**, as the name implies, is the number of times that a response occurs. For example, we might discuss the frequency of absences for members of your class (the number of students who failed to attend class today). A frequency can be reported as a total (two out of twenty students were absent today) and as a percentage (10% of the twenty students were absent today).

We can also group responses so that we can report the information in more manageable terms. For instance, we might group the annual income of the families of incoming freshmen into five categories, as in table 10.2, rather than reporting a list of the one hundred responses.

Measures of Central Tendency

Measures of central tendency are a statistic (number) that is used to represent a set of responses for a variable. A **central tendency** is an estimate of the center of a distribution of values. You can think of central

TABLE 10.2: ANNUAL INCOME OF FAMILIES OF INCOMING FRESHMEN

FREQUENCY	INCOME	PERCENTAGE
50	Less than $25,000	50%
20	$25,000–$50,000	20%
15	$50,000–$75,000	15%
10	$75,000–$100,00	10%
5	Over $100,00	5%

tendencies as the means to determine what is most typical, common, and routine. There are three major types of estimates of central tendency—mean, median, and mode—of which the mean is the most often used measure of central tendency.

A **mean** is a statistical average. You can use a mean for any variable that is collected through interval-level or ratio-level responses (e.g., weight, miles driving, grade point average, age). The mean is a precise way to detect what is typical because it calculates the middle score by taking all scores into account. If you wanted to find the typical or average age of people in your class, you could simply add the ages of each person together and divide the sum by the number of people in your class.

The second measure of central tendency is the **median.** The median is simply the midpoint of a set of numbers. In order to get an accurate median, you must first order the data from low to high and then find the number that falls in the middle. For instance, if you have a set of numbers from 1 to 5, the median would be 3 because 3 falls directly in the middle, with two numbers below it (1 and 2) and two numbers above it (4 and 5). However, if your numbers ranged from 1 to 4, then the median would be 2.5 (the midpoint between 1 and 4).

The final measure of central tendency is the **mode.** The mode is the most frequently occurring response found for a variable. Let us assume for a moment that in seeking the mean for your classmates' ages, the number 21 kept occurring more than any other number. Then 21 would be the mode, or the most frequently occurring number in the variable of age. Modes are most commonly reported when the researcher has used a nominal measure of a variable, such as the number of Catholics, Protestants, and Muslims in a study.

Because measures of central tendency attempt to represent how data are grouped around what is average for a variable, it is highly probable that you use these methods without realizing it. For example, if you have ever paid attention to your grade point average, you are examining a measure of central tendency (the mean of your class grades).

Make sure that when choosing a statistical measure, you are using the appropriate level of measurement. For example, it would not make sense to report the average for a nominal- or ordinal-level variable (e.g., reporting the average sex for a group of people would be impossible). A second important point is that a statistical mean is very sensitive to outliers. An **outlier** is an anomaly or result that is far different from most of the results for the group. An outlier is a number or variable that has extreme values that can skew the overall results (especially in a statistical average). For example, let us imagine for a moment that you want to measure the mean income of consumers in your agency. Most of the consumers your agency serves are poor (as measured by the federal poverty guidelines). However, you have one consumer whose annual income is above $100,000. This one person would be considered an outlier, and including his or her income would skew the overall mean income and make it appear greater than what is actually true. The question arises as to what to do about outliers—do you simply ignore them? Do you throw them out? There is no one answer. One solution may be to report the information both ways. For example, you may report that the average income of the consumers in your agency is $25,201; however, there is one consumer who has an income of over $100,000. When this income is removed from the analysis, the average income is $14,287.

In summary, central tendency statistics report how much our data are alike or similar. In other words, how much do the subjects reflect similar characteristics, views, or beliefs? For example, let us say you are trying to decide whether to take a particular elective class. You ask twenty students who have had the class previously to rate the class on a scale from 1 (didn't like it very much) to 10 (liked it a lot). Seven students give the class a 10, eight students give the class a 9, and five students give the class an 8. The mean of the responses is 9.1 (total score of 182 divided by twenty responses). You might conclude that, based on the students you surveyed, students who have taken the class typically liked the class very much. In fact, the mode was 9 (eight students) and the median was also 9 (midpoint between 8 and 10).

Measures of Dispersion

A **measure of dispersion** shows how dissimilar or different the data are from each other and is reported by how the scores fall (i.e., are arranged) around the mean. Measures of dispersion, also referred to as measures of variability, report the overall spread of scores from the mean. Do responses stay close to the mean or do they fall away from what is typical? Put another way, how close do the scores cluster near the typical answer? An example of a distribution with a small dispersion could be the results you obtain from asking everyone in your class what their desired grade is (assuming that everyone wants an A and no one wants to fail). The topic of the legalization of abortion can create a wide dispersion, as many people hold opposing views. Measures of dispersion are only used for studies with interval- or ratio-level data.

The simplest measure of dispersion is range. **Range** is the overall spread or variability of a variable; it tells us the difference between the lowest (minimum) and highest (maximum) values (responses) for a variable. For example, if the ages of the students in your class cover a span from eighteen years old to seventy-three years old, you would say that the range is 55 (the difference between 18 and 73), and that the minimum is 18 and the maximum is 73. A wide range of scores would indicate that responses are more dissimilar to the mean than a narrow range of scores would be. Ranges are easy to calculate, but they tell the reader very little information. For instance, we do not know where the ages of the respondents fall in the 18–73 age continuum.

Variance is a statistical measure used to examine the spread of scores in a distribution. The larger the variance, the farther the scores are from the mean; the smaller the variance, the closer the scores are to the mean. That is, if the scores vary a lot from each other (have a large variance), we can assume the responses vary a lot from the typical response (they are dissimilar from the mean). If the scores do not vary a lot (have a small variance), we can assume that the responses are more typical of the mean.

Figure 10.1 is a **histogram** (a vertical block graph used in statistics to visually present interval- or ratio-level data) that shows a distribution of scores that are closely clumped around the mean. This type of distribution is called **leptokurtosis.** Leptokurtosis is the shape of a distribution of scores that is tall and narrow because the majority of scores closely resemble the mean. Figure 10.1 presents the frequency of AA meetings per month for 406 recovering addicts. The mean number of meetings was 15.5, and the range was 17 with a minimum of 8 and a maximum of 25. Looking at the graph, you can see that most respondents reported a similar number of meetings (13–17), which is very close to the mean (15.5). Very few of the scores fall away from the mean (fewer than 13 or more than 17). This causes the distribution to be tall and narrow, or leptokurtic.

Figure 10.2 is a histogram that shows how a distribution looks if the scores are not similar to the mean. This type of distribution is called platykurtosis. **Platykurtosis** is the shape of a distribution of scores that is flat and wide because the majority of scores differ from the mean. This histogram displays the month of birth of 1,487 respondents. As you can see, the months of birth for this population are dissimilar. Therefore, the distribution is spread wide and flat.

Finally, we will look at the standard deviation. A **standard deviation** is a measure of dispersion that is calculated by taking the square root of variance. It is the most commonly used measure of dispersion. We make two assumptions when looking at standard deviation—first, that we are dealing with interval-level or ratio-level variables, and second, that the data are normally distributed.

FIGURE 10.1: HISTOGRAM WITH LEPTOKURTOSIS

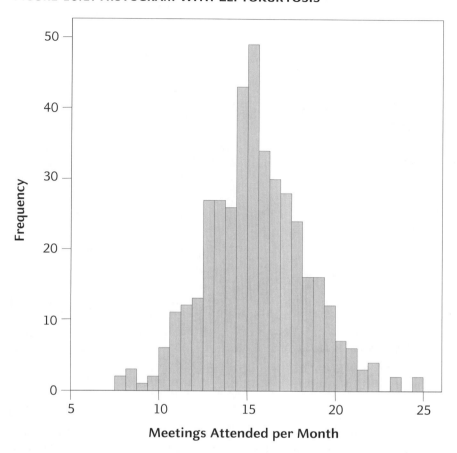

A **normal distribution** of data is the symmetrical distribution of scores around the mean, with the most scores clustered around the mean and tapering off on both sides. Normally distributed data resemble a bell-shaped curve where the mean is 0. If we folded a bell-shaped curve in half, one half would perfectly match the other. Therefore, a bell-shaped curve is the distribution of scores that are symmetrically spread around the mean so that each side of the mean resembles the other. If we assume that our data are normally distributed based on probability distribution theory (the theory that data are equally distributed on both sides of the mean), then we can make other assumptions. Such as, we can be more confident that our sample adequately reflects the population from which it was drawn. For instance, we can assume that 68.26 percent of any population will fall within one standard deviation of the mean. We can assume that 95.44

Figure 10.2: Histogram with Platykurtosis

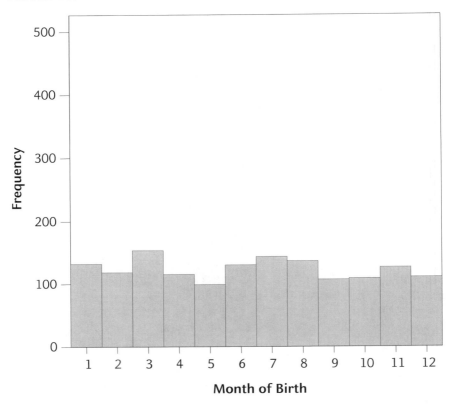

Month of Birth

percent will fall within two standard deviations of the mean. And we can assume that 99.74 percent of the population will fall within three standard deviations of the mean. The more symmetrically the data fall around the mean, the more normally distributed we say they are. When data are arranged less symmetrically around the mean, the more likely it is that the results are out of the norm.

One of the easiest ways to explain this is with IQ tests. It is known that if IQ tests were administered to a large group of people (for example, 1,000 people), 68.26 percent would score within one standard deviation. Average IQ is 100 points (with a standard deviation ± 15 points). Therefore we can be confident that 682.6 people (68.26%) would score 100 ± 15 points (one standard deviation), or between 85 and 115 points. We can be confident that 954.4 people (95.44%) would score 100 ± 30 points (two standard deviations), or between 70 and 130. We can be confident that 997.4 people (99.74%) would score within three standard deviations (100 ± 45 points), or between 55 and 145. This means that less than 1 percent of the population would have an IQ score lower than 55 (considered moderately retarded) and 1 percent would have an IQ above 145 (genius level). Common sense and our own experience also tell us that this is true.

The following example will help you interpret a descriptive analysis: You are asked to interpret the results of a survey conducted with child welfare employees in one hundred agencies throughout the state (table 10.3). In the top row are four variables (education level in years, current salary, months since hire, and minority classification). The first column shows the type of descriptive statistics that were measured (mean, median, mode, variance, standard deviation, and range, with minimum and maximum). The number of people who responded (*n*) for each variable, except current salary, is 474; the number of people who responded for current salary is 473. Keep in mind that some individuals may choose not to answer one or more questions, which would make the *n* different for that variable. Under the *n* are the measures of central tendency (mean, median, and mode) then the measures of dispersion (range, variance, and standard deviation).

Let's examine three variables, starting on the right and working left. Minority classification is coded (i.e., a number is assigned to represent an answer). The code is 0 = "No, not a minority" and 1 = "Yes, a minority." As you can see, this variable provides us with minimal information because it is nominal. Therefore, we cannot interpret this variable using measures

TABLE 10.3: DESCRIPTIVE STATISTICS OF CHILD WELFARE EMPLOYEES

	YEARS OF EDUCATION (*N* = 474)	CURRENT SALARY (*N* = 473)	MONTHS SINCE HIRE (*N* = 474)	MINORITY CLASSIFI-CATION (*N* = 474)
Mean	16.49	$34,419.57	81.11	.22
Median	16.00	$28,875.00	81.00	.00
Mode	16	$30,750.00	81	0
Variance	4.322		101.223	.172
SD	2.885	$17,075.66	10.061	.414
Range	6	$119,250.00	35	1
Minimum	12	$15,750.00	63	0
Maximum	18	$135,000.00	98	1

of dispersion. We can, however, use one central tendency by reporting the mode for this variable (the most frequently reported response is "No, not a minority"). This is still very limited information that does not tell us how many reported minority status as opposed to nonminority status.

The months-since-hire variable shows the same number (or value) for mean, median, and mode. This means that the average, the midpoint, and the most frequently occurring value are 81—that is, eighty-one months (almost seven years) employed in child welfare. The variance for these scores is 101.223. Variance is telling us how closely the numbers are distributed in relation to the mean. Since the mean is 81 and the variance is 101, we might expect the scores to be fairly equally distributed around the mean like a normal bell-shaped curve—not too close and not too far away (see figure 10.3). If the variance were 85, we would expect the scores to be closer to the mean (creating a tall and narrow graph), and if the variance were 130, we would expect the scores to spread farther from the mean

FIGURE 10.3: HISTOGRAM WITH BELL-SHAPED CURVE

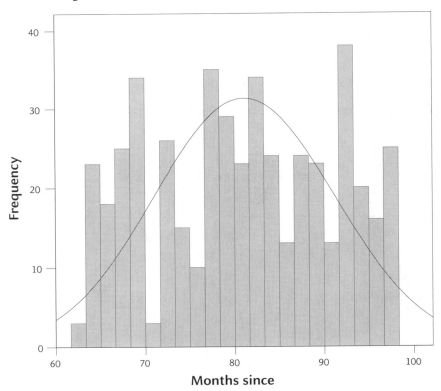

(creating a shorter but wider graph). The standard deviation is 10.061 or, rounded, 10 (1SD = 10). The range is 35 with a minimum of 63 and a maximum of 98 months.

Now we can calculate the following: What is the number of months since hire for 68.26 percent of the employees? To do this, we subtract 1SD (10) from the mean (81), which equals 71. Then we add 1SD (10) to the mean (81), which gives us 91. This gives us our spread on both sides of the mean. Thus it has been between seventy-one and ninety-one months since 68.26 percent of employees were hired.

Keep in mind that we *assume* a normal distribution, but in actuality, a distribution may be skewed (meaning there are more responses on the left or right side of the mean). When plotted on a graph, a **skewed distribution** of scores produces a nonsymmetrical curve. Distributions skewed to the left are said to be negatively skewed, and those skewed to the right are positively skewed. Figure 10.4 is a visual representation of a skewed distribution of 473 responses ($n = 473$) for the variable current salary. The mean is at the top of the curve. As you can see, the majority of responses are at or below the mean average salary of $34,419 (i.e., the most responses

FIGURE 10.4: HISTOGRAM WITH SKEWED DISTRIBUTION

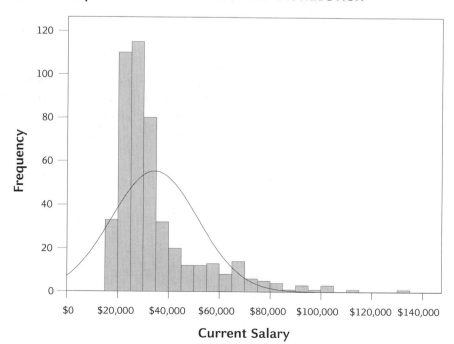

are in the \$20,000–\$35,000 range), while fewer responses fall to the right and farther away from the mean (i.e., there are fewer responses as the salary increases past \$35,000).

Strengths and Limitations of Descriptive Statistics

Descriptive statistics are necessary and valuable. They can provide an overview of general patterns of demographic variables such as sex, age, income, race, and marital status. Descriptive statistics help to organize the data and present information in an understandable form. It is advisable always to include descriptive statistics at the beginning of your results section. One of the major limitations of descriptive statistics, however, is that they offer no insight into the relationships among variables. That is, they fail to explore associations and explanatory issues concerning how variables are connected and whether the results can be generalized outside the sample.

Let us imagine for a moment that you are a case manager working with parents who physically abuse their children. You are interested in investigating the relationship between three independent variables: a ratio-level variable for income, a nominal-level variable for parenting status (single-parent versus two-parent households), and another ratio-level variable for number of children in the home. Your dependent variable (ordinal-level variable) is the type of abuse inflicted on the child. While descriptive statistics can tell you the average income of your consumers, they offer no insight into the relationship between household income and type of abuse. To examine that relationship, we need a more sophisticated statistical approach. In other words, to examine the relationship between independent and dependent variables, we turn to inferential statistics. Inferential statistics will be discussed in the next chapter.

Applied Learning Activity

Using the characteristics of your family members, compute the following statistics:

1. What is the n?

2. What are the range, minimum, and maximum of ages?

3. What is the mean age?

4. Report the percentage of people in your family who are male.

5. What are the frequencies for people who are married, divorced, single, widowed, and living with someone?

Key Points

- Data analysis is the process of using a variety of statistical procedures to analyze data.

- Data analysis is usually conducted in two steps—first the descriptive analysis of the individual variables is conducted, and then inferential statistics are used to analyze the associations between variables.

- Descriptive statistics are ways of organizing, describing, and presenting quantitative data in a manner that is concise, manageable, and understandable.

- Inferential statistics are statistical procedures that are used to examine associations about a population based on the results found in a sample. The five commonly used types of descriptive statistics are the mean, median, mode, range, and frequency.

- Measures of central tendency are statistical measures that report how much our data are alike or similar. The mean (average of the scores), median (midpoint of the scores), and mode (most frequently occurring score) are all measures of central tendency.

- Measures of dispersion, also known as measures of variability, are statistical measures that reflect dissimilarities in our sample.

- Three types of measures of dispersion are range (the overall spread or variability from the minimum score to the maximum score), variance (the spread of scores in a distribution of scores), and standard deviation (the square root of variance and the most commonly used measure of dispersion).

- Normal distribution of data is an assumption used in statistical procedures that scores are probably distributed equally around the mean. Normally distributed data resemble a bell-shaped curve.

Additional Resources

Kirk, R. (2007). *Statistics: An introduction* (5th ed.). Belmont, CA: Wadsworth.

The author strives to help readers understand the basic concepts and terminology of statistics and to develop applications for the concepts that are presented.

Salkind, N. (2004). *Statistics for people who think they hate statistics* (2nd ed.). Thousand Oaks, CA: Sage.
Salkind takes a light-hearted approach to the often daunting subject of statistics. This book makes the subject of statistics at least understandable, if not fun. Salkind does a good job of making the subject matter accessible and understandable for the reader.

Vogt, W. P. (2005). *Dictionary of statistics and methodology* (3rd ed.). Newbury Park, CA: Sage.
Having an excellent dictionary of statistical terms can help you understand much of the confusing vocabulary that is peculiar to research.

CHAPTER ELEVEN

Introduction to Inferential Statistics

THIS CHAPTER WILL INTRODUCE THE USE of inferential statistics. Keep in mind that one chapter is insufficient to cover this topic adequately, and the purpose of including an introduction to inferential statistics is to provide a basic overview for you to consider in developing your research proposal and interpreting statistical outputs in studies that you review. Therefore, we will define inferential statistics and explain how they are used to test hypotheses. We will examine how to measure associations between variables and discuss significance values, which allow us to determine if two variables or two groups are statistically important (significant) to the study. This chapter will also examine two distinct types of inferential statistics— parametric and nonparametric statistics—and provide a description of several of the more common procedures used within these categories.

What Are Inferential Statistics?

Inferential statistics examine associations between variables and use significance tests and other measures to make inferences about the collected quantitative data. For instance, we can look at whether sex and education have a relationship with occupation. That is, in a sample, do more women tend to work in certain occupations, and more men in other occupations? Similarly, is there a relationship between a person's occupation and his or her level of education? Inferential statistics are also used to assess how likely it is that group differences or correlations between the variables in the sample exist in the population.

Any quantitative study can be designed to use inferential statistics but no qualitative studies can use inferential statistics, and many qualitative studies do not describe the sample in numerical terms (i.e., they do not use descriptive statistics). For these studies, it is not how often the participants have had a common experience but the experience itself and how it is being lived that is being examined. In addition, the issue may not be how many individuals are in a sample because the sample may be only one individual. In these exploratory studies, the descriptions are related in words, not numbers.

Four Types of Correlation

A **measure of association** is any of several statistical procedures that allow you to measure the correlation between variables. In simplified terms, this concept deals with the degree of association between variables. Inferential statistics tell the reader how much the change in the dependent variable is related to the change in the independent variable (in our example, how much sex influences the career choice of workers). There are four types of correlations that can exist between variables: no correlation, a positive correlation, a negative correlation, and a curvilinear correlation. While the four types of relationships that can exist might sound complicated, both the articles that you examine in your literature review and the statistical program that you use in your own study analysis will tell you the direction of the relationship.

No Correlation

The first type of relationship is **no correlation** between the two variables—they are simply not related (one variable does not influence the other). For example, let's assume that high school students are taking a class to learn refusal skills that they can use when their friends encourage them to use drugs. After the class, researchers can try to see if the class had any effects on students' use of drugs. A no-relationship situation would mean that roughly the same proportion of students do and do not use drugs before and after the class—these two variables are not related. Another way of stating this is that the class had no relationship with (or effect on) the students' drug use.

Positive Correlation

A second way that two variables can be related is by way of a positive correlation. A **positive correlation** occurs when the dependent variable increases as the independent variable increases. For example, when study-ing the drug use of high school students, a researcher might ask about their parents' drug use or if their friends use illegal substances. If the researcher finds that students who smoke marijuana are more likely to have family members who use drugs, and if students who smoke mari-juana regularly hang out with other users, then the researcher has found positive correlations.

Negative Correlation

The third relationship is known as a negative correlation. A **negative correlation** (also called an *inverse relationship*) means that as one variable increases, the other decreases. For example, research shows that the cost of drugs is related to drug use. An inverse relationship is demonstrated when the cost of drugs increases as the amount of drug use decreases.

Curvilinear Correlation

The last type of relationship is known as a **curvilinear correlation**. This type of relationship can start off as either a positive relationship or a nega-tive relationship and then begins to curve. For instance, it is very possible that test anxiety drops commensurate to amount of time spent studying but at some point begins to level off (i.e., not drop any further). There is probably a point at which the anxiety will still be present regardless how much time one spends studying. In fact, anxiety may even start increasing again as the time when the actual test will take place approaches. This is a curvilinear relationship.

Determining the Strength of the Correlation

Since this book is directed toward students in their first research course, we will focus on how statistical calculations (outputs) help researchers examine the strength of the relationships between independent and depen-dent variables.

The strength of the relationship (or how well the variables fit with each other) is represented by a number between -1 and $+1$. This number indicates whether the correlation between the variables is non-existent, weak, moderate, or strong. Most correlation analyses report a raw value for a relationship between two variables on a scale that ranges from 0 to 1. This means the results will tell you how much the variables relate to each other. A correlation value of 0 tells you that there is absolutely no relationship whatsoever between the two variables. The stronger the relationship between two variables, the closer the analysis findings will be to the number 1. So then, a correlation analysis can yield a value from 0 (meaning the two variables are not correlated) to 1 (meaning they are perfectly correlated). Therefore, a relationship of .5 is a moderately strong positive relationship. For a negative relationship, the same is true, except that numbers range from −1 to 0. The negative sign implies an inverse relationship. Therefore, a relationship of −.5 (as represented in figure 11.1) is a moderately strong inverse or negative relationship. A common error that students make is to assign value to the negative sign—in other words, to assume a negative value yields poor results.

Probability Values and Confidence Intervals

The **probability value** or *p* value is a report of whether the strength of a relationship is statistically significant or whether it could have occurred by chance. Most researchers set the level for statistical significance at .05 or smaller, meaning that there is less than a one-in-twenty chance that the results are due to sampling error. You will see this significance level shown as $p < .05$, where the *p* represents probability, the symbol < means "less than," and .05 represents the level of statistical significance. Thus whenever you see a probability level such as $p < .05$, $p < .01$, or $p < .001$ in a table, you know that the relationship is strong enough to be considered statistically significant. This means that the prediction of the relationship (the hypothesis) was correct and that the relationship between the two variables was so powerful that it could not be considered a fluke.

A **confidence interval** tells us how certain we can be that our sample is reflective of the population from which it was drawn. As a common rule, most researchers establish a confidence interval of 95 percent. This means that they want to be 95 percent certain that the findings from the analysis are not in error. The confidence interval is determined at the time that the analysis is conducted.

Imagine that you recruited fifty volunteers and measured the amount

FIGURE 11.1: NEGATIVE CORRELATION

Perfectly Correlated   **No Correlation**

−1	−.9	−.8	−.7	−.6	−.5	−.4	−.3	−.2	−.1	0

of time they spent studying for their midterm exam. You recorded this and then asked them to report their numerical grade on the midterm. You could then complete a statistical analysis to determine whether a relationship exists between amount of time spent studying and test grades. What if the results showed that the two variables were positively associated at a correlation of .49 and a p value of less than .05 ($p < .05$)? We then could determine that there is indeed a relationship between amount of time spent studying and exam grades, and that it is not likely that it occurred by chance.

Parametric Statistics

The first of the two types of inferential statistics, **parametric statistics**, is based on a set of assumptions or rules that must be met. It assumes that your data are normally distributed. It assumes that the dependent variable is measured at an interval or ratio level. It also assumes that you have a sample size of at least thirty. If the collected data do not meet all these conditions, then parametric statistics should not be used. Some of the most common parametric procedures are Pearson's r, multiple regression (sometimes referred to as linear regression), t-tests, and analysis of variance (ANOVA).

Pearson's r

One of the most common measures of association is known as Pearson's product moment correlation (Pearson's r). **Pearson's r** seeks to determine if a relationship exists between two variables (one independent variable and one dependent variable) and the direction of the relationship. It also shows the degree to which the variables are related and the probability that this relationship occurred by chance. This analysis assumes that both the independent and dependent variables are measured at the interval or ratio level. An example of this might be amount of education attained and salary. When one is trying to determine if these two variables affect each other, Pearson's r is used. Pearson's r is a type of **bivariate analysis** (also called simple regression), or an analysis that examines the relationship between one independent and one dependent variable. There are several other bivariate associations, including eta, gamma, lambda, Kendall's tau, and Spearman's rho. However, the Pearson's correlation is so commonly used that it is associated with the word *correlation*.

Imagine for a moment that you are a caseworker teaching parenting classes to couples. You have noticed that your consumers have different attitudes about the spanking of children. You have also noticed that younger parents seem to be more in favor of spanking than those who have been parenting for a while. After conducting a literature review, you find that research shows a positive relationship between the age a person was when he or she got married and his or her attitudes toward spanking. You decide to test this out. You recruit sixty volunteers from your agency and survey them as to how old they were when they first married and their attitudes about spanking. Table 11.1 shows a correlation procedure that you run, utilizing the Statistical Package for Social Sciences (SPSS). **SPSS** is a statistical program that is commonly used by social science researchers to analyze research data. The table shows that there is a positive relationship (.136) between the two variables of a person's age when he or she first married (AGEWED) and beliefs about spanking children (SPANKING). The N represents the sample size (1,202 respondents). *Sig.* represents significance score, which is .000, and the significance level in this case was set at $\leq$.01. It is clear that the relationship has a significantly positive correlation. This would be noted as $r = .136$, $p < .01$. Therefore, people who marry at a younger age are more likely to condone spanking.

Rarely will you find research studies in which the researchers have used only one independent and one dependent variable. It is clear that nothing is influenced by only one variable. That is, a person's salary is not influenced entirely by his or her educational level, and a person's feelings about spanking are not purely determined by the age at which he or she married. For instance, we can assume that a person's salary is also influenced by a slew of other factors, such as discrimination against women and minority racial groups, the geography of where one lives, and availability of transportation. Much more common is the inclusion of multiple independent

TABLE 11.1: CORRELATIONS BETWEEN AGE WHEN FIRST MARRIED AND ATTITUDES ABOUT SPANKING

		AGEWED	SPANKING
AGEWED	Pearson Correlation	1	.136 **
	Sig.		.000
	N	1202	796
SPANKING	Pearson Correlation	.136 **	1
	Sig.	.00	
	N	796	997

** Correlation is significant at the 0.01 level.

variables (and it is not uncommon for studies to have multiple dependent variables).

Multiple Regression

Multiple regression (or linear regression) is a statistical procedure that measures the correlation between an independent variable and the dependent variable while holding other independent variables constant. Another way of saying this is that it determines the impact of one independent variable on the dependent variable while removing the influence of other independent variables. While multiple regression is important for many reasons, one of the most important reasons is that it is a statistical way to deal with issues of confounding variables, because a researcher can place an endless amount of independent and control variables into the statistical model for a multiple regression.

Let us return for a moment to our study about spanking. Table 11.1 showed that there is a positive relationship between these two variables but they are not perfectly correlated. In fact, the strength of the correlation is only .136, which is a weak relationship. We can say with confidence that a person's age when he or she is first married is associated with views on spanking. Another way to state it is to say that a person's age when he or she first married is a predictor of that person's views on spanking (though not a strong predictor). How can we determine the strength of the relationship more precisely? One way is to control for other variables. A researcher may want to hold constant certain variables within the study. In this example, it was discovered in the literature review that education had a strong effect on people's views on spanking. In fact, researchers found that the more education a person has, the less likely he or she is to spank. Therefore, we will want to control for level of education to reduce the risk of this variable influencing the results. We can accomplish this by using group assignment (when we select our sample) or by using multiple regression.

Let's use another example where we have collected more than one independent variable. If we were to suggest that there is a relationship between amount of education and income, you might agree. On the surface, that would make sense. We could even perform bivariate analysis to test if this hypothesis is true (see table 11.2).

Based on the results from table 11.2, we can see that there is a positive relationship (.342) between education (EDUC) and respondent's income (RINCOM91). This would be noted as $r = .342$, $p < .01$. However, you may be thinking, "Yes, that makes sense, but there is more to predicting income than just education level." And you would be right. For example, we know

TABLE 11.2: CORRELATIONS BETWEEN EDUCATIONAL LEVEL AND INCOME

		EDUC	RINCOM91
EDUC	Pearson Correlation	1	.342**
	Sig.		.000
	N	1496	991
RINCOM91	Pearson Correlation	.342**	1
	Sig.	.000	
	N	991	994

** Correlation is significant at the 0.01 level.

that men, on the whole, have more income than women. And we know that, for the most part, whites are paid more than people of color. So we might run a second analysis that would look at the role of education after controlling for the variables of sex and race. In short, we would run multiple regression (see table 11.3).

You may notice that SPSS gives you a different table for multiple regression than for a simple bivariate analysis. Even though much more information is presented, it is still possible to learn to interpret the results without having to understand all the underlying theory. In the table, you will want to pay attention to the standardized coefficients (known as the *beta* or *beta*

TABLE 11.3: COEFFICIENTS FOR EDUCATIONAL LEVEL AND INCOME, CONTROLLING FOR SEX AND RACE (DEPENDENT VARIABLE = TOTAL FAMILY INCOME)

MODEL		UNSTANDARDIZED COEFFICIENTS		STANDARDIZED COEFFICIENTS	t	SIG.
		B	SE	BETA		
1	(Constant)	7.158	.778		9.202	.000
	Highest Year of School Completed	.756	.042	.429	18.059	.000
	Respondent's Sex	−1.075	.260	−.098	−4.141	.000
	Race of Respondent	−.551	.253	−.052	−2.175	.030

weight). You use the same methods to interpret the beta as for the correlation in the bivariate analysis. This means that you look for beta weight to determine the strength of the relationship. The significance level (Sig.) is reported the same as in bivariate analysis. You would look for a significance of less than .05. In this table, we see that education is the strongest predictor of (has the strongest relationship with) the dependent variable of income because it has the largest beta and a significance level of less than .05 when sex and race are controlled for. This is noted as beta $= .429, p <$ .05. While sex and race are both significant ($p < .05$), they are negative relationships at $-.098$ and $-.052$ respectively, as shown in the output.

t-tests

A *t*-test is a statistical procedure that tests the means of two groups to determine if they are statistically different. There are two common types of *t*-tests—independent and paired samples (also known as dependent samples *t*-tests). We will examine each individually.

The **independent samples *t*-test** is utilized when a researcher needs to compare two groups to see if the independent variable has an effect on the dependent variable. For example, let us assume that you want to measure the difference between a group of males and a group of females and their beliefs about teaching sex education in schools. The hypothesis might be that women and men have different beliefs about teaching sex education in schools. The independent samples *t*-test would be appropriate for this analysis. After we survey a group of males and a group of females, we would compare their answers. Based on tables 11.4 and 11.5, we can conclude that there is no difference in people's attitudes about sex education based on sex. These tables present both a *t*-score and a significance score. The significance should be .05 or smaller, which is not the case in this example. Instead, the researcher would have to accept the null hypothesis and look for other independent variables that might sway opinions about teaching sex education in schools.

TABLE 11.4: INDEPENDENT SAMPLES t-TEST: CORRELATIONS BETWEEN SEX AND ATTITUDES TOWARD TEACHING SEX EDUCATION IN SCHOOLS

	RESPONDENT'S SEX	*N*	MEAN
Sex Education in Public Schools	Male	444	1.15
	Female	540	1.16

TABLE 11.5: INDEPENDENT SAMPLES t-TEST: SIGNIFICANCE RESULTS

	t-TEST FOR EQUALITY OF MEANS	
	t	SIG.
Sex Education in Public Schools	− .458	.647

We might also want to compare a client against him- or herself over time. Perhaps we are interested in administering a pretest to a group of participants and then providing some form of intervention. At the end of the intervention we want to administer a posttest and then compare the pretest scores to the posttest scores to see if the participants' situations improved, remained the same, or became worse after the intervention. For this analysis we would use a paired samples *t*-test. A **paired samples *t*-test** (also known as dependent samples *t*-test) can be defined as a test of significance of the differences between two different sets of scores for the same respondents.

For example, let us assume that you are a drug abuse counselor whose job it is to teach middle school students about the spread of the HIV virus. You administer a pretest designed to test their knowledge about HIV and then you present them with some factual information. At the end of the presentation, you administer the same test as a posttest to see if their scores changed. It would be a simple matter then to measure the pretest results against the posttest results, using a paired samples *t*-test. The results would report a *t*-value, which refers to the standard deviation. In general you want to look for a *t*-value of three standard deviations or greater. In this case, the *t*-value is 26.473, and its significance level is well below .05 ($p < .000$). This finding would be noted as $t = 26.473$, $p < .05$. You would probably be excited to conclude that the intervention was a success. Again, we must caution you that this is a simplified discussion of interpreting *t*-test results. To fully understand how to interpret a *t*-test, you must consider such things as sample size and something called *degrees of freedom* (*df*). We only use this example to give you a rough idea of how a *t*-test can be utilized in the research process.

Analysis of Variance

Analysis of variance (ANOVA) is a parametric statistical procedure that allows us to examine the difference between the mean scores of two or more groups simultaneously. This is an extension of the independent *t*-test in that the *t*-test is limited to only two groups. ANOVA examines and compares the means within each group and then compares those to the means of other groups to see if there is a significant difference. To use ANOVA, you must have an interval- or ratio-level dependent variable.

ANOVA is useful for comparing several measurements between two groups (treatment and nontreatment). To illustrate how to use ANOVA, we will walk through a simple example of a research design that used ANOVA in the analysis of the data.

First, you conduct a literature review, which shows that participating in low-element challenge courses increases group cohesion (i.e., satisfaction) and individual self-esteem. Low-elements challenge courses are a series of sequenced events where group members have to work together to solve problems.

You formulate the research question "Can participating in low-element challenges also increase group satisfaction and individual self-esteem in families?" and develop two hypotheses: (1) families participating in a low-elements challenge course will report a significant increase in family satisfaction after the intervention, compared to the nontreatment group, and (2) individuals participating in a low-elements challenge course will report a significant increase in self-esteem after the intervention, compared to the nontreatment group.

Two measurement surveys are selected to measure family satisfaction: the Self-Report Family Instrument and the Kansas Family Life Satisfaction Scale. The Rosenberg Self-Esteem Scale is selected to measure individual self-esteem.

Your sample is a convenience sample. Families agree either to participate in the treatment group or to simply complete the surveys (nontreatment group). The treatment group receives the low-elements challenge course intervention, and participants are asked to complete the two surveys that measure family satisfaction and one survey that measures self-esteem. The nontreatment group simply completes the three surveys without receiving the intervention. To analyze the data, you use ANOVA to compare the three measures between the two groups, and the results are reported in an SPSS output table. In table 11.6 there are three dependent variables: the results of the Self-Report Family Instrument (SRF), the Kansas Family Life Satisfaction Scale (KFL) and the Rosenberg Self-Esteem Scale (RSE). Notice, first of all, that among other things, SPSS reports an *F* value. The *F* value and the significance score are interpreted together. As a general rule, when interpreting the *F* value, you want the number to be greater than 2, but the important statistic is the significance value, which should be .05 or smaller. A quick glance at the table will show you that all

Table 11.6: ANOVA Comparison between Treatment Group and Nontreatment Group

		df	F	SIG.
SRF	Between Groups	1	22.776	.000
	Within Groups	62		
	Total	63		
KFL	Between Groups	1	59.375	.000
	Within Groups	62		
	Total	63		
RSE	Between Groups	1	58.917	.000
	Within Groups	62		
	Total	63		

the F scores are well above 2 and the significance levels are all .05 or smaller. These results would be noted as $F = 22.77$, $p < .05$ for the Self-Report Family Instrument; $F = 59.37$, $p < .05$ for the Kansas Family Life Satisfaction Scale; and $F = 58.91$, $p < .05$ for the Rosenberg Self-Esteem Scale. Without going into too much detail about the interpretation of results, we can infer from these results that the results of the treatment group were inherently different from those of the comparison group in all three measures. In short, the treatment group showed a significant increase in family satisfaction and self-esteem after the intervention, compared to the nontreatment group.

Nonparametric Statistics

Nonparametric statistics are used when the data depart from the criteria established for parametric statistics. For instance, you might have a small sample size and do not meet the assumption of a normal distribution or you may have a nominal- or ordinal-level dependent variable. For analyzing this type of data, you would use nonparametric statistics.

There are actually several different types of nonparametric statistics. To explore each and every one of them is far beyond the scope of this text; therefore, we will present the most commonly used of the nonparametric statistics, which is the cross-tabs analysis. Cross-tabs is a procedure that forms two-way tables and provides a variety of tests and measures of association for these tables. The structure of the table and whether categories are ordered determine what test or measure to use.

Chi-square is a nonparametric statistical procedure that is commonly used when a researcher has a small sample size and a dependent variable that is nominal or ordinal level to determine if there is truly a difference in groups. An example of such a situation is when a researcher seeks to determine if people from different races are drawn to different sorts of religions (Catholicism, Protestantism, Judaism, Islam, Buddhism, etc.). Chi-square is represented as x^2 in the documentation of results. Therefore, when reading a study, you know that the symbol x^2 means that the authors are reporting the significance of a finding for which they used Chi-square. The Chi-square statistic predicts what would have happened in a normally distributed set of data and then compares what really happened to determine whether the two are significantly different. Chi-square is easier to interpret than other statistics—you simply compare the expected frequencies (what the statistical program projects would have occurred) against what was actually observed (from the data collected).

For example, respondents in a study were asked whether they favor or oppose laws that require gun owners to hold permits (see tables 11.7, 11.8, and 11.9). The hypothesis is that there would be a significant difference between women's and men's opinions concerning gun laws.

In table 11.7, it was expected that 492 (half of those responding) would

TABLE 11.7: CROSS-TABS ANALYSIS: OBSERVED AND EXPECTED SCORES

	OBSERVED N	EXPECTED N	RESIDUAL
1 Favor	811	492.0	319.0
2 Oppose	173	492.0	−319.0
Total	984		

TABLE 11.8: CROSS-TABS ANALYSIS: SEX AND OPINION ON GUN PERMIT LAWS

		FAVOR OR OPPOSE GUN PERMITS		
		FAVOR	OPPOSE	TOTAL
Respondent's Sex	Male	314	111	425
	Female	497	62	559
Total		811	173	984

TABLE 11.9: CROSS-TABS ANALYSIS: SIGNIFICANCE RESULTS

	SEX	GUNLAW
Chi-Square[a,b]	31.683	413.663
df	1	1
Asymp. Sig.	.000	.000

a. 0 cells (.0%) have expected frequencies less than 5. The minimum expected cell frequency is 750.0.
b. 0 cells (.0%) have expected frequencies less than 5. The minimum expected cell frequency is 49.20.

favor laws requiring gun permits and the other half would oppose these laws. However, what was observed in this sample was that 811 of all respondents favored gun permit laws and 173 of all respondents opposed them. Table 11.8 shows us that females significantly favored gun permit laws (497) over males (314). In table 11.9, the Chi-square significance (Asymp. Sig.) shows that these findings were significant (.000) for both the gun permit law variable and the sex variable. The Chi-square value (31.683) would be reported in the following manner: $x^2 = 31.68$, $p < .05$.

Strengths and Limitations of Inferential Statistics

Inferential statistics are both necessary and valuable. They provide a level of sophistication that goes well beyond anything that is possible when one is describing individual variables. For instance, simple regression can help us to determine the strength of a relationship between variables, and an independent samples *t*-test can help us to know whether one group is statistically different from another. Let's say that you want to know if one group (who studied twice as much as another group for an entire semester) did better than the other group on a final exam. Inferential statistics can help you to know whether the difference occurred because the first group studied more or is simply a result of chance.

There are limitations with statistics, just as there are limitations with anything. Statistics, especially inferential statistics, deal with probability. While we can establish confidence levels as high as one in a thousand if we so desire, no statistical significance can be absolutely infallible (i.e., absolutely certain that the results did not happen by chance). A second limitation is the issue of causality. We have stated several times in this text that correlation does not imply causation. This bears repeating. However, keeping those things in mind, we can still gain much useful information from inferential statistics.

Which Statistical Program Is Right for Me?

As it becomes increasingly necessary for social workers to learn some basic techniques for evaluating their own practice, many social workers have begun to use statistical programs in their workplaces and private practices. Some of the most popular statistical programs on the market today are SPSS, SAS, and MicroCase. The question arises, then, which statistical package is the best for you? The answer to that question depends on several things. Do you (or your agency) have a particular statistical program already, or are you already familiar with one statistical program? If you are currently using one program and you are familiar with that program, it is often easier to purchase upgrades than to switch to another program. Secondly, how much are you going to use a statistical program? Many people use Microsoft Excel for all their statistical needs. The advantages to this are that this program is already installed on most office and home computers and there is no need to purchase a new program. The downside is that there can be a steep learning curve before new users can create the formulas for statistical analysis with Excel. Finally, how much do you want to spend? Some statistical programs can be quite expensive (running into the thousands of dollars for multiple site installations). These are questions to consider as you decide which program is best for your needs.

Applied Learning Activities

Activity #1

You are a researcher who wishes to determine if a relationship exists between violent video games and aggression in children. You conduct a literature review and find literature that supports this hypothesis. After conducting a research study in which you examine the amount of time a child spends playing violent video games (independent variable) and the amount of aggression he or she exhibits (dependent variable), you find the two variables are related ($r = .47, p < .05$).

1. What conclusions can you draw about these statistics?

2. What type of statistical procedure was conducted?

3. Was this an appropriate procedure? Why or why not?

4. Can you trust your findings? Why or why not?

Activity #2

You are a hospital social worker who conducts an educational group for people addicted to nicotine. You want to determine empirically whether your participants are learning anything about the effects of tobacco on the body. You develop a test and administer the test before your participants begin their first group session and again at the end of the last group session. You compare the results and find the following results: $t = 12.71$, $p < .05$.

1. What type of statistical procedure was conducted?

2. What, if anything, can you conclude about the statistical procedure?

3. Was this an appropriate statistical procedure? Why or why not?

Activity #3

You are a caseworker who helps consumers obtain food vouchers. You have noticed that a large percentage of your consumers have not graduated from high school. You decide to collect data from several of your consumers' files and conduct a statistical analysis to see if education and income are associated.

1. What type of statistical analysis would you run?

2. How would you expect to interpret the results?

3. Would you run a different statistical procedure if you were examining sex and education?

Key Points

· There are two types of inferential statistics—parametric and non-parametric.

· Parametric statistics have a set of assumptions or rules that must be met: they assume that your data are normally distributed, that the dependent variable is measured at an interval or ratio level, and that you have a sample size of at least thirty.

- Nonparametric statistics are used when the data depart from the criteria established for parametric statistics.

- The probability value is used to determine whether the strength of the relationship is statistically significant or whether it could have occurred by chance.

- Multiple regression measures the impact of a dependent variable and an independent variable on each other while removing the impact of the other variables in the study.

- A t-test is a statistical procedure that compares the means of two groups to determine if they are significantly different.

- Analysis of variance (ANOVA) is a statistical procedure that allows us to compare the mean scores of two or more groups simultaneously.

- Cross-tabs is a nonparametric statistical procedure commonly used when a researcher has a small sample size and a dependent variable that is nominal or ordinal to determine if there is a significant difference between groups.

Additional Resources

Abu-Bader, S. (2005). *Using statistical methods in social work practice: A complete SPSS guide.* Chicago: Lyceum Books.
Abu-Bader provides a text that not only focuses on social work (using examples and illustrations that are geared toward the profession) but discusses SPSS with many screen captures and illustrations.

Asadoorian, M. (2004). *Essentials of inferential statistics* (4th ed.). Lanham, MD: University Press of America.
The author begins with basic definitions and guides the reader through such concepts as hypothesis testing and linear regression. The text includes sample exercises (along with answers) and a quick reference guide.

CHAPTER TWELVE

Now What? Practicing Your Research Skills

AT THE RISK OF STATING THE OBVIOUS, we want to stress that the best way to hone your research skills is to become involved in research. It has been our experience that when social workers do not regularly practice some type of research activity, they quickly lose many of their skills. There are probably more opportunities for you to do this that do not require you to conduct your own study than you realize. Once it is known that you have an interest in research and are willing to help others out for the sake of the experience, many opportunities will present themselves to you. You may want to work with one of your professors on his or her research projects. There are many ways for you to be helpful, such as by entering data, helping to collect information, or conducting literature reviews. Along with working as a research assistant, you may want to assist colleagues in some of their own research. If you look around, you may find other social workers conducting single-subject research studies, program evaluations, and their own qualitative or quantitative studies. Researchers love talking about their research, and most would be happy to have a volunteer assist them.

The second way is by conducting your own research studies. There are many practical ways that you can use your knowledge; one is to help your personal practice by evaluating programs and interventions. Hopefully, by now, you understand that research is not conducted in giant leaps, but in small incremental steps. As a practitioner, you can add to the overall level of knowledge by evaluating evidence-based practices. It is perfectly acceptable if the studies you undertake are small and limited in design—remember, there is no such thing as a study without limitations. The more research you conduct, the more confident you will become in your abilities. It is our hope that as a professional in the field of social work, you will regard your social work degree as an opportunity to contribute to your profession. An example research proposal that you can use as a guide to structure your own research proposals is shown in Appendix B.

One of the fundamental truths about the helping professions is that you will never know it all. Just as you become proficient in one area and begin to feel that you have gained competence and confidence, you will begin to realize that not only is there more to learn, but new knowledge is emerging daily. Additionally, in this modern world, our knowledge base is expanding rapidly through technological advances. Because of this, it is important for you as a professional to stay current. This leads to a philosophy of lifelong learning.

One of the ways that you can stay current is by continuing to read, learn, and explore new ideas. One of the ways to stay current is to join one of the many social work organizations that exist, such as the National Association of Social Workers, the Society for Social Work and Research, and the Clinical Social Work Association. Membership to these organizations often includes a subscription to the social work periodical produced by the organization. Make it a point to read at least one research article each month. As you read, critically evaluate what you are reading. You may ask yourself, "Does this research deepen our understanding of the concept under study?" "Is this research methodologically sound (e.g. demonstrate validity)?" "Is it ethically conducted?" "What are the strengths of this research design?" "What are the weaknesses?" and "Can the findings truly generalize to the population to which the authors say it does?" By critically analyzing articles, not only do you gain new knowledge, but you are also keeping your own analytical skills honed and fresh. By reading and staying current with the literature, by working with others, and by conducting your own research, you will be well on your way to becoming a competent practitioner—someone who combines practice wisdom with empirical evidence.

Additional Resources

American Geriatrics Society: http://www.americangeriatrics.org/
American Professional Society on the Abuse of Children: http://www .apsac.org/mc/page.do
Child Welfare League of America: http://www.cwla.org/defaultskip.htm
Clinical Social Work Association: http://www.associationsites.com/main-pub.cfm?usr = cswa
Council on Social Work Education: http://www.cswe.org/CSWE/

Dudley, J. (2005). *Research methods for social work: Becoming consumers and producers of research.* Boston: Pearson/Allyn and Bacon.

This well-constructed text offers another look at the process of basic research methods for social work practitioners.

National Association of Social Workers: http://www.naswdc.org/

Seltzer, R. (1996). *Mistakes that social scientists make: Error and redemption in the research process.* New York: St. Martin's Press.

This text covers common mistakes in social science research. This is a good resource that can help you, as a consumer of research, identify flaws in published research studies and prevent mistakes in the research process.

Society for Social Work and Research: http://www.sswr.org/

Substance Abuse and Mental Health Services Administration: http://www.samhsa.gov/

Ethical Standards of the National Association of Social Workers

The following ethical standards are relevant to the professional activities of all social workers. These standards concern (1) social workers' ethical responsibilities to clients, (2) social workers' ethical responsibilities to colleagues, (3) social workers' ethical responsibilities in practice settings, (4) social workers' ethical responsibilities as professionals, (5) social workers' ethical responsibilities to the social work profession, and (6) social workers' ethical responsibilities to the broader society.

Some of the standards that follow are enforceable guidelines for professional conduct, and some are aspirational. The extent to which each standard is enforceable is a matter of professional judgment to be exercised by those responsible for reviewing alleged violations of ethical standards.

1. Social Workers' Ethical Responsibilities to Clients

1.01 COMMITMENT TO CLIENTS

Social workers' primary responsibility is to promote the well-being of clients. In general, clients' interests are primary. However, social workers' responsibility to the larger society or specific legal obligations may on limited occasions supersede the loyalty owed clients, and clients should be so advised. (Examples include when a social worker is required by law to report that a client has abused a child or has threatened to harm self or others.)

Source: National Association of Social Workers. (1999). *Code of Ethics of the National Association of Social Workers.* Washington, DC: NASW Press. Reprinted with permission.

1.02 SELF-DETERMINATION

Social workers respect and promote the right of clients to self-determination and assist clients in their efforts to identify and clarify their goals. Social workers may limit clients' right to self-determination when, in the social workers' professional judgment, clients' actions or potential actions pose a serious, foreseeable, and imminent risk to themselves or others.

1.03 INFORMED CONSENT

(a) Social workers should provide services to clients only in the context of a professional relationship based, when appropriate, on valid informed consent. Social workers should use clear and understandable language to inform clients of the purpose of the services, risks related to the services, limits to services because of the requirements of a third-party payer, relevant costs, reasonable alternatives, clients' right to refuse or withdraw consent, and the time frame covered by the consent. Social workers should provide clients with an opportunity to ask questions.

(b) In instances when clients are not literate or have difficulty understanding the primary language used in the practice setting, social workers should take steps to ensure clients' comprehension. This may include providing clients with a detailed verbal explanation or arranging for a qualified interpreter or translator whenever possible.

(c) In instances when clients lack the capacity to provide informed consent, social workers should protect clients' interests by seeking permission from an appropriate third party, informing clients consistent with the clients' level of understanding. In such instances social workers should seek to ensure that the third party acts in a manner consistent with clients' wishes and interests. Social workers should take reasonable steps to enhance such clients' ability to give informed consent.

(d) In instances when clients are receiving services involuntarily, social workers should provide information about the nature and extent of services and about the extent of clients' right to refuse service.

(e) Social workers who provide services via electronic media (such as computer, telephone, radio, and television) should inform recipients of the limitations and risks associated with such services.

(f) Social workers should obtain clients' informed consent before audiotaping or videotaping clients or permitting observation of services to clients by a third party.

1.04 Competence

(a) Social workers should provide services and represent themselves as competent only within the boundaries of their education, training, license, certification, consultation received, supervised experience, or other relevant professional experience.

(b) Social workers should provide services in substantive areas or use intervention techniques or approaches that are new to them only after engaging in appropriate study, training, consultation, and supervision from people who are competent in those interventions or techniques.

(c) When generally recognized standards do not exist with respect to an emerging area of practice, social workers should exercise careful judgment and take responsible steps (including appropriate education, research, training, consultation, and supervision) to ensure the competence of their work and to protect clients from harm.

1.05 Cultural Competence and Social Diversity

(a) Social workers should understand culture and its function in human behavior and society, recognizing the strengths that exist in all cultures.

(b) Social workers should have a knowledge base of their clients' cultures and be able to demonstrate competence in the provision of services that are sensitive to clients' cultures and to differences among people and cultural groups.

(c) Social workers should obtain education about and seek to understand the nature of social diversity and oppression with respect to race, ethnicity, national origin, color, sex, sexual orientation, age, marital status, political belief, religion, and mental or physical disability.

1.06 Conflicts of Interest

(a) Social workers should be alert to and avoid conflicts of interest that interfere with the exercise of professional discretion and impartial judgment. Social workers should inform clients when a real or potential conflict of interest arises and take reasonable steps to resolve the issue in a manner that makes the clients' interests primary and protects clients' interests to the greatest extent possible. In some cases, protecting clients' interests may require termination of the professional relationship with proper referral of the client.

(b) Social workers should not take unfair advantage of any professional relationship or exploit others to further their personal, religious, political, or business interests.

(c) Social workers should not engage in dual or multiple relationships with clients or former clients in which there is a risk of exploitation or potential harm to the client. In instances when dual or multiple relationships are unavoidable, social workers should take steps to protect clients and are responsible for setting clear, appropriate, and culturally sensitive boundaries. (Dual or multiple relationships occur when social workers relate to clients in more than one relationship, whether professional, social, or business. Dual or multiple relationships can occur simultaneously or consecutively.)

(d) When social workers provide services to two or more people who have a relationship with each other (for example, couples, family members), social workers should clarify with all parties which individuals will be considered clients and the nature of social workers' professional obligations to the various individuals who are receiving services. Social workers who anticipate a conflict of interest among the individuals receiving services or who anticipate having to perform in potentially conflicting roles (for example, when a social worker is asked to testify in a child custody dispute or divorce proceedings involving clients) should clarify their role with the parties involved and take appropriate action to minimize any conflict of interest.

1.07 PRIVACY AND CONFIDENTIALITY

(a) Social workers should respect clients' right to privacy. Social workers should not solicit private information from clients unless it is essential to providing services or conducting social work evaluation or research. Once private information is shared, standards of confidentiality apply.

(b) Social workers may disclose confidential information when appropriate with valid consent from a client or a person legally authorized to consent on behalf of a client.

(c) Social workers should protect the confidentiality of all information obtained in the course of professional service, except for compelling professional reasons. The general expectation that social workers will keep information confidential does not apply when disclosure is necessary to prevent serious, foreseeable, and imminent harm to a client or other identifiable person. In all instances, social workers should disclose the least amount of confidential information necessary to achieve the desired purpose; only information that is directly relevant to the purpose for which the disclosure is made should be revealed.

(d) Social workers should inform clients, to the extent possible, about the disclosure of confidential information and the potential consequences, when feasible before the disclosure is made. This applies whether social workers disclose confidential information on the basis of a legal requirement or client consent.

(e) Social workers should discuss with clients and other interested parties the nature of confidentiality and limitations of clients' right to confidentiality. Social workers should review with clients circumstances where confidential information may be requested and where disclosure of confidential information may be legally required. This discussion should occur as soon as possible in the social worker-client relationship and as needed throughout the course of the relationship.

(f) When social workers provide counseling services to families, couples, or groups, social workers should seek agreement among the parties involved concerning each individual's right to confidentiality and obligation to preserve the confidentiality of information shared by others. Social workers should inform participants in family, couples, or group counseling that social workers cannot guarantee that all participants will honor such agreements.

(g) Social workers should inform clients involved in family, couples, marital, or group counseling of the social worker's, employer's, and agency's policy concerning the social worker's disclosure of confidential information among the parties involved in the counseling.

(h) Social workers should not disclose confidential information to third-party payers unless clients have authorized such disclosure.

(i) Social workers should not discuss confidential information in any setting unless privacy can be ensured. Social workers should not discuss confidential information in public or semipublic areas such as hallways, waiting rooms, elevators, and restaurants.

(j) Social workers should protect the confidentiality of clients during legal proceedings to the extent permitted by law. When a court of law or other legally authorized body orders social workers to disclose confidential or privileged information without a client's consent and such disclosure could cause harm to the client, social workers should request that the court withdraw the order or limit the order as narrowly as possible or maintain the records under seal, unavailable for public inspection.

(k) Social workers should protect the confidentiality of clients when responding to requests from members of the media.

(l) Social workers should protect the confidentiality of clients' written and electronic records and other sensitive information. Social workers should take reasonable steps to ensure that clients' records are stored in a secure location and that clients' records are not available to others who are not authorized to have access.

(m) Social workers should take precautions to ensure and maintain the confidentiality of information transmitted to other parties through the use of computers, electronic mail, facsimile machines, telephones and telephone answering machines, and other electronic or computer technology. Disclosure of identifying information should be avoided whenever possible.

(n) Social workers should transfer or dispose of clients' records in a manner that protects clients' confidentiality and is consistent with state statutes governing records and social work licensure.

(o) Social workers should take reasonable precautions to protect client confidentiality in the event of the social worker's termination of practice, incapacitation, or death.

(p) Social workers should not disclose identifying information when discussing clients for teaching or training purposes unless the client has consented to disclosure of confidential information.

(q) Social workers should not disclose identifying information when discussing clients with consultants unless the client has consented to disclosure of confidential information or there is a compelling need for such disclosure.

(r) Social workers should protect the confidentiality of deceased clients consistent with the preceding standards.

1.08 ACCESS TO RECORDS

(a) Social workers should provide clients with reasonable access to records concerning the clients. Social workers who are concerned that clients' access to their records could cause serious misunderstanding or harm to the client should provide assistance in interpreting the records and consultation with the client regarding the records. Social workers should limit clients' access to their records, or portions of their records, only in exceptional circumstances when there is compelling evidence that such access would cause serious harm to the client. Both clients' requests and the rationale for withholding some or all of the record should be documented in clients' files.

(b) When providing clients with access to their records, social workers should take steps to protect the confidentiality of other individuals identified or discussed in such records.

1.09 SEXUAL RELATIONSHIPS

(a) Social workers should under no circumstances engage in sexual activities or sexual contact with current clients, whether such contact is consensual or forced.

(b) Social workers should not engage in sexual activities or sexual contact with clients' relatives or other individuals with whom clients maintain a close personal relationship when there is a risk of exploitation or potential harm to the client. Sexual activity or sexual contact with clients' relatives or other individuals with whom clients maintain a personal relationship has the potential to be harmful to the client and may make it difficult for the social worker and client to maintain appropriate professional boundaries. Social workers—not their clients, their clients' relatives, or other individuals with whom the client maintains a personal relationship—assume the full burden for setting clear, appropriate, and culturally sensitive boundaries.

(c) Social workers should not engage in sexual activities or sexual contact with former clients because of the potential for harm to the client. If social workers engage in conduct contrary to this prohibition or claim that an exception to this prohibition is warranted because of extraordinary circumstances, it is social workers—not their clients—who assume the full burden of demonstrating that the former client has not been exploited, coerced, or manipulated, intentionally or unintentionally.

(d) Social workers should not provide clinical services to individuals with whom they have had a prior sexual relationship. Providing clinical services to a former sexual partner has the potential to be harmful to the individual and is likely to make it difficult for the social worker and individual to maintain appropriate professional boundaries.

1.10 PHYSICAL CONTACT

Social workers should not engage in physical contact with clients when there is a possibility of psychological harm to the client as a result of the contact (such as cradling or caressing clients). Social workers who engage in appropriate physical contact with clients are responsible for setting clear, appropriate, and culturally sensitive boundaries that govern such physical contact.

1.11 SEXUAL HARASSMENT

Social workers should not sexually harass clients. Sexual harassment includes sexual advances, sexual solicitation, requests for sexual favors, and other verbal or physical conduct of a sexual nature.

1.12 DEROGATORY LANGUAGE

Social workers should not use derogatory language in their written or verbal communications to or about clients. Social workers should use accurate and respectful language in all communications to and about clients.

1.13 PAYMENT FOR SERVICES

(a) When setting fees, social workers should ensure that the fees are fair, reasonable, and commensurate with the services performed. Consideration should be given to clients' ability to pay.

(b) Social workers should avoid accepting goods or services from clients as payment for professional services. Bartering arrangements, particularly involving services, create the potential for conflicts of interest, exploitation, and inappropriate boundaries in social workers' relationships with clients. Social workers should explore and may participate in bartering only in very limited circumstances when it can be demonstrated that such arrangements are an accepted practice among professionals in the local community, considered to be essential for the provision of services, negotiated without coercion, and entered into at the client's initiative and with the client's informed consent. Social workers who accept goods or services from clients as payment for professional services assume the full burden of demonstrating that this arrangement will not be detrimental to the client or the professional relationship.

(c) Social workers should not solicit a private fee or other remuneration for providing services to clients who are entitled to such available services through the social workers' employer or agency.

1.14 CLIENTS WHO LACK DECISION-MAKING CAPACITY

When social workers act on behalf of clients who lack the capacity to make informed decisions, social workers should take reasonable steps to safeguard the interests and rights of those clients.

1.15 INTERRUPTION OF SERVICES

Social workers should make reasonable efforts to ensure continuity of services in the event that services are interrupted by factors such as unavailability, relocation, illness, disability, or death.

1.16 TERMINATION OF SERVICES

(a) Social workers should terminate services to clients and professional relationships with them when such services and relationships are no longer required or no longer serve the clients' needs or interests.

(b) Social workers should take reasonable steps to avoid abandoning clients who are still in need of services. Social workers should withdraw services precipitously only under unusual circumstances, giving careful consideration to all factors in the situation and taking care to minimize possible adverse effects. Social workers should assist in making appropriate arrangements for continuation of services when necessary.

(c) Social workers in fee-for-service settings may terminate services to clients who are not paying an overdue balance if the financial contractual arrangements have been made clear to the client, if the client does not pose an imminent danger to self or others, and if the clinical and other consequences of the current nonpayment have been addressed and discussed with the client.

(d) Social workers should not terminate services to pursue a social, financial, or sexual relationship with a client.

(e) Social workers who anticipate the termination or interruption of services to clients should notify clients promptly and seek the transfer, referral, or continuation of services in relation to the clients' needs and preferences.

(f) Social workers who are leaving an employment setting should inform clients of appropriate options for the continuation of services and of the benefits and risks of the options.

2. Social Workers' Ethical Responsibilities to Colleagues

2.01 RESPECT

(a) Social workers should treat colleagues with respect and should represent accurately and fairly the qualifications, views, and obligations of colleagues.

(b) Social workers should avoid unwarranted negative criticism of colleagues in communications with clients or with other professionals. Unwarranted negative criticism may include demeaning comments

that refer to colleagues' level of competence or to individuals' attributes such as race, ethnicity, national origin, color, sex, sexual orientation, age, marital status, political belief, religion, and mental or
physical disability.

(c) Social workers should cooperate with social work colleagues and
with colleagues of other professions when such cooperation serves
the well-being of clients.

2.02 CONFIDENTIALITY

Social workers should respect confidential information shared by colleagues in the course of their professional relationships and transactions.
Social workers should ensure that such colleagues understand social workers' obligation to respect confidentiality and any exceptions related to it.

2.03 INTERDISCIPLINARY COLLABORATION

(a) Social workers who are members of an interdisciplinary team
should participate in and contribute to decisions that affect the well-
being of clients by drawing on the perspectives, values, and experiences of the social work profession. Professional and ethical obligations of the interdisciplinary team as a whole and of its individual
members should be clearly established.

(b) Social workers for whom a team decision raises ethical concerns
should attempt to resolve the disagreement through appropriate
channels. If the disagreement cannot be resolved, social workers
should pursue other avenues to address their concerns consistent
with client well-being.

2.04 DISPUTES INVOLVING COLLEAGUES

(a) Social workers should not take advantage of a dispute between a
colleague and an employer to obtain a position or otherwise advance
the social workers' own interests.

(b) Social workers should not exploit clients in disputes with colleagues
or engage clients in any inappropriate discussion of conflicts
between social workers and their colleagues.

2.05 CONSULTATION

(a) Social workers should seek the advice and counsel of colleagues
whenever such consultation is in the best interests of clients.

(b) Social workers should keep themselves informed about colleagues'
areas of expertise and competencies. Social workers should seek

consultation only from colleagues who have demonstrated knowledge, expertise, and competence related to the subject of the consultation.

(c) When consulting with colleagues about clients, social workers should disclose the least amount of information necessary to achieve the purposes of the consultation.

2.06 REFERRAL FOR SERVICES

(a) Social workers should refer clients to other professionals when the other professionals' specialized knowledge or expertise is needed to serve clients fully or when social workers believe that they are not being effective or making reasonable progress with clients and that additional service is required.

(b) Social workers who refer clients to other professionals should take appropriate steps to facilitate an orderly transfer of responsibility. Social workers who refer clients to other professionals should disclose, with clients' consent, all pertinent information to the new service providers.

(c) Social workers are prohibited from giving or receiving payment for a referral when no professional service is provided by the referring social worker.

2.07 SEXUAL RELATIONSHIPS

(a) Social workers who function as supervisors or educators should not engage in sexual activities or contact with supervisees, students, trainees, or other colleagues over whom they exercise professional authority.

(b) Social workers should avoid engaging in sexual relationships with colleagues when there is potential for a conflict of interest. Social workers who become involved in, or anticipate becoming involved in, a sexual relationship with a colleague have a duty to transfer professional responsibilities, when necessary, to avoid a conflict of interest.

2.08 SEXUAL HARASSMENT

Social workers should not sexually harass supervisees, students, trainees, or colleagues. Sexual harassment includes sexual advances, sexual solicitation, requests for sexual favors, and other verbal or physical conduct of a sexual nature.

2.09 IMPAIRMENT OF COLLEAGUES

(a) Social workers who have direct knowledge of a social work colleague's impairment that is due to personal problems, psychosocial distress, substance abuse, or mental health difficulties and that interferes with practice effectiveness should consult with that colleague when feasible and assist the colleague in taking remedial action.

(b) Social workers who believe that a social work colleague's impairment interferes with practice effectiveness and that the colleague has not taken adequate steps to address the impairment should take action through appropriate channels established by employers, agencies, NASW, licensing and regulatory bodies, and other professional organizations.

2.10 INCOMPETENCE OF COLLEAGUES

(a) Social workers who have direct knowledge of a social work colleague's incompetence should consult with that colleague when feasible and assist the colleague in taking remedial action.

(b) Social workers who believe that a social work colleague is incompetent and has not taken adequate steps to address the incompetence should take action through appropriate channels established by employers, agencies, NASW, licensing and regulatory bodies, and other professional organizations.

2.11 UNETHICAL CONDUCT OF COLLEAGUES

(a) Social workers should take adequate measures to discourage, prevent, expose, and correct the unethical conduct of colleagues.

(b) Social workers should be knowledgeable about established policies and procedures for handling concerns about colleagues' unethical behavior. Social workers should be familiar with national, state, and local procedures for handling ethics complaints. These include policies and procedures created by NASW, licensing and regulatory bodies, employers, agencies, and other professional organizations.

(c) Social workers who believe that a colleague has acted unethically should seek resolution by discussing their concerns with the colleague when feasible and when such discussion is likely to be productive.

(d) When necessary, social workers who believe that a colleague has acted unethically should take action through appropriate formal channels (such as contacting a state licensing board or regulatory body, an NASW committee on inquiry, or other professional ethics committees).

(e) Social workers should defend and assist colleagues who are unjustly charged with unethical conduct.

3. Social Workers' Ethical Responsibilities in Practice Settings

3.01 SUPERVISION AND CONSULTATION

(a) Social workers who provide supervision or consultation should have the necessary knowledge and skill to supervise or consult appropriately and should do so only within their areas of knowledge and competence.

(b) Social workers who provide supervision or consultation are responsible for setting clear, appropriate, and culturally sensitive boundaries.

(c) Social workers should not engage in any dual or multiple relationships with supervisees in which there is a risk of exploitation of or potential harm to the supervisee.

(d) Social workers who provide supervision should evaluate supervisees' performance in a manner that is fair and respectful.

3.02 EDUCATION AND TRAINING

(a) Social workers who function as educators, field instructors for students, or trainers should provide instruction only within their areas of knowledge and competence and should provide instruction based on the most current information and knowledge available in the profession.

(b) Social workers who function as educators or field instructors for students should evaluate students' performance in a manner that is fair and respectful.

(c) Social workers who function as educators or field instructors for students should take reasonable steps to ensure that clients are routinely informed when services are being provided by students.

(d) Social workers who function as educators or field instructors for students should not engage in any dual or multiple relationships with students in which there is a risk of exploitation or potential harm to the student. Social work educators and field instructors are responsible for setting clear, appropriate, and culturally sensitive boundaries.

3.03 PERFORMANCE EVALUATION

Social workers who have responsibility for evaluating the performance of others should fulfill such responsibility in a fair and considerate manner and on the basis of clearly stated criteria.

3.04 CLIENT RECORDS

(a) Social workers should take reasonable steps to ensure that documentation in records is accurate and reflects the services provided.

(b) Social workers should include sufficient and timely documentation in records to facilitate the delivery of services and to ensure continuity of services provided to clients in the future.

(c) Social workers' documentation should protect clients' privacy to the extent that is possible and appropriate and should include only information that is directly relevant to the delivery of services.

(d) Social workers should store records following the termination of services to ensure reasonable future access. Records should be maintained for the number of years required by state statutes or relevant contracts.

3.05 BILLING

Social workers should establish and maintain billing practices that accurately reflect the nature and extent of services provided and that identify who provided the service in the practice setting.

3.06 CLIENT TRANSFER

(a) When an individual who is receiving services from another agency or colleague contacts a social worker for services, the social worker should carefully consider the client's needs before agreeing to provide services. To minimize possible confusion and conflict, social workers should discuss with potential clients the nature of the clients' current relationship with other service providers and the implications, including possible benefits or risks, of entering into a relationship with a new service provider.

(b) If a new client has been served by another agency or colleague, social workers should discuss with the client whether consultation with the previous service provider is in the client's best interest.

3.07 ADMINISTRATION

(a) Social work administrators should advocate within and outside their agencies for adequate resources to meet clients' needs.

(b) Social workers should advocate for resource allocation procedures that are open and fair. When not all clients' needs can be met, an allocation procedure should be developed that is nondiscriminatory and based on appropriate and consistently applied principles.

(c) Social workers who are administrators should take reasonable steps to ensure that adequate agency or organizational resources are available to provide appropriate staff supervision.

(d) Social work administrators should take reasonable steps to ensure that the working environment for which they are responsible is consistent with and encourages compliance with the NASW Code of

Ethics. Social work administrators should take reasonable steps to eliminate any conditions in their organizations that violate, interfere with, or discourage compliance with the Code.

3.08 CONTINUING EDUCATION AND STAFF DEVELOPMENT

Social work administrators and supervisors should take reasonable steps to provide or arrange for continuing education and staff development for all staff for whom they are responsible. Continuing education and staff development should address current knowledge and emerging developments related to social work practice and ethics.

3.09 COMMITMENTS TO EMPLOYERS

(a) Social workers generally should adhere to commitments made to employers and employing organizations.

(b) Social workers should work to improve employing agencies' policies and procedures and the efficiency and effectiveness of their services.

(c) Social workers should take reasonable steps to ensure that employers are aware of social workers' ethical obligations as set forth in the NASW Code of Ethics and of the implications of those obligations for social work practice.

(d) Social workers should not allow an employing organization's policies, procedures, regulations, or administrative orders to interfere with their ethical practice of social work. Social workers should take reasonable steps to ensure that their employing organizations' practices are consistent with the NASW Code of Ethics.

(e) Social workers should act to prevent and eliminate discrimination in the employing organization's work assignments and in its employment policies and practices.

(f) Social workers should accept employment or arrange student field placements only in organizations that exercise fair personnel practices.

(g) Social workers should be diligent stewards of the resources of their employing organizations, wisely conserving funds where appropriate and never misappropriating funds or using them for unintended purposes.

3.10 LABOR-MANAGEMENT DISPUTES

(a) Social workers may engage in organized action, including the formation of and participation in labor unions, to improve services to clients and working conditions.

(b) The actions of social workers who are involved in labor-management disputes, job actions, or labor strikes should be guided by the profession's values, ethical principles, and ethical standards. Reasonable differences of opinion exist among social workers concerning their primary obligation as professionals during an actual or threatened labor strike or job action. Social workers should carefully examine relevant issues and their possible impact on clients before deciding on a course of action.

4. Social Workers' Ethical Responsibilities as Professionals

4.01 COMPETENCE

(a) Social workers should accept responsibility or employment only on the basis of existing competence or the intention to acquire the necessary competence.

(b) Social workers should strive to become and remain proficient in professional practice and the performance of professional functions. Social workers should critically examine and keep current with emerging knowledge relevant to social work. Social workers should routinely review the professional literature and participate in continuing education relevant to social work practice and social work ethics.

(c) Social workers should base practice on recognized knowledge, including empirically based knowledge, relevant to social work and social work ethics.

4.02 DISCRIMINATION

Social workers should not practice, condone, facilitate, or collaborate with any form of discrimination on the basis of race, ethnicity, national origin, color, sex, sexual orientation, age, marital status, political belief, religion, or mental or physical disability.

4.03 PRIVATE CONDUCT

Social workers should not permit their private conduct to interfere with their ability to fulfill their professional responsibilities.

4.04 DISHONESTY, FRAUD, AND DECEPTION

Social workers should not participate in, condone, or be associated with dishonesty, fraud, or deception.

4.05 Impairment

(a) Social workers should not allow their own personal problems, psychosocial distress, legal problems, substance abuse, or mental health difficulties to interfere with their professional judgment and performance or to jeopardize the best interests of people for whom they have a professional responsibility.

(b) Social workers whose personal problems, psychosocial distress, legal problems, substance abuse, or mental health difficulties interfere with their professional judgment and performance should immediately seek consultation and take appropriate remedial action by seeking professional help, making adjustments in workload, terminating practice, or taking any other steps necessary to protect clients and others.

4.06 Misrepresentation

(a) Social workers should make clear distinctions between statements made and actions engaged in as a private individual and as a representative of the social work profession, a professional social work organization, or the social worker's employing agency.

(b) Social workers who speak on behalf of professional social work organizations should accurately represent the official and authorized positions of the organizations.

(c) Social workers should ensure that their representations to clients, agencies, and the public of professional qualifications, credentials, education, competence, affiliations, services provided, or results to be achieved are accurate. Social workers should claim only those relevant professional credentials they actually possess and take steps to correct any inaccuracies or misrepresentations of their credentials by others.

4.07 Solicitations

(a) Social workers should not engage in uninvited solicitation of potential clients who, because of their circumstances, are vulnerable to undue influence, manipulation, or coercion.

(b) Social workers should not engage in solicitation of testimonial endorsements (including solicitation of consent to use a client's prior statement as a testimonial endorsement) from current clients or from other people who, because of their particular circumstances, are vulnerable to undue influence.

4.08 Acknowledging Credit

(a) Social workers should take responsibility and credit, including authorship credit, only for work they have actually performed and to which they have contributed.

(b) Social workers should honestly acknowledge the work of and the contributions made by others.

5. Social Workers' Ethical Responsibilities to the Social Work Profession

5.01 INTEGRITY OF THE PROFESSION

(a) Social workers should work toward the maintenance and promotion of high standards of practice.

(b) Social workers should uphold and advance the values, ethics, knowledge, and mission of the profession. Social workers should protect, enhance, and improve the integrity of the profession through appropriate study and research, active discussion, and responsible criticism of the profession.

(c) Social workers should contribute time and professional expertise to activities that promote respect for the value, integrity, and competence of the social work profession. These activities may include teaching, research, consultation, service, legislative testimony, presentations in the community, and participation in their professional organizations.

(d) Social workers should contribute to the knowledge base of social work and share with colleagues their knowledge related to practice, research, and ethics. Social workers should seek to contribute to the profession's literature and to share their knowledge at professional meetings and conferences.

(e) Social workers should act to prevent the unauthorized and unqualified practice of social work.

5.02 EVALUATION AND RESEARCH

(a) Social workers should monitor and evaluate policies, the implementation of programs, and practice interventions.

(b) Social workers should promote and facilitate evaluation and research to contribute to the development of knowledge.

(c) Social workers should critically examine and keep current with emerging knowledge relevant to social work and fully use evaluation and research evidence in their professional practice.

(d) Social workers engaged in evaluation or research should carefully consider possible consequences and should follow guidelines developed for the protection of evaluation and research participants. Appropriate institutional review boards should be consulted.

(e) Social workers engaged in evaluation or research should obtain voluntary and written informed consent from participants, when appropriate, without any implied or actual deprivation or penalty for refusal to participate; without undue inducement to participate; and with due regard for participants' well-being, privacy, and dignity. Informed consent should include information about the nature, extent, and duration of the participation requested and disclosure of the risks and benefits of participation in the research.

(f) When evaluation or research participants are incapable of giving informed consent, social workers should provide an appropriate explanation to the participants, obtain the participants' assent to the extent they are able, and obtain written consent from an appropriate proxy.

(g) Social workers should never design or conduct evaluation or research that does not use consent procedures, such as certain forms of naturalistic observation and archival research, unless rigorous and responsible review of the research has found it to be justified because of its prospective scientific, educational, or applied value and unless equally effective alternative procedures that do not involve waiver of consent are not feasible.

(h) Social workers should inform participants of their right to withdraw from evaluation and research at any time without penalty.

(i) Social workers should take appropriate steps to ensure that participants in evaluation and research have access to appropriate supportive services.

(j) Social workers engaged in evaluation or research should protect participants from unwarranted physical or mental distress, harm, danger, or deprivation.

(k) Social workers engaged in the evaluation of services should discuss collected information only for professional purposes and only with people professionally concerned with this information.

(l) Social workers engaged in evaluation or research should ensure the anonymity or confidentiality of participants and of the data obtained from them. Social workers should inform participants of any limits of confidentiality, the measures that will be taken to ensure confidentiality, and when any records containing research data will be destroyed.

(m) Social workers who report evaluation and research results should protect participants' confidentiality by omitting identifying information unless proper consent has been obtained authorizing disclosure.

(n) Social workers should report evaluation and research findings accurately. They should not fabricate or falsify results and should take steps to correct any errors later found in published data using standard publication methods.

(o) Social workers engaged in evaluation or research should be alert to and avoid conflicts of interest and dual relationships with participants, should inform participants when a real or potential conflict of interest arises, and should take steps to resolve the issue in a manner that makes participants' interests primary.

(p) Social workers should educate themselves, their students, and their colleagues about responsible research practices.

6. Social Workers' Ethical Responsibilities to the Broader Society

6.01 SOCIAL WELFARE

Social workers should promote the general welfare of society, from local to global levels, and the development of people, their communities, and their environments. Social workers should advocate for living conditions conducive to the fulfillment of basic human needs and should promote social, economic, political, and cultural values and institutions that are compatible with the realization of social justice.

6.02 PUBLIC PARTICIPATION

Social workers should facilitate informed participation by the public in shaping social policies and institutions.

6.03 PUBLIC EMERGENCIES

Social workers should provide appropriate professional services in public emergencies to the greatest extent possible.

6.04 SOCIAL AND POLITICAL ACTION

(a) Social workers should engage in social and political action that seeks to ensure that all people have equal access to the resources, employment, services, and opportunities they require to meet their basic human needs and to develop fully. Social workers should be aware of the impact of the political arena on practice and should advocate for changes in policy and legislation to improve social conditions in order to meet basic human needs and promote social justice.

(b) Social workers should act to expand choice and opportunity for all people, with special regard for vulnerable, disadvantaged, oppressed, and exploited people and groups.

(c) Social workers should promote conditions that encourage respect for cultural and social diversity within the United States and globally. Social workers should promote policies and practices that demonstrate respect for difference, support the expansion of cultural knowledge and resources, advocate for programs and institutions that demonstrate cultural competence, and promote policies that safeguard the rights of and confirm equity and social justice for all people.

(d) Social workers should act to prevent and eliminate domination of, exploitation of, and discrimination against any person, group, or class on the basis of race, ethnicity, national origin, color, sex, sexual orientation, age, marital status, political belief, religion, or mental or physical disability.

Example Research Proposal

Abstract

This quantitative explanatory study proposes an intervention that utilizes a challenge course to increase employee cohesion among family support and child protection employees of a ten-county region. Supervisors will solicit convenient volunteers for the four-hour experience, and participants will be asked to sign an informed consent form to protect their rights. An eight-item survey tool will be used to survey the employees who participate in the challenge course on their levels of cohesion both pre- and post-intervention. Results of this quasi-experimental study will indicate whether employee cohesion was significantly increased immediately after participation in the challenge course intervention. In addition, a follow-up survey will be offered through e-mail to participants two weeks post-intervention to determine whether the effect of the intervention remained. Descriptive statistics will be used to describe demographics of the sample, and inferential statistics (paired sample t-test) will be used to compare means for both the pre- and post-surveys and the post- and follow-up surveys.

Key words: employee cohesion, challenge course, family support, protection workers

Introduction

Employees working in human services in every state must work in highly stressful situations and must utilize multiple resources to assist consumers needing their services. This requires a high degree of cooperation and coordination within agency programs. Reorganizations, reduced funds leading to limited resources, increased caseloads, and employee turnover are issues that create on-the-job stress and conflict. Increasing perceived cohesion among employees may reduce the feelings of stress and isolation, in turn leading to more stability on the job and better services to families. This research study will determine if a simple intervention called a challenge course increases cohesion among family support and protection workers within ten counties.

To fully understand the importance of employee cohesion, one only has to review the demographics and employment situation of Appalachia. The region of study is primarily rural; only 17 percent of the population is urban, according to the U.S. Census Bureau (2002). Five of the counties in the region are considered completely rural, meaning there are not any communities with a population of at least 2,500 people within the counties. It needs to be noted that approximately 28 percent of the people in the study region live below the poverty line, compared to the national average of 12.4 percent. The per-capita income of $13,453 is 36 percent below the national average. Self-employment and farm incomes have been standard components of the economic dynamics in the study region; an additional 30 percent of workers are employed by private businesses, and only 9 percent of workers are employed by the public sector, which includes state, federal, and local government agencies. The high employment rate is an important factor that keeps the communities economically viable even though per-capita incomes are low. Employee cohesion is one means of maintaining the relatively high level of employment and low employee turnover.

This study is supported by the top administrator of family support and protection services in a ten-county region. Employee cohesion is a broad concern as a result of a major reorganization of family support and protection workers within the ten counties. The sharing of office spaces to reduce the regional budget caused many staffing concerns, as some employees chose early retirement, and staff conflicts led to threats of terminated employment. In addition, the high poverty rate in the area already places multiple demands upon the regional workers struggling to survive on limited resources. A final concern is the lack of social workers (individuals with a social work degree) to replace employees who leave. Many of the current positions were already filled with individuals with other degrees (sociology, psychology, general studies) due to the lack of social workers in this area. It is anticipated that increasing employee cohesion would reduce some of these concerns.

Literature Review

The ability of challenge courses to increase group cohesion of individuals brought together for the short-term experience has been well documented. However, there are little data measuring the effect on employee cohesion. Long (1987) discusses the use of ropes courses by multinational corporations such as AT&T and IBM to foster team building, problem solving, and personnel management. These companies have made challenge courses a part of their overall management programs. In a similar empirical study, Wilde (1997) reported that an exercise called the "Leap of Faith" was incorporated into a day-long ropes course for business executives and midlevel managers. The results were increased trust and a greater sense of teamwork among the participants.

While perceived employee cohesion has not been examined, studies on challenge course interventions among a variety of treatment groups have demonstrated positives outcomes. Teaff and Kablach (1987) outlined a list of positive psychological outcomes for participants in a ropes course that included increased trust and improved problem solving, goal setting, discipline, team work, decision making, self-confidence, and self-esteem. Other benefits included the ability to communicate thoughts and feelings to others. Smith (1991) demonstrated similar results for a ropes course that was used with psychiatric inpatients. In addition, Faulkner (2002) demonstrated that a low-elements challenge course could be effective in increasing communication and problem solving skills in a case study of substance abusers.

Family groups have also reported increased cohesion after challenge course intervention. Increasing the cohesion among family groups has been linked to a number of positive outcomes, including improved overall functioning of adolescents, reduction in suicidal behavior, and increased feelings of bonding and closeness (Faulkner, 2001; Golins, 1978; Hibner, 1987; Rubinstein, Halton, Kasten, Rubin, & Stechler, 1998).

The research question to be addressed in this study is twofold: Will a low-elements challenge course have an effect on increasing perceived employee cohesion, and if so, will the effect remain significant later?

Methods

Design

This study will use a quasi-experimental pretest/posttest and posttest/follow-up design to test the effect of the challenge course experience on perceived employee cohesion. The dependent variable, perceived employee cohesion, is defined as an individual's sense of belonging to a particular group, or an individual's appraisal of his or her relationship to the group (Chin, Salisbury, & Gopal, 1996). The construct of cohesion has been used numerous times in various research studies connected to group dynamics.

For this study, perceived employee cohesion is operationalized by an Employee Cohesion Scale developed by Faulkner, Faulkner, and Hesterberg (2007) after consulting the existing literature. The Employee Cohesion Scale (Addendum A) will be given to employees before and after completion of the four-hour challenge course experience. In addition, an e-mail asking employees to complete the scale again will be sent to all employees two weeks later. By clicking on a link in the body of the request, they will be able to complete the scale online and send it back to the researchers at the click of a button. The items for the instrument are:

- On the whole I am satisfied with the people I work with.
- My coworkers and I work together to find solutions to problems.
- I feel a sense of closeness with my coworkers.
- When I make suggestions, my coworkers listen to me.
- In general, I like the people I work with.
- In general, I feel free to share my opinions and ideas with my coworkers.
- My coworkers are receptive to feedback and criticism.
- My coworkers attempt to include me at work.
  The items will be ranked on a scale of 1 to 5, where 1 = "Not at all," 3 = "Neutral," and 5 = "Very much."

The independent variables for this study are the intervention (the challenge course), eight demographic variables, and the respondent's level of participation. A challenge course is defined as a series of non-competitive activities designed to allow participants to build employee cohesiveness through the use of group problem-solving games and activities that require individuals to help each other to complete the challenge. The challenges chosen for this study are borrowed from various sources within the experiential learning community. It is the sequencing of the challenges, from initiatives to more physical challenges, that was of considerable importance. Descriptions of the specific challenges are included in Addendum B.

Initiatives are challenges that are used as precursors to more physically demanding activities. The amount of skills needed for these challenges increases as the group progresses. All initiatives require the following skills: problem-solving skills, cooperation, and communication. There were nine initiatives for this intervention: "Helium Hula Hoop," "Hula Hoop Pass," "Group Juggle," "Warp Speed," "Tug of Peace," "Human Knot," "Tank," "People to People," and "Willow in the Wind."

Physical challenges are designed to provide more intense opportunities for cooperation, communication, and problem-solving skills. Using ropes, beams, boards, and platforms, these activities also involve various degrees of physical skills. This intervention consisted of three physical challenges: "All Aboard," "Traffic Jam," and "Alligator Crossing."

Eight challenge course sessions will be conducted within a two-month period with the ten counties participating in the study. Each session will take approximately four hours and will be led by both co-investigators.

Each participant will be asked to read and sign an informed consent form (Addendum C) to protect his or her right to refuse to participate or to stop participating in the intervention at any time. With the pretest, participants will also be given a questionnaire (Addendum D) asking for specific demographic information to determine if these variables have an effect on the results. These eight independent demographic variables were age, sex, job title, county of employment, total time with the agency, total time in current position, race, and educational level.

With the posttest, respondents will be given a list of the challenges (Addendum E) that were presented and asked to place a check mark beside any challenge in which they did not participate.

Hypotheses

For this study, two hypotheses were developed: a low-elements challenge course intervention will significantly increase perceived employee cohesion and the effect of the challenge course intervention will remain significant after two weeks.

Participants

The sample for this research is by convenience. Participants will be asked to attend the challenge course by their county supervisors; however, participation will be on a voluntary basis. The challenge courses will be held on Fridays and employees will receive continuing education units for attending.

Pre- and Post-Survey Samples

Eight of the ten counties will participate as a separate group, and two counties will join together to form one group, each due to small employee count. For the joined sessions, employees will be paired together with their own coworkers as often as possible and will be asked to complete the scale with their coworkers in mind (as opposed to the group as a whole). Participants will be recruited by their county supervisors to participate and receive four hours of training credit (twelve hours required annually), and all challenge courses will be held in local community buildings. Only participants who complete both the pre- and post-surveys will be included in the sample.

Follow-Up Survey Sample

A follow-up survey will be offered through e-mail to participants two weeks post-intervention to determine whether the effect of the intervention remained. Only participants who completed the pre- and post-surveys will be included in the follow-up sample.

Analysis

Independent Variables

DEMOGRAPHICS

There are eight demographic variables that will be used to describe the sample. The means of participants' ages, total time with the agency, and total time in current position, and percentages of race, educational level, sex, job title, and county of employment, will be calculated.

PARTICIPATION LEVEL

Because the activities are "challenge by choice" (i.e., participants may choose whether or not they wish to participate), participation in the challenges will be documented for each participant. Participation in each challenge will be entered as 1 = yes (participated) and 0 = no (did not participate). These data will be used to calculate the percentage of participants who engage in each challenge.

Dependent Variable: Perceived Cohesion Outcomes

Inferential statistics will be used to accept or reject the two hypotheses. Paired samples t-test will be used to compare mean difference between the scores of the pre- and post-survey respondents and the post- and follow-up survey respondents. A significant increase in scores from the pretest to the posttest will accept the first hypothesis: A low-elements challenge course intervention will significantly increase perceived employee cohesion. No significant change in mean scores between posttest and follow-up will accept the second hypothesis: The effect of the challenge course intervention will remain significant after two weeks.

Multivariate Analysis

Linear regression will be used to determine if any demographic variables are significant predictors to account for the difference in scores between pre- and posttest or the difference in scores between posttest and follow-up.

Discussion

Implications

This study has implications for social work on several levels. Social workers are charged with promoting individual welfare and helping people achieve their maximum potential. As agencies are placed under increasing monetary restraints, resources are taxed, and employees are asked to do more, interventions that help people work together assume even greater significance. Thus any intervention that helps people bond together into a cohesive unit is important and should be explored. Interacting positively together, communicating with one another, and solving benign problems, all in the spirit of play, can create a sense of cohesion. Games such as those presented in the challenge course training are one way to facilitate increased cohesion.

The implications for practice, then, are that this study hopes to demonstrate that challenge courses should be offered as part of continuing education. Facilitating the challenges is fairly simple, and the cost for supplies is minimal. Therefore, designated employees can offer the training at little expense to the agency.

Implications for policy are equally significant. In times of budget constraints, shrinking resources, and expanding demands, administrators are often faced with the daunting tasks of getting more productivity out of their staff, with fewer resources to accomplish the job. However, before managers can adopt informed practices and implement new programs, a workforce needs to have communication, cooperation, and cohesion. As more corporations, agencies, and businesses move toward a total quality management approach to service provision, policies that foster cohesion become even more salient. One positive aspect of challenge course training is that the techniques are easy to learn and can be incorporated into a staff meeting or short workshop—participants do not have to spend hours away from their office to develop cohesion.

The implications for research are twofold. First, exploration of the effect of the intervention on perceived cohesion immediately as well as two weeks after it occurs will be breaking the ground for further studies.

Strengths and Limitations

This study has several strengths. The follow-up survey is the first attempt to look at the long-term effect of the intervention. Secondly, this study examines the intervention on cohesion within a long-term group (employees), as opposed to spontaneous or short-term groups, as is seen mostly in the literature. In addition, the literature supports the contention that increased cohesion has positive outcomes for retention and productivity. Finally, the risk for harm to individuals is minimal, while the potential benefits are large.

Weaknesses of this study are the lack of a comparison or control group and the fact that sampling is done by convenience. Any results from the study will not be generalizable outside the sample. Finally, while the follow-up survey measures the effect two weeks post-intervention, it does not provide information on how long the effect will ultimately last.

References

Chin, W. W., Salisbury, W. D., & Gopal, A. (1996). *Perceived cohesion in groups: A confirmatory factor analysis of the dimension of belonging and morale.* Retrieved July 12, 2008, from http://faculty.cob .ohiou.edu/salisbury/research/cohedion.html

Faulkner, C., Faulkner, S., & Hesterberg, L. (2007). Immediate and short-term effects of challenge course training on perceived employee cohesion within human services workers in ten rural counties. *Journal of Education and Human Development, 1*(2). Retrieved July 12, 2008, from http://www.scientificjournals.org/journals2007/articles/1241.pdf

Faulkner, S. (2001). Ropes course as an intervention: The impact on family cohesion and self-esteem for adolescents in therapeutic foster care and their foster families. *Dissertation Abstracts International, A: The Humanities and Social Sciences, 2002, 62,* 7, Jan, 2570-As.

Faulkner, S. (2002). Low-elements ropes course as an intervention tool with alcohol/other drug dependent adults: A case study. *Alcoholism Treatment Quarterly, 20*(2), 83–90.

Golins, G. (1978). How delinquents succeed through adventure based education. *Journal of Experiential Education, 1*(2), 26–29.

Hibner. B. (1987). Learning the ropes family style. *Network, 17*(5).

Long, J. (1987). The wilderness lab comes of age. *Training and Development Journal, 3,* 30–39.

Rubenstein, J., Halton, A., Kasten, L., Rubin, C., & Stechler, G. (1998). Suicidal behavior in adolescents: Stress and protection in different family contexts. *American Journal of Orthopsychiatry, 68*(2), 274–284.

Smith, T. (1991). *An investigation of the usage and effectiveness of adventure ropes course programs in psychiatric hospitals.* Master's thesis. Georgia College, Milledgeville, GA.

Teaff, T., & Kablach, J. (1987). Psychological benefit of outdoor adventure activities. *Journal of Experiential Education, 10*(2), 43–46.

U.S. Census Bureau. (2002). *Census 2000 summary file 3.* Retrieved October 15, 2005, from http://www.census.gov/Press-Release/www/2002/sumfile3.html

Wilde, C. (1997). Learning the ropes. *Computerworld, 83*(6).

Addendum A Employee Cohesion Scale

Please respond to the statements below by circling the number (1 = Not at all, 3 = Neutral, 5 = Very much) that best indicates the degree to which you agree with each statement.

1. On the whole I am satisfied with the people I work with.

      1   2   3   4   5

2. My coworkers and I work together to find solutions to problems.

      1   2   3   4   5

3. I feel a sense of closeness with my coworkers.

      1   2   3   4   5

4. When I make suggestions, my coworkers listen to me.

      1   2   3   4   5

5. In general, I like the people I work with.

| 1 | 2 | 3 | 4 | 5 |

6. In general, I feel free to share my opinions and ideas with my coworkers.

| 1 | 2 | 3 | 4 | 5 |

7. My coworkers are receptive to feedback and criticism.

| 1 | 2 | 3 | 4 | 5 |

8. My coworkers attempt to include me at work.

| 1 | 2 | 3 | 4 | 5 |

Addendum B Challenge Course Activities

Initiatives

These challenges are to be used as precursors to more physically demanding activities. The skills needed for these challenges are listed and increase as the group progresses. All activities require the following skills: problem-solving skills, cooperation, and communication.

Helium Hula Hoop (Additional skills: bending)
All members stand in a circle and point their index fingers, on top of which a hula hoop is placed. Together, they must lower the hoop to the ground while keeping it horizontal.

Hula Hoop Pass (Additional skills: holding hands)
The object of this game is to pass a hula hoop around the group with everyone holding hands and not letting go. Start by having everyone stand in a circle. Place the hula hoop over the shoulders of one member. Have the group join hands. Pass the hoop around by going through it. The hoop cannot touch the ground.

Group Juggle (Additional skills: hand-eye coordination)
Group Juggle is an introductory activity that serves two purposes. First, it breaks the ice by introducing participants to the concepts behind challenge activities, and second, it promotes group unity and cooperation. The activity starts off with the group standing in a circle. A ball is passed from

person to person until a pattern is established. Eventually, this simple activity becomes more challenging as more balls are introduced into the pattern.

Warp Speed (Additional skills: hand-eye coordination)
The object of Warp Speed is to move one ball through an established pattern of people in the least amount of time. The group is encouraged to think through many solutions to the problem. Most groups significantly beat the times they originally project for completing the activity. The rules of the game are:

1. The ball must always travel in the same order.
2. The group may do anything they like to improve their time as long as the ball contacts each participant in the original order.

Tug of Peace (Additional skills: movement and stretching, pulling)
A rope is stretched out, and two groups are lined up on each side of the rope, sitting down. While pulling the rope at the same time, both groups stand up at the same time.

Human Knot (Additional skills: physical contact, movement, and stretching)
The object of the Human Knot is to form a circle from a knot of crossed hands. This activity promotes communication among group members and presents a challenge that can easily be met with effort from participants. The rules of the game are:

1. The group must form a circle. Each participant holds the hands of two different participants facing him or her.
2. Each group member may not let go of the other participants' hands until the activity is complete.
3. The group is told to form a circle without letting go of one another's hands.

Tank (Additional skills: physical contact, movement and stretching, use of blindfolds)
Members of the group form pairs. One (the tank) is blindfolded, and his or her partner gives commands to direct where the blindfolded person should go to locate ammunition that has been placed on the ground. Once the tank finds the ammunition, he or she must throw it at other tanks to put them out of the game.

People to People (Additional skills: physical contact, movement and stretching)
This is a game that involves a lot of touching. Everyone gets a partner and forms a circle. Everyone stands next to his or her partner. One person is "It" and stands in the middle of the circle, instructing the pairs to perform actions. An example is "Elbow to foot." Usually four or five directions are given before the person in the center calls out, "People to people." At this time, everyone runs to get a new partner, and the person left without a partner becomes "It."

Willow in the Wind (Trust Fall) (Additional skills: trust, physical contact)
Group members stand shoulder to shoulder in a circle with their hands "spooned." The person in the center of the circle has eyes closed eyes and arms crossed in front of his or her chest. The person in the center keeps his or her body rigid and gently falls back. The other members of the group catch the person in the center and gently move him or her around the circle.

Physical Challenges

These challenges are designed to provide more intense opportunities for improving cooperation, communication, and problem-solving skills. These activities use ropes, beams, boards, and platforms and involve various degrees of physical skills.

All Aboard (platforms)
In All Aboard, groups try to get all members onto a small platform so that no one's feet are touching the ground. Platforms can get smaller, and a metaphor can be used (decreasing resources, family size, etc.) to represent the challenge.

Traffic Jam (boards)
Two groups line up on opposite ends of several feet of boards laid out in a straight line so they are facing each other. The object is for the two groups to switch places without stepping off the boards.

Alligator Crossing (boards, platforms)
The object is to use boards placed on platforms to move the entire group across a "river" from point A to point B. Platforms are placed strategically apart from each other. All participants enter from point A of the course.

Everyone has to be on the platforms or boards before anyone can exit point B of the course. The rules of the game are:

1. The participants must cross using only the boards given to them. These boards may not be slid across the floor, thrown, or tossed to teammates.
2. A participant must have some sort of body contact at all times with any board placed in the river. If a board is left unattended, then the current of the river may sweep it away.
3. If a person falls into the river, he or she must return to the beginning. If he or she falls again, then the entire team must return and start over again.
4. The entire team must reach the other side of the river.

Addendum C Informed Consent

Dear Participant:

I am requesting your help with a research project I am conducting on the effects of a challenge course. Let me emphasize that you do not have to take part in anything that makes you uncomfortable. If you do not wish to take part in this project (or any of the activities), you do not have to participate. This is true for the attached questionnaires as well. You are free to refuse to answer any (or all) of the questions. Completing the survey is voluntary (up to you), and you can withdraw from the study at any time.

If you agree to participate in the challenge course experience, you will be asked to participate in games and activities that require you to work with others as a group to solve certain problems. The group leader will explain each activity before you begin.

The potential benefits for those who participate in the challenge course are an increased sense of self-worth and trust among group members.

This study has been reviewed to determine that participants' rights are safeguarded, and there appears to be minimal risk or discomfort associated with completion of the intervention. You may choose to discontinue your participation at any time, and you may refuse to answer any of the questions in the surveys.

The answers you provide will be kept strictly confidential, and all your responses on the completed surveys will be stored in a locked file cabinet accessible only to the researcher (Jane Doe). This means that no one will be able to find out how you answered any of the questions. These records will be kept secured in a locked cabinet at the social work office. Please feel free to ask for help if something does not make sense to you or if you have any questions. If you experience any discomfort, you may contact: (Jane Doe, 123 Main Street, Springfield, Anystate, 98765; 123-456-7890).

If you decide to volunteer, please be sure to **PRINT** your name on the form and to **SIGN** it to indicate your willingness to participate. This will indicate that you understand the purpose of the survey and that you are willing to participate.

Name (Print): _____

Signature: _____

Date Signed: _____

Addendum D Demographics

Your Name _____ **Today's Date** _____

Your E-mail Address: _____

Your Age _____   **Sex:**   Male   Female

Please tell us the *county* **or** *office site* **you are currently assigned to:**

_____

Please tell us the title of your *current position***:**

Amount of *total* **time employed by this agency**   ____Years   ____Months

Amount of time at current job site and position (working with the people you are here with today) _____Years _____Months

Your primary race (Circle only one)

White	0	Asian/Pacific Islander	3
Hispanic	1	Alaskan/American Native	4
African American	2	Other	5

Your highest educational level (Circle only one)

Some high school	0	Undergraduate degree	4
High school graduate/GED	1	Some graduate school	5
Some college/technical degree		Graduate degree	6
	2		
Associate's degree	3		

Addendum E Opt-Out Participation Choices

Please place an X beside any game in which you did *not* participate.

☐ **Helium Hula Hoop** Participants stand in a circle and place a hula hoop on top of their fingers. The hula hoop is lowered to the ground.

☐ **Hula Hoop Pass** Everyone holds hands and does not let go as a hula hoop is passed around the circle.

☐ **Group Juggle** The group stands in a circle, and a ball is passed from person to person. Eventually more balls are introduced.

☐ **Warp Speed** A ball is moved from person to person as quickly as possible.

☐ **Tug of Peace** Two groups sit facing each other on each side of a rope. While pulling on opposite ends of the rope, groups stand up at the same time.

☐ **Human Knot** Participants must untangle a knot of crossed hands.

☐ **Tank** One person is blindfolded and his or her partner gives commands to the blindfolded person indicating where he or she should go to locate ammunition.

☐ **People to People** Everyone stands next to his or her partner and forms a circle. One person is "It" and stands in the middle of the circle giving directions to the partners (e.g., "Knee to elbow").

☐ **Willow in the Wind** Members stand shoulder to shoulder with hands "spooned" to catch the person in the middle and gently move him or her around the circle.

☐ **All Aboard** Groups try to get all members onto a small platform with no one's feet touching the ground.

☐ **Traffic Jam** Two groups are lined up facing each other on opposite ends of several feet of boards laid out in a straight line and switch places without stepping off the boards.

☐ **Alligator Crossing** The group moves across a "river" from point A to point B, using boards placed on platforms.

Glossary

Abstract   A brief summary of the research and its findings, usually no more than 250 words

Aggregate   To compile data in a concise, manageable, and understandable manner so that they can be examined relatively quickly

Analysis of variance (ANOVA)   A statistical procedure that allows us to examine the difference between the mean scores of two or more groups simultaneously by computing a statistical average for one group as a whole and comparing it to another group or groups

Anonymity   Assurance that the researcher will not collect any information that can identify the subject

Baseline   A beginning point in research that establishes an initial sense of how a program, group, or individual is currently functioning and allows researchers to track progress over time

Bell-shaped curve   The distribution of scores that are symmetrically shaped around the mean where the majority of the scores are clustered around the mean and each side of the mean resembles the other

Beneficence   The obligation in research to do no harm and maximize benefits while minimizing possible harm

Benefits   Positive values related to health or well-being that is expected, in research, to outweigh the risks

Bias   The unknown or unacknowledged error created during the design of the study, in the choice of problem to be studied, over the course of the study itself, or during the interpretation of findings

Bivariate analysis   An analysis that examines the relationship between one independent and one dependent variable (also known as simple regression)

Case study   A detailed analysis of a single person or event (or sometimes a limited number of people or events)

Causal relationship   A relationship in which three conditions must be met: (1) the independent variable must come before the dependent variable (known as temporal ordering), (2) the independent and dependent variables must be correlated, and (3) the correlation between the independent and dependent variables cannot be explained by the impact of another variable

Central tendency   An estimate of the center of a distribution of values

Chi-square   A nonparametric statistical procedure that is commonly used when a researcher has a small sample size and a dependent variable that is nominal or ordinal to determine if there is truly a difference in groups

Citation   Means of giving credit to the authors for what is being reported; is organized by last name then date

Cluster sampling   A method for drawing a sample from a population in two or more stages through a process of listing naturally occurring clusters within the population and sampling the clusters (sometimes referred to as multi-stage sampling)

Coefficient   The number by which a variable is multiplied

Conceptualizing a variable   How we translate an idea or abstract theory into a variable that can be used to test a hypothesis or make sense of observations

Concurrent validity   How well a measure correlates with some other measure of the same variable that is believed to be valid

Confidence interval   An indication of what level of certainty we can have that our sample accurately depicts the real world; usually established at 95 percent (or .05) in statistical analysis

Confidentiality   Assurance that a researcher provides to subjects that all information about them, and all answers they provide, will remain in the hands of the investigator and that no person outside the research process will have access to this information

Confounding variable   A variable that obscures the effect of another variable

Construct   The concept or the characteristic that an instrument is designed to measure

Construct validity   A form of validity related to the extent to which the items of an instrument accurately sample a construct

Content validity   A form of validity related to how well the items in a measurement represent the concept that is being measured

Control for   A means of subtracting the effects of certain independent variables on the dependent variable by holding those variables constant

Control variable   Any variable that researchers control for (i.e., hold constant)

Convenience sampling   Reliance on available subjects; one of the most frequently used sampling techniques in social work research

Convergent validity   How well the measures of a construct (e.g., depression or alcoholism) that you expect to be related to each other are, indeed, found to correspond to each other (measure the same construct)

Correlational relationship   A relationship between two or more variables in which a change in one variable may be associated with some degree of change in the other variable

Criterion-related validity   A form of validity related to a measure's ability to make accurate predictions (also called predictive validity)

Cross-sectional design   A research design that looks at a cross-section or subset of a population at one point in time

Curvilinear correlation   A statistical relationship that starts off as either a positive relationship or a negative relationship and then begins to curve

Debriefing   The process of fully informing subjects of the nature of the research when some form of deception has been employed

Deductive research   The process of reasoning that moves from a general hypothesis or theory to specific results through the use of quantitative methods

Demographics   The physical characteristics of a population, such as age, sex, marital status, family size, education, geographic location, and occupation

Dependent variable   The variable that is changed or predicted by another variable or is said to depend on the other variable (the independent variable)

Descriptive inquiry   A strategy used in qualitative research to develop a greater understanding of issues by describing individual experiences

Descriptive research design   A research design that uses descriptive language (how many, how much, what is the statistical average, how do people view a topic, etc.) to describe a population or phenomenon

Descriptive statistics   Ways of organizing, describing, and presenting quantitative (numerical) data in a manner that is concise, manageable, and understandable

Dichotomous variable   A variable with only two responses to choose from, such as yes or no or treatment group or nontreatment group

Discriminate validity   The degree to which the measures of a construct that you would not expect to be related are indeed measuring different constructs

Distribution   A summary of the frequency of individual values or ranges of values for a variable

Elements   Individual members of a population or sample

Enumeration unit   A unit containing one or more units listed in the sampling frame

Equivalent form reliability   A measure of consistency between two versions of a measure

Ethnography   A type of qualitative research design that is centered on cultural behavior and seeks to record the cultural aspects of a group

Evaluative research design   A type of research design that draws from both qualitative and quantitative research methods

Evidence-based practices   Practices whose efficacy is supported by evidence

Explanatory research design   A type of research design that looks at the correlation between two or more variables and attempts to determine if they are related, and if so, in what way and how strongly they are related

Exploratory research design   A type of research design that allows us to use our powers of observation, inquiry, and assessment to form tentative theories about what we are seeing and experiencing; generally used to explore understudied topics

External validity   The extent to which a study's findings are applicable or relevant to a group outside the study (also called generalizability)

Face validity   A form of validity related to whether a measure seems to make sense (be valid) at a glance

Faking data   Making up desired data or eliminating undesired data in research findings

Focus group   An open discussion in which individuals share their opinions about or emotional responses to a particular subject

Frequency   The number of times that a response occurs

Grand tour questions   Large, overarching questions that identify the broad intent of a research study and are based on the existing knowledge (i.e., experience, knowledge from others, tradition, and prior research)

Grounded theory   A type of research design that utilizes a recursive form of question and analysis

Histogram   A vertical block graph used in statistics to visually present interval- or ratio-level data

Hypothesis   A research statement about relationships between variables that is testable and that can be accepted or rejected based on the evidence

Independent samples **t-test**   A type of *t*-test that is utilized when a researcher needs to compare two groups to see if the independent variable has an effect on the dependent variable

Independent variable   A variable that is controlled or manipulated by the researcher

Inductive research   The gathering of information based upon observations and quotes that is organized into common themes

Inferential statistics   Statistical procedures that examine associations between variables and use significance tests and other measures to make inferences about the collected quantitative data

Informed consent   The process of educating potential research participants about the basic purpose of the study, informing them that their participation is voluntary, and obtaining their written permission to participate in the study

Institutional review board   A committee mandated by the federal government to oversee the protection of human and animal subjects in research

Internal consistency   The consistency among the responses to the items in a measure; the extent to which responses to items measuring the same concept are associated with each other

Internal validity   A measure of how confident the researcher can be about the independent variable truly causing a change in the dependent variable (as opposed to outside influences)

Interobserver reliability   A measure of reliability that is used when two or more observers rate the same person, place, or event

Interval-level variables   Variables that are measured in such a way that there are equal gradations between each item, items are rank ordered, and each item is mutually exclusive and exhaustive

Intraobserver reliability   A measure of reliability that is used when one observer rates a person, place, or event two or more times

Justice   An ethical research principle regarding the fairness of distribution of benefits and risks among all individuals, which can be formulated in four ways:

to each person an equal share, to each person according to individual need, to each person according to individual effort, and to each person according to merit

Key words   Words that are found in the abstract of an article, and again as identifiers for the article, and that can be used as search terms in a database search

Laundering data   A way of statistically manipulating the data collected to reduce errors and make the findings more accurate

Leptokurtosis   The shape of a distribution of scores that is tall and narrow because the majority of scores closely resemble the mean

Literature review   A search of the published research that allows you to synthesize what is known about the topic you are studying

Longitudinal design   A research study that follows one cohort over a period of time

Mean   The statistical average of a set of numbers

Measure   A tool or instrument that is used to gather data and has two parts: the item (stimulus) and the response

Measure of association   Any of several statistical procedures that allow you to measure the correlation between variables

Measure of dispersion   A statistical measure that shows how dissimilar or different the data are from each other and is reported by how the scores fall (i.e., are arranged) around the mean

Median   The midpoint of a set of numbers

Methodology   The research methods, procedures, and techniques used to collect and analyze information in research

Mixed-method design   A research design that uses both qualitative and quantitative methods

Mode   The most frequently occurring response for a variable

Multiple regression   A statistical procedure that measures the correlation between an independent variable and the dependant variable while holding other independent variables constant (also known as linear regression)

Negative correlation   A statistical relationship that occurs when one variable increases when the other decreases (also called an inverse relationship)

No correlation   The absence of a relationship between variables—one variable does not influence the other

Nominal-level variables   Variables that are measured in such a way that items are mutually exclusive and exhaustive

Nonparametric statistics   Statistics that are used when the data depart from the criteria established for parametric statistics, the most common of which is the Chi-square

Non-probability sampling   Techniques for selecting a sample in which every individual does not have a greater-than-zero chance of being selected

Non-standardized methods   Informal methods of collecting data, such as the use of broad and open-ended question (recorded for accuracy) or a journal or field notes

Normal distribution   The symmetrical distribution of scores around the mean, with the most scores clustered around the mean and tapering off on both sides

Open-ended question   An inquiry that is worded in a way that allows the respondent to answer in a his or her own words as opposed to merely soliciting a yes-or-no response

Operationalizing   How we define a concept so that it can be measured

Ordinal-level variables   Variables that are measured in such a way that items must be mutually exclusive, exhaustive, and rank ordered

Outcome evaluation   An external evaluation that measures the overall effectiveness of a program by looking at the goals and objectives established by the program to answer the question "Did this program accomplish what it set out to do?"

Outlier   An anomaly or result that is far different from most of the results for the group and can skew the overall results (especially in a statistical average)

Paired samples t-test   A test of significance of the differences between two different sets of scores for the same respondents (also known as dependent samples *t*-test)

Parametric statistics   A type of inferential statistics in which a certain set of assumptions or rules must be met: data must be normally distributed, the dependent variable must be measured at an interval or ratio level, and a sample size of at least thirty must be used

Pearson's r   An analysis of correlation that seeks to determine if a relationship exists between two variables (one independent variable and one dependent variable) and the direction of the relationship

Peer review   Review of an article's content, accuracy, and methodological concerns by experts in the field that occurs before an article is accepted for publication

Phenomenology   A type of research design that seeks to understand the lived experience of the individuals who are being studied (their perceptions, thoughts, ideas, and experiences)

Plagiarism   The act of taking credit for work that is not one's own, either in whole or in part

Platykurtosis   The shape of a distribution of scores that is flat and wide because the majority of scores differ from the mean

Population   A set of entities from which a sample can be drawn to either describe a subsection of that population or generalize information to the larger population

Positive correlation   A statistical relationship in which the independent variable increases as the dependent variable increases

Probability distribution theory   The theory that data are equally distributed on both sides of the mean in a normal bell-shaped curve and that 68.26 percent of the population will probably fall within one standard deviation, 95.44 percent will probably fall within two standard deviations, and 99.74 percent will fall probably within three standard deviations of the mean

Probability sampling   A sampling technique in which each and every member of the population has a non-zero chance of being included in the sample

Probability sampling theory   A theory that requires the researcher to select a set of elements from a population in such a way that those elements accurately portray the parameters of the total population

Probability value   A report of whether the strength of a relationship is statistically significant or whether it could have occurred by chance; generally set at .05 or lower

Problem statement   An open-ended statement that tells you what a study is intended to do but does not predict what the results might be

Process evaluation   An internal evaluation process that is initiated in the early stages of a program and has three main goals: to construct a program description, to monitor a program, and to assess the quality of services being provided

Program description   The delineation of the setup, routines, and consumer characteristics of a program

Program evaluation   A type of research design and analysis that evaluates specific characteristics of a program within an agency

Program monitoring   A program evaluation method that is used to examine what happens after people receive services from a program

Program objective   A measurable, objective, specific, and time-lined goal that allows the effectiveness of a piece of a program goal to be evaluated

Purposive sampling   Selection of a sample based on knowledge of a population or with some predetermined characteristics in mind

Qualitative research   A field of research that is largely exploratory but can also involve the use of descriptive methods that is employed when little or nothing is known about a subject or phenomenon

Quality assurance   Means of determining the level of satisfaction of both services for consumers and programmatic issues for the staff

Quantitative data analysis   The process of analyzing data utilizing a variety of statistical procedures including descriptive and inferential statistics

Quantitative research   A field of research that is used when a sufficient amount of information has been acquired that the researcher can develop hypotheses about what is being studied

Quota sampling   A means of selecting a stratified non-random sample in which a researcher divides a population into categories and selects a certain number (a quota) of subjects from each category

Random assignment   the selection and placement of individuals from the pool of all potential participants to either the experimental group or the control group, which increases internal validity and reduces the likelihood of bias

Random selection   Means of selecting a sample from a larger population in which each member of the population has an equal chance of being selected for a study

Range   The overall spread or variability of a variable that tells us the difference between the lowest (minimum) and highest (maximum) values (responses) for a variable

Ratio-level variables   Variables that are measured in such a way that items are mutually exclusive and exhaustive, they are rank ordered, there are equal gradations between items, and there is an absolute zero

Reference page   The alphabetical list of studies cited in a summary of a literature review

Reliability   The stability and consistency of a measurement

Representativeness   A condition that is met when characteristics of the sample are similar to those of the population from which the sample was drawn

Research   The process of systematically gaining information; assimilating knowledge and gathering data in a logical manner in order to become informed about something

Respect for individuals   An ethical research principle according to which the autonomy of an individual is acknowledged and those with diminished autonomy are protected

Risk   The possibility that psychological, physical, legal, social, or economic harm may occur; sometimes expressed in levels, such as "no risk," "little risk," "moderate risk," and "high risk"

Sample   A group of subjects (elements) selected from a larger population

Sampling error   An error that occurs because only part of the population is directly contacted

Sampling frame   A list of all elements or other units containing the elements in a population

Sampling unit   A population selected for inclusion within a sampling frame

Semi-structured interview   Prepared research questions that are used to start the interview process but allow additional information to be solicited

Simple random sampling   A method of sampling in which a sample is generated randomly from a population in which each person has been assigned a number

Single-subject design   A method for evaluating an individual's progress over time that measures whether a relationship exists between an intervention and a specific outcome

Skewed distribution   A distribution of scores that produce a nonsymmetrical curve because there are more responses on the left or right side of the mean

Snowball sampling   A method of sampling in which the researcher starts with one or more members of the group being studied to gain access to other members of the same group, through a referral system, for the purpose of building the sample

Speculative inquiry   A strategy used in qualitative research to generate a theory based on common experiences

SPSS (Statistical Package for Social Sciences)   A statistical program that is commonly used by social science researchers to analyze research data

Standard deviation   The most commonly used measure of dispersion, which you calculate by taking the square root of variance

Standardized measure   A measurement or instrument that has been given to enough people that we can compare one person's scores to those of other test takers

Stratified random sampling   A method of sampling in which the population is divided into subgroups (strata) and a sample is drawn from each stratum

Structured interview   An interview that is limited to the research questions the researcher wants answered

Systematic random sampling   A method of sampling in which every nth number is selected at random (for example, every third person or every tenth person)

Target outcome   The goal of the intervention

Test-retest reliability   A method of examining the consistency of your measure from one time to the next to establish reliability

Theory   A statement or set of statements designed to explain a phenomenon based upon observations and experiments and often agreed upon by most experts in a particular field

Theoretical perspective   A model that makes assumptions about something, attempts to integrate various kinds of information, gives meaning to what we see and experience, focuses on relationships and connections between variables, and has inherent benefits and consequences

t-test   A statistical procedure that compares the means of two groups to determine if they are statistically different

Univariate analysis   A descriptive statistical method that involves the examination across cases of one variable at a time

Validity   How much a measurement tool measures what it is meant to measure

Variable   Any attribute or characteristic that changes or assumes different values

Variance   A statistical measure that is used to examine the spread of scores in a distribution

References

Barton, B. (2006). *Stripped: Inside the lives of exotic dancers.* New York: New York University Press.

Fischer, J., & Corcoran, K. (2007). *Measures for clinical practice: A sourcebook* (4th ed.). New York: Oxford University Press.

Gorovitz, S. (1985). *Doctors' dilemmas: Moral conflict and medical care.* New York: Oxford University Press.

Haney, C., Banks, C., & Zimbardo, P. (1973). Interpersonal dynamics in a simulated prison. *International Journal of Criminology and Penology, 1,* 69–97.

Haney, C., & Zimbardo, P. (1998). The past and future of United States prison policy: Twenty-five years after the Stanford Prison Experiment. *American Psychologist, 53*(7), 709–727.

Ingelfinger, F. (1972). Informed (but uneducated) consent. *New England Journal of Medicine, 287,* 465–466.

Ingram, B., & Chung, R. (1997). Client satisfaction data and quality improvement in managed mental health care organizations. *Health Care Management Review, 22,* 40–52.

Jones, J. (1981). *Bad blood: The Tuskegee syphilis experiment.* New York: Free Press.

Milgram, S. (1963). Behavioral study of obedience. *Journal of Abnormal and Social Psychology, 67,* 371–378.

National Association of Social Workers. (1999). *Code of ethics of the National Association of Social Workers.* Washington, DC: NASW Press.

Seltzer, M. L. (1971). The Michigan Alcoholism Screening Test: The quest for a new diagnostic instrument. *American Journal of Psychiatry, 127,* 89–94.

Sinetar, M. (1986). *Ordinary people as monks and mystics: Lifestyles for self-discovery.* New York: Paulist Press.

Index